COMRADE
ROCKSTAR

COMRADE ROCKSTAR

The Life and Mystery of Dean Reed,
the All-American Boy Who Brought
Rock 'n' Roll to the Soviet Union

REGGIE NADELSON

WALKER & COMPANY
NEW YORK

Published in 2006 by Walker & Company
Distributed to the trade by Holtzbrinck Publishers

All papers used by Walker & Company are natural, recyclable products made from
wood grown in well-managed forests. The manufacturing processes conform to the
environmental regulations of the country of origin.

Library of Congress Cataloging-in-Publication Data has been applied for.

ISBN-10: 0-8027-1555-9
ISBN-13: 978-0-8027-1555-5

First published in the UK by Chatto & Windus Ltd.
Revised edition published in the UK in 2004 by Arrow Books
First published in the U.S. in 2006 by Walker & Company

Visit Walker & Company's Web site at www.walkerbooks.com

Printed in the United States of America by Quebecor World Fairfield

2 4 6 8 10 9 7 5 3 1

For Richard David Story

Acknowledgements

I'd like to thank Artemy Troitsky for his absolutely unique insights into the business of Soviet rock and roll and pop culture and just about everything else back in the USSR. Vladimir Pozner's special perceptions of the relationship between East and West were irreplaceable.

Many others helped enormously during the writing of this book, and I'm grateful to all of them: Svetlana Kunetsina, Jo Durden-Smith, Yelena Zagrevskaya, Xenia Golubovitch, Anatoly Schevshenko, Renate Blume-Reed, Russell Miller, and Johnny and Mona Rosenburg.

I'd also like to thank Mike Wallace at 60 *Minutes* and Anthony Wall, Alan Yentob, and the late Nigel Finch at the BBC. At William Heinemann: Ravi Mirchandani, Caroline Knight, Susan Sandon, Richard Cable, Cassie Chadderton and Emily Sweet.

And, of course, Leslie Woodhead.

Introduction

More than anything, this is a tale from the Cold War. It began for me on a Sunday night at home in New York in April, 1986. I was only half-watching as 60 *Minutes* began and the little clock on the logo went tick-tick-tick and the title of the piece came up on the TV screen. "The Defector," it was called, and then there was Mike Wallace in shot, describing the piece, his voice familiar, resonant; no one in America has a more hypnotic voice than Mike Wallace, and he was talking about a rock star named Dean Reed. I'd never heard of Dean Reed.

The man in the frame now was tall, slim, and improbably handsome, all that thick good hair, the blue eyes, the juicy lips and promiscuous smile, and he was strumming a guitar and singing "Heartbreak Hotel" fit to bust.

I couldn't take my eyes off him. What made it so intriguing was that Reed appeared to be an all-American boy, yet he was in Red Square, being mobbed by Soviet fans, people plucking at his clothes, throwing flowers, begging for autographs—and this during the Cold War. People gazed at him adoringly and behind this big American, a man whose presence was obviously so addictive, so adhesive that everyone wanted a piece, was the Kremlin, heart of the Evil Empire, as Ronald Reagan who was President at the time called it. By now I was crouched near the TV set, transfixed.

The scene shifted as Wallace sketched in the life. Born in Wheat Ridge, Colorado, in 1938, Dean Reed was an American kid with an itch for stardom. At twenty, he set out for Hollywood to try his luck. He had a nice singing voice and he looked great. One of his tunes went gold in Latin America and Reed, always restless, headed south. In Chile, he became a superstar. He also saw the misery in which most people he met lived, and he got politics. By then it was the Sixties and, like millions of other young Americans, Reed was ripe for conversion.

"Come with me, Dean Reed," said a talent scout from Moscow, who heard him sing at a peace conference in Helsinki. He took Dean back to Moscow and made him a star in the Soviet Union, where tens of thousands of kids thronged to his concerts. Dean, they shouted, Dean Reed!

He sang "Rock around the Clock," he did the Twist in Minsk, he touched people and made them touch each other, and he radiated good health and good looks. His voice wasn't much, but he could carry a tune and whack a guitar, and all of it electrified the audience.

On my TV screen now was a sea of young Russian kids, prim in their white blouses and Young Pioneer scarves, and Dean among them, giving off body heat so potent you could almost feel it through the television. And at his feet, the girls swooning, blushing, throwing red carnations and their neckerchiefs, as he swiveled his narrow hips and preached peace and love, offering them sex and politics and rock and roll all tied up together.

For almost twenty years, he held the East in thrall. He was their American—their first.

"He was the embodiment of the whole country's dream about America," said a young woman in Moscow. "He came and was a smashing success," a Soviet official said. "He became a celebrity.

Here it was like it was with the Beatles for that time in England." A fan I met in a Moscow record shop said, "The girls, young girls, are crying, just crying, 'Dean Reed! Dean Reed!'"

Reed's albums went gold from Berlin to Bulgaria. He made cowboy movies, Eastern Westerns with stand-in Indians cast in Uzbekistan. He played the radical circuit, too—South America and the Middle East. He sang "Ghost Riders in the Sky" to Yasser Arafat.

Dean Reed settled in East Berlin, where he married an East German movie star, but he kept his American passport and he filed his tax return annually with the Internal Revenue Service. In fact, he was not technically a defector at all. He called himself an American patriot.

Hard to remember now that, even in 1986, the USSR was still Communist—Gorbachev had been in power only a year—and the rest of Eastern Europe still practically invisible behind the Iron Curtain. It is hard to remember how amazing this seemed: An American rocker in Red Square. Fans clinging to him, throwing flowers.

"Dean was as big a star over there as I'd ever seen anywhere," said an American friend who visited him in the East. "We were never anywhere without him being recognized. Every child, every old lady, everybody knew him."

Artemy Troitsky, Russia's premier rock critic, remembered, "His name was everywhere. Our dear American friend, Dean Reed, was on TV. He was on radio. He was in the papers. His mug was even on paper bags."

Six weeks after I saw the piece about Dean Reed on *60 Minutes*, I saw his obituary in the *New York Times*. It was a short obit down the page that I wouldn't have noticed if I hadn't seen *60 Minutes*. Drowned in the lake behind the house in suburban East Berlin where he lived, the obituary said. I wanted more.

It was 1986, the Berlin Wall was still up, and information was hard to come by. I started making phone calls. Looking for people who had known Reed. Getting hold of clips from foreign newspapers. Waiting. Obsessing. After a while, a tiny trickle of material about Reed's mysterious death turned into a stream of speculation. Nothing firm. Nothing satisfying.

"Accidental death by drowning" was the official East German report, but the follow-up stories concluded that this was pretty fishy. Dean Reed had been an excellent swimmer. He was in great shape. He was only forty-seven.

The Cold War. Rock and Roll. Sex and Death! I was pretty sure that Dean Reed, the life, the way he died, had the potential for a great movie. I tried it out on Leslie Woodhead, a director at Granada Television who had worked in Eastern Europe a lot and a rock fan who had made the *Stones in the Park* with the Rolling Stones. I told him the story and it took him about two minutes to commission a drama-documentary.

Then came a year and a half of research and, though the drama-documentary never happened, I wrote the first version of this book.

The Berlin Wall was still up and information at a premium. Rumors ran wild. All kinds of people came out of the woodwork: people who had known Reed, or met him once, or slept with him, or said they did. Because Dean Reed was dead before I began, the tales were as often about the tellers, people whose lives were changed, made thrilling or terrible—or both—by their connection with Dean Reed.

For every event, personal and political, there were at least two versions, sometimes three or four or five. Some people were difficult to reach or didn't want to talk. My own obsession was with the East and the Soviet Union. For that reason some of the people, Reed's first wife Patty, his daughter Ramona, who were extremely important to him, barely appear here.

This isn't a conventional biography; it isn't really a biography at all. I think of it as a kind of travel book through a now half-lost time and place. My search for Dean Reed took place at the end of the Cold War, as the socialist empire cracked up and the monolith began to topple like those statues of Lenin pulled down by the crowds in Moscow.

From the moment in June 1986 when I saw Dean Reed's obituary, I followed his ghost, trailing the evidence, mired in the big rich fruitcake of a life. Dean moved through it singing "Bye-Bye Love" with Phil Everly in East Berlin and Woody Guthrie songs on the Siberian Express, and making spaghetti westerns with Yul Brynner. He was part Forrest Gump, part political hustler, part American hero.

Comic, triumphal, tragic, incredible, here were all the things about the East that I'd never read in any newspaper, these tales about music and style and sex and teenage life, about what rock and roll meant to them, about what the Beatles meant in the USSR. Above all, here was the story of the yearning for the West. Here was a Cold War sideshow invested in one handsome American boy from Colorado who, guitar on his back, struck out in search of fame and fortune and found it on the other side of the world. And even after I had finished this book and it was published in England and Leslie Woodhead made a BBC documentary based on it, the story stuck to my life. In 1999, I got a call from Hollywood.

"I've sold your book to Tom Hanks," my agent said.

And it was true, as it turned out, and eventually I met Tom Hanks, but that came later.

Sixteen years have passed now since the Berlin Wall came down on November 9, 1989, and Dean Reed will soon have been dead for twenty years. So it seems like a good time to take another look at his life. After the Berlin Wall fell, I was able to track down information about Reed that I couldn't access before. Based on this, I reworked the original book, incorporating things as I saw them on the road in those astonishing years. It is now finally published in the United States for the first time.

Looking back, what I feel most now is how exciting it was as late as the late 1980s: the still thrilling, still terrifying crossing over the Berlin Wall, the look behind the Iron Curtain, the sudden contact with the so-called enemy and the realization that, for many, all they wanted was our music. Give us rock and roll! Dean Reed gave it to them.

Here was a guy who lived at the intersection of East and West, them and us. The crossing over gave Dean Reed glamour, and made him Comrade Rockstar.

Reggie Nadelson
New York
February 2006

One

1

DEATH IN BERLIN FOR DEFECTOR WHO CHANGED HIS TUNE

MYSTERY OF POP STAR IN LAKE: IT WAS MURDER SAYS MANAGER

DEAN REED, THE SINGER WHO WENT EAST AND THEN WANTED
TO COME IN FROM THE COLD

The crumpled newspaper cuttings dated June, 1986 were in my bag as I climbed up the viewing platform near Checkpoint Charlie and looked down at the Berlin Wall on the first day of my search for Dean Reed. How he died, and who he was; most of it lay on the other side of the Wall that split the world for as long as I could remember. It was November, 1988.

Down a jumble of gray streets fifteen minutes from the center of West Berlin, the Berlin Wall wasn't marked on a lot of Berlin maps, but it felt like the border of the world. Whenever I heard the phrase "Iron Curtain," in my mind's eye I always saw the Berlin Wall.

I saw it for real now, in front of me, this curtain of fortified concrete, eight feet high, twenty-nine miles long, topped with balls of barbed wire, covered on the Western side with graffiti, splattered in the East with blood. I was on my way to the other side, to East Berlin, where Dean Reed lived and died, to see his house, to find his albums, to try to get a sense of who he was, this man who had haunted my dreams since I had first seen him on *60 Minutes.*

Dean Reed's death had been the subject of plenty of speculation. People variously believed that he had been murdered by the East German Stasi, the KGB, the CIA, and neo-Nazis.

From the top of the viewing platform at Checkpoint Charlie, I could see not just the Berlin Wall but the other side. I looked at the unsmiling border guards in a watchtower peering through binoculars at the tourists, who looked back through their cameras. Between us was the dead zone of no-man's-land. A few months later, a twenty-two-year-old waiter jumped over the Wall because he could no longer wait, and he was shot dead. He was the last person to die there.

On the platform near me, a West German woman was showing the Wall to an English friend. Turning to me, she said, "Do you think they shall take this down? They are sometimes talking so."

"I hope so. Wouldn't it be great?!" I exclaimed.

She smiled knowingly, tucked her beautifully cut blonde hair behind her pink shell of an ear, and shouldered her Gucci bag.

"If they take it down, there will be trouble," she said. "First Turks shall come over, and then German nationals. These East Germans shall take our jobs. They will invade our department stores."

That's what really got to her: if they dismantled the Wall, the East Germans might charge into the KaDeWe, denuding it of most of its 400 varieties of sausage and all of the handbags. She didn't have to worry. Two years later, on the Sunday in

4

November when the Wall was sliced open and East Germans raced into the West, the *New York Times* reported: "The big department stores such as KaDeWe were closed, despite recently passed legislation that would have allowed them to stay open."

"You know what I am thinking?" she asked.

"What?"

"If the East Germans take the Wall down, we in the West will have to build another."

I climbed down from the platform and got back in the car.

The line of cars moved slowly into the border crossing. Leslie Woodhead, who was hoping to make a drama-documentary out of the Dean Reed story, was with me on this first trip East and I was glad. He had worked in Eastern Europe a lot and I figured he was knowledgeable when it came to doing business in Communist countries. As we pulled into the crossing proper, passing from West to East, then stopped, a man pushed a little mirror on wheels underneath the car in front of us.

"The spy's carpet sweeper," Leslie said.

My stomach turned over as we edged forward. A pale border guard put his head out of his cubicle like a jack-in-the-box and stared into the car. I had never been to the East before, but I'd seen all the movies.

The building where you showed your passport reminded me of a drive-through confessional; the young soldier, like an angry priest, snatched my passport, then snapped his window shut, leaving us to wait without any identity under a sickly white light in no-man's-land.

Eventually, the guard returned our passports and we bought day visas inscribed on what felt like cheap toilet paper, stiff, slick, brown, foreign.

Creep, I thought silently. "Have a nice day," I said, and the guard looked startled.

Whenever Dean Reed went through Checkpoint Charlie, though, he apparently always said "hi" to the guards, and Hans, or Heinz, or Hermann, whoever was on guard duty, would go home and say, "Dean Reed passed by today." He was so famous that for years you could just write DEAN REED, EAST BERLIN on a postcard and it would get to him.

The empty streets that led away from the border were full of potholes. The walls of the dank gray buildings that lined the roads were still pocked with shell marks from a war that had been over for more than forty years. I was expecting posters with socialist slogans or banners or stylized graphics of Lenin's head, but here were none, only the crappy streets with half the streetlights broken, crumbling buildings stained by the insistent rain, and shop windows that featured maybe a sparkly nylon blouse or a can of Spreewald pickles or some fancy china no one wanted. Still there was something thrilling about being here; I had crossed the Berlin Wall. How could I have known then that, in two years' time, the Wall would be a pair of earrings in Bloomingdale's?

"I want a Dean Reed record, please," I said to the clerk at the Melodia record shop on the Leipzigerstrasse, where "Winter Wonderland" was playing. The saleswoman, who had thick ankles and thick glasses, ignored me. I shouted at her the way you do when you don't speak a language and feel that if you say it loud enough in English someone will understand.

"Dean Reed, please. *Bitte?*" I added and pointed vaguely at the albums.

"Winter Wonderland" was more her sort of thing. It was the

most popular song in East Germany that year except for "Baa Baa Black Sheep." "Oh Tannenbaum" was also high on the charts, but it was almost Christmas.

"Dean Reed, Dean Reed," I insisted, my voice rising. A man with a little green fedora shot me a disapproving look.

"Shhh," he hissed.

The woman with thick glasses turned away impatiently, nodding brusquely towards the door, and so I began to speculate that, even dead, Dean Reed was a non-person, a subject not for discussion in this country where you could not discuss much, not out loud anyway.

Outside, in the streets, the shoppers plodded by, their expressions dour and disengaged. On the Alexanderplatz, a brutal piazza big enough for an army to maneuver in, a wind came up and drove the freezing rain in slanted sheets against us.

"Be Our Guest" in German flickered in neon on the Stadt Hotel. The doorman there loomed up out of the gloom, wielding his umbrella like a Kalashnikov.

"Nein! Nein! Nein!"

He was absolutely furious. We were not hotel guests. Only hotel guests were allowed inside. There were rules. He was the doorman. This was his door.

"Go," he shrieked and hid under the umbrella.

Across the square we found a forlorn espresso bar. Its walls were a sort of distempered duck-egg blue and the table tops were covered in scratched linoleum. But the Flying Pickets were on the sound system and the espresso machine, which had clearly been lovingly cared for, gleamed. It shimmered with the suggestive promise of sunny countries and laughter and good coffee.

"Halifax," Leslie said.

"What?"

"This is Halifax, 1951. Where I grew up. The Bon Bon Coffee Bar on Commercial Street. You could listen to Guy Mitchell and Frankie Laine and Ruby Murray on the jukebox . . . you don't know what I'm talking about, do you?"

I ordered something from the menu. It was some kind of chopped beef on toast. Minced, minced beef, I thought. Leslie shuddered.

"That looks like dog's vomit."

The Dog's Vomit Café was how I came to think of the duck-egg blue espresso bar on the Alexanderplatz.

"How could Dean Reed have lived here?" Leslie asked, his voice full of disbelief and some despair. "What could he have wanted badly enough to live in this bloody place?"

East Berlin must have had something, something to entice a man like Dean Reed, I thought to myself. Maybe this was just façade; maybe it was too soon to understand. After all, I had friends in London who preferred East Berlin to West, who talked about the opera and museums, the Berliner Ensemble, and the socialist ideals. Maybe it was too soon for me to get it. People in the west sometimes spoke of the quality of friendship in the GDR, the way you could take the time to sit and talk because no one was rushing to work in a country where everyone was always fully employed. A couple of years later, however, when the Wall came down, everyone saw that what lay behind the façade was much worse that it had seemed that first day. Not only ugly, but polluted, impoverished, run by gray-faced old despots with a vicious secret police so ubiquitous that one in every three or four citizens was involved with it.

Right now, though, I wanted a record. There were none in the

West because Dean Reed had never played in the West or recorded there.

On the Alexanderplatz was a second record store; in the drizzle, a line had formed outside it. A couple of muscular black American GIs, presumably stationed in West Berlin, passed us and held out their hands, palms up in despair as if to say, "They told us you could get cheap stuff here, but there's nothing to buy."

I could see the record shop was almost empty. Still, our line of forlorn customers stood in the rain because you were not allowed inside without one of the orange plastic shopping baskets which were in short supply. As one customer left the shop, he handed on his basket to the next person in line.

The baskets were too small for the records, though, I realized when I got one and went into the shop. The clerks didn't care if you bought anything either and they were irritated if you didn't have the right change; there was nothing much to want anyway.

Right there in the dreary record shop, I lost whatever was left of my political virginity, of any vestige of the socialist fantasies I was raised on as a "Red Diaper Baby" in Greenwich Village. My mother had been in the Communist Party when she was young, and I came of age in the Sixties when everyone believed in peace and love and universal disarmament. Even in the late 1980s, I probably clung to some kind of sentimental version of it all. I had friends whose parents still stood up when they heard the "Internationale," in one case during a performance of *Reds* at the movies. ("Down in front," somebody shouted from the balcony. "We want to see them kiss!")

So my absolute conversion to capitalism came with a small orange plastic shopping basket in a record store on the Alexanderplatz in East Berlin. Simple-minded, maybe, but the practical effects, the everyday results of a system, were always a lot more potent than any theory.

Rock records were scarce in the East, though before long rock and roll would be the soundtrack for the revolutions of the late eighties. Swaying mobs with lighted candles would appear in Gorky Park in Moscow; the crowd in Prague's Wenceslas Square in 1989 would rattle their key chains like a cheery punk band to celebrate the Velvet Revolution; in East Berlin, as early as 1987, kids climbed into the trees near the Wall to listen to concerts in the West, or to look at the new Soviet premier who was a lot like a rock star.

"Gorby, Gorby," the kids hanging in trees near the Berlin Wall would shout, as if the Soviet premier were that year's rock star. And, in a way, he was.

Over that year, during my first encounters with the world where Dean Reed lived, I finally saw why. He had been a star. He was an American guy singing the music that everyone yearned for, the music that made you feel alive if you were young. It was the best, most joyful expression of the sedition which was the only way to keep from shriveling up in an oppressive society. In West Berlin, I met a man who smuggled synthesizers and cassettes past Checkpoint Charlie, not for profit, but as a gesture of solidarity with the rock and roll underground.

In the record store on the Alexanderplatz, flipping albums methodically, front to back, in bin after bin, long after I had given up, Leslie scanned each cover and found nothing. Not for the first time that day I had the eerie sense that Dean Reed had never existed in this strange country, where the rules were made to fence people in, to make them conform, to keep them quiet. How could the exuberant cowboy I'd seen on TV have been part of it?

Suddenly, Leslie whispered at me, "Over here."

The album was titled *Country Songs* and Dean Reed's picture was on the cover. He wore a cowboy hat and he was smiling and he looked wonderful, full of life. I held the album. I touched his hat. I carried it gently in the orange plastic basket to the cashier, who glared at me because I didn't have the right change. I didn't care. Dean was real now; I could touch him.

Outside, we located the rental car and climbed in and decided to risk the trip to Schmockwitz, where Dean Reed had lived. It was not on the map of places you were permitted to visit, according to the day visa printed on the stiff oily paper. All day we had discussed if we should risk it. But it seemed innocent enough, the half-hour drive into the suburbs, and Leslie turned the key in the ignition.

I propped the Dean Reed album on the dashboard. My feet were soaked and I took off my shoes and hung my socks on the radiator to dry. Outside a thick mist, a kind of soaking drifting fog clung to the windshield. In an endless tangle of suburban streets, we got lost.

Then, all at once, we bumped over the cobblestones into the village of Schmockwitz itself. I had assumed that Schmockwitz must be the Graceland of the East. There would, I hoped, be souvenirs, mugs and keyrings, albums and posters, all with Dean's face on them, maybe even a replica of his guitar or a talking Dean doll.

We pulled up in front of a tavern, one of those Berlin pubs with lace curtains in the window. As I opened the door, the buzz of voices went silent. Everyone looked up from their food. I felt like an interloper as, in unison, a half-dozen hefty burghers stopped their Sunday lunch and stared at my bare feet. No one smiled. There were no Dean Reed beer mugs.

Backing off, I got in the car and Leslie drove down a narrow road between bare birch trees. Slush spattered the window. The rain, heavy now, fell from a greasy leaden sky. We took a wrong turn. We ended up in front of a large building that was shuttered for the winter. A sign I could just decode announced that it was a Communist Party Rest House. The car wheels squealed and we backed out in a hurry. We were lost in the dark. The woods seemed to close in from both sides of the road. It was completely deserted.

Paranoia turned on the projector in my head and the movie flickered into life: it was in black and white with a creepy grain and the pulsing soundtrack of an irregular heartbeat. Whoever had it in for Dean Reed, whoever killed him, was somewhere down this road. Someone who was looking for us.

We would miss closing time at Checkpoint Charlie; we were way out of bounds, beyond the limits of our visa. We would spend the night in an East Berlin jail among officials who were not only Communists but also Germans, and perhaps there was a small concentration camp still open somewhere . . . that would be it, a small camp. Rigid with fear, I sat, watching my socks flutter on the radiator. I thought I heard the wail of a German police car siren rise and fall. It was coming closer.

6A Schmockwitzer Damm was a low-lying, white stucco house with an orange tiled roof, a garage, a lawn. A large carved wooden R was perched on a post in the yard as if it were a ranch: the Double-R ranch; the Dean Reed Dude Ranch of Schmockwitz.

On the other side of the house from the road was a stretch of lake the color of tin, where Dean Reed's body lay for four days before it had been dragged to shore in June of 1986. The place felt deserted, lonely, desolate.

I took the newspaper clippings out of my bag and read the article by Russell Miller, a British journalist. Miller, by chance, had arranged to interview Dean Reed for a magazine the weekend he died. From West Berlin, where Miller was staying, he had called the house at Schmockwitz. The interview was scheduled for the next day, but Mrs. Reed told him that Dean was ill and could not see him. In the middle of the conversation, a man came on the line—it seemed to Miller that he had snatched the phone away from Mrs. Reed. He told Miller that Dean was in the hospital and that he should go home and would be contacted. Then he gave Miller his name and a telephone number in Potsdam. He was Mr. Weiczaukowski, he said.

Puzzled, Russell Miller went back to London and, on the following Tuesday, when he heard the news that Dean Reed was dead, he called Potsdam. There was no Mr. Weiczaukowski at the number he had been given. He wrote a story for the *Sunday Times*, and so the mystery was cranked up. It grew and leaked and multiplied.

"I have over 2000 scenarios," Dean Reed's mother would tell me. "And it's about up to 3000 now, I think . . . each scenario brings up a new way I think he was killed."

"I read something about maybe there being drugs, or that there were some political implications," a friend of Reed's told me. "I've heard the CIA whack," said someone else. "I've heard killed by a jealous lover. Or the KGB."

And so it went. Eventually, the rumors spread so that nobody could unpick the truth about his death from the rumors. KGB, CIA, eventually I became hooked on the creepy network of conspiracy buffs. Already, for months, I'd been trying to get a fix on it, had talked to Russell Miller, who was as perplexed as I was. Now, finally, on this dank December day in 1987, I was here in this silent, cold place. The house was shut up. No answers.

I said, "Let's go."

It was wet and dark and I was frightened; we had seen the house. I wanted to go. I felt we were out on a limb with no back-up, no way back if we got lost. But Leslie insisted on getting out of the car to take pictures of the house because, if he made a drama-documentary, his production designer would need them. He took his time while I sat in the car. It wasn't just for the production designer, I could see that. It was an obsession for him, this part of the world, this other place across the Wall. In a way he was addicted to Eastern Europe. It tested you and then you could go home, a no-exit with a revolving door, an adventure with a return ticket, he always said.

"Cheer up," he said now, turning to take yet one more picture, then getting back in the car and revving up the motor of the car loud enough to wake the dead. "Listen, honestly, this is nothing at all compared to when I was filming a documentary about torture in Brazil."

Down that country road, in the encroaching gloom on the other side of the Berlin Wall was where I seriously began looking for Dean Reed. The Berlin Wall had gone up in August, 1961, which was just about the time Dean Reed had left America. He never lived there again, and he died in this lake in East Berlin. Who killed him? Who was he? A true believer? A spy? Just a guy, an American with a guitar and great looks and a lot of ambition?

14

Leslie drove a few hundred yards and stopped and got out of the car. I followed him to the little cemetery by the side of the road. A few wet flowers lay on a headstone. It seemed incredibly sad somehow that the dazzling American I'd seen on TV should end up in this lonely place. I bent down. On the headstone, in German, was inscribed simply: *Dean Reed. Born Colorado, 1938. Died Berlin, 1986.*

2

When Dean Reed was seventeen, he raced a mule 110 miles for a quarter. He did it on a dare, his mother told me, and he nearly dropped dead and so did the mule. Some people said it showed his tenacity and grit, but she figured it was just a funny thing a kid would do. Anyway, Reed won and someone caught him in a photograph. At the end of the race Dean's face glowed with triumph. Racing that mule was ambitious, brave, and hokey, and it had the feel of one of those old folk songs where heroic men in bare feet race locomotives.

"I still have that quarter somewhere," said Dean's mother, Ruth Anna Brown.

Mrs. Brown lived in a condo on the north shore of Oahu in Hawaii. I went to see her because I wanted her to tell me how her son had died. Instead, for a while, we talked about his childhood: how, born in 1938, he grew up in Wheat Ridge, Colorado. We talked about the mule race and she looked for the quarter.

Hawaii seemed as far away as you could get from East Berlin and the Dog's Vomit Café. The islands were like a trail of denatured but delectable crumbs, nibbled off the coast of California and flung far away across the South Pacific. The sun shone, holiday-makers tanned their plump flesh, girls in bars wiggled their hips and their straw hula skirts, and everyone drank things from huge pineapples with pink plastic parasols in them.

Up near Wahiawa, where Mrs. Brown lived with her fond husband, Ralph, the air smelled of pineapples. The fruit, whose smell made you giddy, grew on plantations that were as plush and tidy as wall-to-wall carpeting, but the mountains just beyond the fields were raw and imposing. The settlements had a breezy ramshackle charm, and on my way to Mrs Brown's I'd seen plenty of surfers with heavy tans and hard bodies and pale vacant blue eyes lounging outside the bars and burger joints.

Mrs. Brown got up suddenly from her chair and went to the windows, one at a time, fastening the wooden shutters, then closing the windows. There was a storm coming and you could hear the wind and somewhere a flag flapping in it like wet laundry.

I liked Mrs. Brown. She was a handsome woman with fine, powdery white skin and hair, but she wasn't a fragile old lady. She was tough and funny, and some of the time she (Well, my goodness!) camped it up, her hands on her hips, full of self-mockery and good humor. Her back was straight and she wore a sweatshirt from the University of Hawaii, where she had just finished her doctorate in women's peace studies. At seventy-four, she was immensely hospitable and naturally wary, and she had an unbending determination to see right done by her boy who was dead in East Berlin. At first we made small talk.

Mrs. Brown was no fool. Courteously, she asked who I was. Leslie Woodhead, who was there too, talked about the drama-documentary he hoped to make, and I mumbled something about writing for the *Guardian* and tried, shamelessly, to refer to my right-on past on various picket lines and peace marches. Ho Ho

Ho Chi Minh, I almost said. It was OK; Mrs. Brown got the point.

"I had that child for a special reason. I always thought that Dean was born under a magic star," she said.

Mrs. Brown sat on the carpet between the television set and a brass-bound trunk. I sat beside her. The trunk was full of memorabilia. Every so often, she reached into it and brought out pieces of Dean; there were record albums and tapes, videos and scrapbooks, and copies of Dean's autobiography, a small book with dark blue covers, written in German. Everyone I met had a copy of Dean's little blue book and in each, on the flyleaf inside the blue covers, was an inscription in his big childish hand, invariably wishing the recipient peace and love and all good things for a socialist future. And then there were the photographs of Dean: Dean in his high school letter sweater, Dean and the mule, Dean with his guitar, Dean with his white Chevrolet Impala convertible. His mother next to me, his images spilled on the carpet, I began to feel I knew him a little; already I was thinking of him as Dean.

She was rueful. In spite of the trunk, she felt she had so little of Dean left. She said that she possessed not so much as his belt buckle—Dean's widow would not give it to her, she said. So, when a year or two later, the Colorado Historical Society organized the Dean Reed Collection, she was happy. Eventually I met Stan Olliner, the curator of the collection, a bespectacled man who carefully put on white cotton gloves before showing me the Reed archive, which included film scripts and pictures and diaries, as well as a plaster casting of Dean's teeth. Dean had always carried the cast with him in case he should break a tooth on the road, Olliner explained. "Dean was a pack rat, thank goodness," he added. "He literally saved everything."

All of it had been donated by Dean's widow, Renate. She even apparently offered Olliner Dean's dog, Emu, for when the dog died and could be stuffed. Olliner said, no thanks.

"In no way could I justify a stuffed Emu to the Colorado Historical Society," its director told the *Denver Post*. Mrs. Brown thought it was all perfectly wonderful anyway.

"I think Dean's looking down and saying, 'Wow! I just knew I'd come back to Colorado, no matter what.'"

All day long, as we sat with Mrs. Brown on her living-room floor, the television was on, and images of Dean—some from contraband videos of television specials he'd made, others from documentary films about his life—flickered across it. Pictures of Dean lay on the carpet in black and white and color. 1938—1986. I knew I should get to the point and ask Mrs. Brown about Dean's death, but it made me feel like an intruder. Anyway I didn't want to stop her from telling the stories that poured out of her in random order as she turned over the photos and glanced up at the videos and talked about her kid. I couldn't turn away from the images, either.

On the wall was a large glossy photograph of Dean; in it he was wearing a beaded Indian neckband and the eyes looked a little mournful. It had been taken not long before his death, and as I stared at it, I found myself dredging up a poem by e. e. cummings. The verse that I'd loved as a moony teenager came back and it reminded me of Dean Reed:

Buffalo Bill's
defunct
     who used to
     ride a watersmooth-silver
          stallion

and break onetwothreefourfive pigeonsjustlikethat

                                   Jesus

he was a handsome man

                    and what I want to know is

how do you like your blueeyed boy

Mister Death

Dean Reed was born on September 22, 1938, in Wheat Ridge, Colorado. It was one of a string of small towns on the fringe of Denver when Denver was still a cow town. Wheat Ridge was resolutely rural, not yet eaten by Denver's urban sprawl. Ladies put on their hats for a day out in Denver.

"All we had was just a very small house and two enormous chicken houses at the back, where we kept the chickens," said Ruth Anna Brown. "We had a cow—I made my own butter and whipping cream—and a pig. I think the kids enjoyed it very very much. I don't think I did. I wasn't meant to be a farm wife," she said, laughing. "I never did care for those chickens."

In Wheat Ridge, everywhere you looked were the mountains; everything was diminished by their presence. The Rocky Mountains dominated the town where Dean Reed was born; the mountains formed him. Sometimes during the summers when he was a teenager, Dean cruised the mountain passes at night, aboard his Chevrolet. He put down the top, stuck his foot flat on the accelerator, climbed the steep, curving roads, and, turning off the radio, sang at the stars. Sometimes, he turned out the car's lights and steered by the light of the moon.

All around Denver, the Rockies were the horizon, a huge presence, waiting to test you or trick you. The mountains could make you feel tiny, a scrap of nothing on God's turf.

Dean went to the local schools and joined the Boy Scouts and the Future Farmers of America. At the local military academy he attended, he was good at sports, a keen gymnast, and a fine horseman.

At Wheat Ridge High, he set the record for the mile-and-a-half cross-country run. In his senior year there was the mule race. Also, as his mother pointed out, he could eat more ice cream than any kid in town—all his life he was crazy about ice cream. In the afternoons after school, he worked at the local dairy. His ears bugged him, though. They were as big as jug handles. He thought they made him ugly, and he worried about getting girls. He got a guitar, figuring it would help get with girls, the ears notwithstanding. He played the high school auditorium; he played Phipps Auditorium in Denver; he played the Harmony Guest Ranch up in the mountains at Estes Park.

Mrs. Reed stuck a video in the VCR. A documentary titled *American Rebel* flickered into life.

"Dean's dad, Cyril," Mrs. Brown explained.

Cyril was on camera, a big man with glasses. He talked about Dean's first musical performance, how he was a little guy in a big auditorium. He said Dean was called Slim Reed back then. He said he knew that his kid, that Dean, was scared as could be.

Dean Reed always claimed that he had been a shy boy, an insecure boy who learned to play the guitar at twelve to help him meet girls. A more important theme of his life, though, was wanting his father's love. He had two brothers, Vern and Dale. Dale, the younger, lived in Alaska. Vern, who was a committed libertarian, lived in Seattle where, although he was employed at Boeing, he refused to work on military aircraft. Dean thought this was very brave and often boasted about what a good engineer

21

Vern was. But Dean was not at all close to his brothers; most of all, he wanted his father to love him best.

"Dean's father did believe in whipping," Ruth Anna Brown said. "And Dean would never cry. Which is very irksome to a person if you're trying to prove your point to them and they just sit there smiling at you."

On film, wearing thick black glasses, Cyril, who had the politics of Genghis Khan, had cast himself as a lovable rogue; he was very funny. And in his way, Cyril cared for the boy, and the first time Dean got up to play for an audience, the old man worried himself sick. Still, although Dean sent his dad money for a ticket to come see him perform in the East, Cyril never went.

"I had no use for those countries," he said in his corn-pone accent, laying it on good and thick for the cameras, and it was easy to see how Dean got his star quality from those two old country hams, Cyril and Ruth Anna.

I'd heard somewhere that when General Jimmy Walker founded the John Birch Society in 1961, Cyril joined up. BETTER DEAD THAN RED. What sweet revenge for his son to finish up a dedicated Communist, if revenge was what Dean was after. Better dead than red. Poor Dean was red and dead.

"Well, Cyril was a cantankerous creature," said Mrs Brown, who divorced him as soon as the boys were grown up.

She searched for her spectacles, found them on top of her head, put them on and peered at the screen where there was a picture of Dean as a boy with some of Mrs. Brown's chickens.

"Like I said, I kept them back in Wheat Ridge to earn extra money," Mrs. Brown said. "I never did care much for those chickens. Come to think of it, I didn't much care for Cyril, either."

* * *

The late 1940s, when Dean was a boy, and especially the 1950s, when he was a teenager, were, on the surface, triumphant and remorselessly upbeat, when any boy, even in provincial America, even in a place like Wheat Ridge, could grow up to be President if he tried hard enough, so long as he was white and obeyed the rules. The War was over, the country was on the move. Dean tried plenty hard. Dean practiced positive thinking. *The Power of Positive Thinking* by Dr. Norman Vincent Peale was the biggest seller of the euphoric fifties, when the country was in its prime and it was un-American to be a failure and small town values were practically a religion.

The 1950s were a time when kids competed at hula-hoops; kids stuffed themselves into phone booths and ate goldfish; winning was what counted, but so did charity. Sometimes Dean got a little money for playing his guitar and, when he did, he gave it to the American Cancer Society.

"He always shared that way," Mrs. Brown said.

The soundtrack for Dean's teen years would have been peppy and bland, hit parade tunes like "How Much Is that Doggy in the Window" by Patti Paige and "Oh, Mein Papa" by Eddie Fisher. By the mid-1950s though, a whiff of rock and roll and things to come arrived, with Bill Haley and "Rock around the Clock"; and after that: Elvis.

Anyhow, at first it sounded like a typically all-American childhood, the sunny uplands of life that Hollywood let us believe all good Americans inhabited. This version did not include racial segregation or Senator Joe McCarthy's House of Un-American Activities Committee or the desolating conformity parents preached to their kids.

In Hawaii that day in her condo, Mrs. Brown suddenly looked up from Dean's photographs and said, "Dean's dad killed himself, did you know that?" She let it pop out of her mouth by the by, as if she did not want it to count for much.

Injured in a wheat combine accident, Cyril lost a leg, and, in 1984, he killed himself because he could not afford a new one, it was rumored. Dean told reporters that his daddy had died because he couldn't afford medical care and he, Dean, deeply embedded in his socialist beliefs by then, never forgave America for failing his father. Again and again, he told the story.

"Why didn't you give him the money for a leg?" one reporter finally asked.

Dean said his dad was too proud.

By now the rain was battering the roof of Mrs. Brown's condo. She stopped the video and left her boy frozen in time. She peered hard at him as he'd been once, forever crew-cut, forever smiling.

Fumbling in her trunk of memories, Mrs. Brown was like a woman trying to get unstuck from a chaotic dream. Outside, the tropical storm smashed open the shutters; they banged incessantly against the window frames. As she got up to fix them, she lurched slightly, whether from age or grief was hard to tell, then she sat down heavily in a chair, her legs falling apart a little. Leslie reached out to take her arm to help her. I wanted to ask her about the death. I wanted it badly. Who killed Dean Reed? I wanted to say. But the intrusion was too great, and, anyhow, she was well defended against it.

"You about ready for us, Ralph?" she called out towards the kitchen to her husband.

Ralph, who was wearing a Hawaiian sarong, was making lunch.

"Give me a few minutes," he called back.

As we set the table for lunch, I learned, among other things: that, right up to the end of his life, Dean could walk on his hands; that he whistled when he was nervous; that he could juggle brilliantly. He adored spaghetti and Skippy crunchy peanut butter, which Mrs. Brown sent him by mail to East Berlin; and turquoise was his favorite color (not red, he often cracked). He also had medical problems. As a boy—here she grew vague—he'd had some sort of major operation and by twenty he had ulcers and trouble sleeping.

"He took a sleeping pill every night of his life," Mrs. Brown said. "But only one. He never took more than one sleeping pill," she said, and then Ralph appeared from the kitchen to say he was ready with the lunch.

He was apparently known for his fruit salad and was a dab hand with pineapple sherbet, which he produced from a white plastic gadget. We sat down at the table.

"There's a little something we like to do before meals," Mrs. Brown said.

I froze. They were going to say grace and I had already attacked the food. I was embarrassed. I wanted to do the culturally correct thing. But Ruth Anna Brown just smiled her smart, wry smile and reached for Leslie's hand.

"We like to hold hands and wish each other peace and love and friendship," she said.

After lunch, the rain stopped and the sun twirled some droplets into a rainbow on the window pane. All around the apartment complex, which resembled a two-storey motel made of poured concrete, people were throwing open their windows, getting ready to go out to do the Saturday chores. There was the scraping and banging of front doors and car doors as the place came alive after the storm. Fit-looking old people in Bermuda shorts went outside, sucked in the fresh washed air, hailed each other, arranged dates to eat dinner and play Scrabble, and set off in their cars for the supermarket.

In the late Hawaiian afternoon, we listened to "Our Summer Romance" on Ruth Anna Brown's record player. It had been Dean's first hit tune.

Mrs. Brown said, "You have to understand, Dean always did everything he did for a woman. First he married Patty in Hollywood. Then Wiebke and Renate in East Berlin. But I guess you could say I was the original model."

Mrs. Brown showed me a photograph of the Dean Reed School, which had been dedicated recently in East Berlin. She had also written to Erich Honecker, the East German boss, to tell him to change the name of the cemetery where Dean was buried to the Dean Reed Cemetery.

"Dean knew Honecker. He knew everyone," she said.

She put a video of Dean's last concert into the VCR and side-stepped any talk about his death.

In a single spotlight, Dean sat on a stool on a bare stage in Germany, picked up his guitar and, a cappella, sang a song he said was for his mother. It was called "Mom's Song."

Mrs. Brown's eyes filled with tears and Mrs. Brown turned away and then looked at us and said, "When I first saw that video, he was already dead and I thought he was trying to tell me goodbye."

3

In 1958, Dean Reed went to Hollywood. Somehow, during that long day on the north shore of Oahu, Mrs. Brown summoned up the energy to tell one more story and, as she told it, she was recharged because this was a good story, an exciting story, a family legend about how her boy sought fame and fortune on the road to Hollywood.

In her hand was a blurred black-and-white snapshot. Dean Reed smiled up out of it. He was twenty and almost unbearably hopeful and handsome. In a white Chevrolet Impala convertible, big as a boat, he had a big stiff crew-cut and he wore a skinny tie. It was taken the year he left home for California.

His father was not happy about it. Dean had been studying to be a meteorologist and then he just picked up and went West, and his dad, Cyril, was mad because he wasn't at all crazy about this "singing stuff." Dean had planned on becoming a TV weatherman after he finished college. But at the end of summer after his sophomore year and, instead of heading back to school, Dean went West.

What the heck, he probably said to himself. He was pretty good with the guitar. He had racked up a few successes playing

27

Estes Park, a resort town up in the Colorado Rockies. Dean wanted a look at the big time.

Driving down the endless desert highway, he was having a ball, maybe singing or listening to the radio or day-dreaming. Anything was possible. Then Dean saw a guy by the roadside thumbing a lift.

The guy—the bum, as Mrs. Brown called him—at the roadside looked forlorn and miserable. Dean, always up for a good deed, pulled over. According to his mother, the incident might have played like this:

"Hop in," Dean said.

"Where are you going?" the bum asked.

"Hollywood," replied Dean.

Clocking the guitar in the front seat, the bum knew a good thing when he saw one.

He said, "I'll tell you what. You pay for a night at a motel, maybe give me a spare pair of pants, and I'll give you a name of someone in the music business."

Skeptical, Dean laughed. But he was a good kid with a good heart, and he thought, what the heck.

Dusk fell over the desert. The neon came on outside the motels. Dean agreed to pay for the bum's room. He gave him a pair of pants, too, although it was his only spare pair, according to his mother.

Mrs. Brown went on. "And this fellow said to stop by and see Capitol Records, and he gave Dean the name of a person to see. And Dean did. And what do you know? He was for real. Dean got a recording contract." Ruth Anna Brown beamed.

In Hollywood, the Capitol Records building was pretty easy to find because it was built in the shape of a stack of records.

Inside, sweet-talking the receptionist, Dean evetually got in to see Mr. Voyle Gilmore, who turned out to be the genuine article. The bum on the road was, in fact, a musician and a pal of Gilmore's from the old days. Gilmore was also a top producer for, among others, Frank Sinatra.

Dean got a try-out. Next thing you knew, he was on the phone back to his mom telling her to come on out and sign him to a seven-year contract with Capitol. He wasn't twenty-one yet and his mother had to sign.

"Come on out to California, Mom," he said, shouting because he was on long distance, which was still a novelty, used only for death and celebration.

It was 1958. He was twenty. He had a great smile. He could shake his hips and girls thought he was very sexy.

Dean's dad was mad as hell that Dean had quit his education and gone to Hollywood. Dean didn't care. He was on the move now, recording songs, appearing on TV. Now, on Ruth Anna Brown's television set, I watched a clip from an old program. In it, a girl bobbed on to the stage, her pony-tail bouncing.

"How about everyone coming over to my house. I've got the new Dean Reed album and it's a real gasser," she said.

The girl on the screen had the knowing look of a TV pro, even at fifteen. She wore a party dress with a big skirt and she had the calculated innocence of the 1950s.

"But here he is himself in person. It's Dean Reed!"

Bright as a button, he bounced up to the mike in that loose-jointed way that was considered slick, snapping his fingers, dancing, jumping. He wore a white sports coat and he had all the moves. He was quite polished; he knew his stuff. He was accompanied by a group of similarly hip boys, snapping their fingers.

"I went to a football game and I never will forget that pretty little, pretty little, pretty little majorette," he sang as he smiled his million watt smile. The boys joined in the refrain: "Twirly Twirly," they sang. "Twirly Twirly."

Then a couple of plump majorettes in little white booties came on and pranced around, tossing their batons, eyeing Dean Reed.

"Twirly Twirly," Dean sang again.

Leslie and I looked at each other; I could see that, like me, he could barely sit still he was so excited, that he wanted to say, as he did after we left, "This is it! This is the key. This is the root of the story, the beginning of the Dean Reed we've been looking for. He was on his way to being an early American idol and, if he'd stuck it out, he could have been, well, Fabian."

"Dean's life, it was just like a movie," Mrs. Brown said, as she reached over to shut off the TV.

For a minute I was silent. Mrs. Brown was clearly ready for us to go. I wasn't going.

Finally, I said, "So who do you really think killed him? How did your son die?"

"Well, I went to see one of their policemen over in East Germany, you can just imagine." Mrs. Brown was not as reticent as I had expected. "My goodness, he was a pompous man. I asked who he thought did it and he looked at me as if I were just plain crazy. I'll never forget it. He said to me, 'There are three things to consider. First, crime. Second, suicide. Third, accident.'" She hesitated. "Then he said, 'One. We do not have crime in the GDR. Two. We know Dean well and he would never have committed suicide. Three, therefore, it was an accident.'

"So tell me this," Mrs. Brown continued. "If it was an accident, why was Dean pinned under the pilings of the pier in the lake? Why were his arms stretched out so that he was pinned in a

Christ-like position? Why was he wearing two jackets in the middle of summer? Why?"

Notions poured from her like hope: that Dean got into trouble because he knew something about Chernobyl—he had been due to start filming that summer in Yalta, which was not far away; that he was dissatisfied with the system—she had a letter from him as far back as 1985 saying so; that he knew things about Oliver North and the Contras. He was intending to call a press conference for the Saturday he died, he said.

"There was always an agent assigned to Dean to do a 'wet job', in case he got out of line," she said.

"A wet job?"

The scenarios of his death, as Mrs. Brown called them, came on faster and faster. She could handle something dramatic, brave, important, a death that had meaning. The only unspeakable thing was an accidental death. She whispered to me of the CIA. From her trunk she took a folder and handed it to me. It was the coroner's report on Dean's death.

Back at the Kahala Hilton in Honolulu, I sat on my balcony—my *lanai*, as they called it—and watched people on the terrace below feed peanuts to the birds. Dolphins in the man-made lagoon sang for their supper. Holiday-makers, dolphins, we were all tourists locked in a palmy conspiracy of good times. In the souvenir shop were toy rescue dogs with barrels of macadamia nuts around their neck, plastic pineapples with clocks in them, and motorized plastic dolphins to swim in your bath.

All of Hawaii seemed a comfy lagoon where old people, tourists and children relaxed in the sun. Everyone who tended to the visitors appeared as cheery as could be, putting on muu-muus, cooking pig luaus, driving pedi-cabs, carrying suitcases, selling nuts at the macadamia nut museum, working the army bases, frying McNuggets at McDonald's, dancing the hula, though a waiter at the Kahala Hilton restaurant did tell me that when Imelda Marcos came for lunch—she had her own personalized silver napkin ring—it was an awful lot of trouble. Security men had to be posted everywhere and local reporters came by to see what kind of shoes Imelda was wearing.

There were a lot of realtors, too, selling real estate to the Japanese, who were buying up the islands even faster than the native culture was disappearing. Every hotel had numerous courteous Japanese on the staff.

Much of the most desirable real estate the Japanese were buying was around Honolulu, within spitting distance of Pearl Harbor and the Arizona Monument. The sunken battleship, entombed in the waterborne shrine, preserved World War II in a plastic box; visitors, ferried out into the harbor to look at it, looked down fearfully and imagined the dead and dying, December 7, 1942, when the Japanese attacked Pearl Harbor. Dean Reed was four years old.

I got out the police file Mrs. Brown had given me, along with the coroner's autopsy report. These were the banal summaries of officialdom—the police and the forensic experts in Berlin—their brutal expressionless accounts of what had happened to a human being. It was labeled "The Final Report Concerning the Death Under Suspicious Circumstances of United States Citizen Dean Cyril Reed."

Taking into account the autopsy and the criminal investigation, so-called, the report stated that there was "no evidence of traumatic violence," "no evidentiary basis for suicide," that "the suspicion of crime has not been confirmed." Officials of the German Democratic Republic concluded: "It can be presumed that Dean Reed died by accidental drowning."

In the grim medical log that was the autopsy, the only anomaly was a reference to "so-called Canuto's trial cuts . . . in a typical place as can often be seen in cases of suicide." The cuts were very superficial, the report noted. Nothing conclusive.

Mrs. Brown was certain Dean's death was not a suicide. He had everything to live for: he was at the height of his career; he loved his wife; he was preparing his biggest movie role ever.

Before I left Hawaii, Ruth Anna Brown called to say that she wanted Leslie Woodhead to help her produce a television series about the Reed family; she had a sort of American *Upstairs, Downstairs* in mind. There wasn't much I could do in the way that she wanted me to, so I sent flowers by way of thanks for her time. She wrote to say that she had placed them on the Korean Peace Memorial in Hawaii in memory of her son, Dean Reed, the American singer who died in East Berlin.

She missed her son whose grave was on the other side of the world. So she made do by putting out flowers for him and communing with his spirit at a Korean shrine. But she failed to find the quarter he had won for racing a mule when he was seventeen.

4

"Dean did not kill himself," said Phil Everly when I met him in Burbank a week after I saw Ruth Anna Brown in Hawaii. "He was a good laugher and a guy that laughs does not kill himself," Everly added.

After Dean got to California in 1958, he not only got himself a recording contract, he got a screen test and a contract with Warner Brothers, where he studied to be a movie star. Among his new friends was Phil Everly of the Everly Brothers and, according to Ruth Anna Brown, they remained friends for life.

The day was bright and hot. Inside El Torito, a Mexican restaurant, it was dark and wonderfully cool. The maître d' had a moustache and a red vest. I whispered that we were waiting for Phil Everly and he smiled. "Of course," he said, "we know Señor Everly."

Leslie Woodhead was there; he was in California on business and, as a serious rock and roll guy, he wasn't going to pass up a chance to meet Phil. We watched through the window as outside Everly disembarked from a long, low powder-blue Cadillac with tail fins, and sauntered across the parking lot to the restaurant.

A handsome man with a thick shock of brown hair and a baby

face, he came through the door, removing his sunglasses as he walked slowly into the restaurant, ducking slightly to avoid the hanging plants. He looked around in a leisurely way, not because he expected anyone to pay particular attention to him, but because he was a man who moved slowly with that easy, hot-weather grace southerners often have. With him was a middle-aged man with a bald spot. They paused for a moment, conferring, squinting, canvassing the room.

Phil Everly took the center of the floor naturally and, star-struck, like teenagers, Leslie and I fumbled towards him.

Then Phil saw us. He smiled, walked forward, and stuck out his hand.

"Hi," he said, "I'm Phil Everly."

"Hi," said Leslie. "I'm Leslie Woodhead."

The nice man with the bald spot was Phil's friend, Joe. Once Joe had played bass for Phil. In Phil's company, he'd once met Dean Reed, which was why he was there, I guessed, or maybe he served as Phil's entourage. Joe sold real estate somewhere around Burbank.

Phil's had not been an easy phone number to come by, which had added to the anticipation. Getting it had required a couple of dozen phone calls back to London, to friends at the BBC, who once had made a documentary for *Arena* about the Everly Brothers and their reunion concert at the Albert Hall. On the phone, Phil Everly who had a sweet, southern wispy voice, had said he was seeing us just because he liked the guys from the BBC so much. He had had a nice time with them. He liked those English guys. But during the whole, long, boozy lunch that followed, Phil Everly never once mentioned the reunion concert. He never mentioned his brother, Don, either.

* * *

We settled, the four of us, in a booth towards the back and drank frozen margaritas out of huge glasses. Phil advised on certain dishes with the assurance and concern of an expert—this burrito or that quesadilla or whatever other fried, cheesy, spicy, tasty Mexican item that was a specialty of the house.

Phil was an easy talker, and he described how, in 1946, his folks, Ike and Margaret Everly, took their kids and left Tennessee for a better life, first in Chicago, then in California. Their two boys, Don and Phil, were already making records together. In the restaurant in Burbank, a song ran through my head: "Bye-bye, love. Bye-bye, happiness. Hello, loneliness."

As far back as 1957, the year they recorded "Wake Up Little Susie," Phil and Don were stars. But everyone wanted to be in movies. The studios, awed by the success of Elvis Presley on the big screen and terrified by television, which was a dirty word in Hollywood, grabbed at new talent wherever they could find it.

"We had signed with Warner Brothers Records," Phil said, blowing out smoke from a Marlboro. "And in the process, we also went to the Warner Brothers Drama School," he added and said it was where he met Dean.

"Dean was a real all-rounder. He could sing, he could act. I was a lousy actor." Phil laughed. "The acting class was taught by a man named Paton Price, and to know Dean you had to know about Paton Price. Paton was a real important guy for all of us," Phil said. "He taught us it didn't so much matter what your politics were so long as you used your art to further what you believed in. He was what you might call a life teacher," Phil added. "He was also a surrogate father for Dean who lived with him and his wife, Tillie, for a while. Tillie still lives here in Burbank."

Paton Price was a man of impeccable liberal credentials. Although Hollywood had been badly wounded by the anti-Communist witch-hunts of the early fifties, there remained a sturdy left-wing community of which Price was a mainstay. A pacifist, he had gone to jail during World War II. A fierce opponent of segregation and, later, of the Vietnam War, he was a deeply political man.

Anyway, clearly Paton Price was the first to influence Dean Reed's politics.

In the booth at El Torito, Phil Everly finished his drink and lit up another Marlboro.

"I was about as far away as you can get politically from Dean, I guess," Phil said. "He was a socialist and I'm a Reagan supporter. But it didn't matter. You could talk politics, you know? I respected Dean's political views because Dean had political views that he lived."

In interviews Dean Reed said he considered that the best part of his time in Hollywood was finding Paton Price, that because of Paton he acquired a life-long friend, and because of Paton he kept his integrity.

Price was dead by the time I started looking for people who knew Dean Reed. The only pictures I saw of him were in a filmed interview. He had a tense, intense, intelligent face, a high forehead and a goatee, but he was dying by then and you could see the skull beneath the skin.

He told his classes at Warner Brothers that you could not be a good artist unless you were a good human being. He told them that they had to dedicate their fame, if they were lucky enough to have fame, to make this world a better place to live in. Among his students, along with Dean and Phil Everly, were Jean Seberg, Don

Murray, the Smothers Brothers, and Dick Clark. Dick Clark, who had gone on to invent *American Bandstand*, one of the first rock and roll shows on TV, became a very rich man. I wondered what he thought about Dean now, if he thought of him at all, but I couldn't get hold of him.

In spite of Phil Everly's fond words about Paton Price, there were also those people I met over the months when I went looking for Dean who thought Price was a manipulative man, a mentor and teacher, but also a godfather who pulled Dean's strings.

At Warner Brothers, in his acting class, at his house, which was a kind of salon for his students, Price always undertook to preach his beliefs. Because of Paton's teachings, Dean turned down the chance to star in a TV show that was coming up then; it was called *Wanted Dead or Alive*. (There was some confusion over whether it was a show called *Killer Diller*, about a cowboy who would rather sing than fight, but most people thought it was *Wanted Dead or Alive*.) Dean did not want to carry a gun on screen; instead of Dean, a young unknown named Steve McQueen was cast.

On one occasion, when Dean was having trouble with his lines, Paton apparently told him he was having problems because he was sitting next to an attractive woman and both of them wondering what was under their clothes. Price made both of them strip naked and told them they could now both concentrate on putting some emotion into their acting. It embarrassed the hell out of Dean.

I remembered Dean's mother's bitter words: "Most often, in later years when Dean came on a visit to America, he stayed with Paton and Tillie in Burbank," she had said in Hawaii. "Paton had a lot of influence with Dean. Paton blamed me for the fact Dean was a virgin when he got to Hollywood. Well, just what in the world did he think I could do about that? I think what Paton taught him, was he taught him about sex."

I heard other versions—with Dean's life there were always other versions—about how Price asked Dean to do a love scene with Jean Seberg in class. About how Price felt Dean didn't know what to do and said to him, "You're a virgin, aren't you?" He took him to a brothel and got him the best prostitute, who was black. And afterwards the girl apparently said to Dean, "You're a natural." Or maybe that was only rumor.

Along with Paton Price and his lessons, there were other requirements for the students who were contract players at Warner Brothers. Dean learned to fence and act and wear nice clothes. He and the other kids worked as bit players and walk-ons. When big shots toured the studio, they posed with them. Movie magazines pictured them dressed to the nines, the girls in evening gowns with big skirts, the boys in white dinner jackets, all of them smiling and dancing at restaurants and nightclubs like Chasen's or the Brown Derby. Hollywood wallpaper.

In Hollywood, things were changing. A handsome young truck driver changed his name to Rock Hudson and became a big star, so it could happen to anyone. Universal produced movies made by Ross Hunter where the titles always seemed to appear on padded satin cushions and seemed always to feature Agnes Moorhead and Deborah Rush. On the screen, married couples slept in separate beds and starlets had their dresses glued to their breasts because a starlet was not permitted to show her cleavage, although she could show the mounds on either side. It was the 1950s. The Eisenhower Years.

Did you hear the one about the Eisenhower doll? people would say. You wind it up and it does nothing for eight years. But the country was prosperous, secure and confident, and scared. The McCarthy period had only just ended. Fear of Communism remained; people were actually literally scared of it, especially if they were Catholic. The Church actually instructed them to pray for the souls of the poor commie children. They probably would have worried less if they knew how Nikita Khrushchev felt when he visited California in 1959.

Forbidden to visit Disneyland, the Khrushchevs went to 20th Century Fox. There, they watched a rehearsal of *Can Can*, disapproved of it, and met the stars and starlets. Among them was Marilyn Monroe. Having learned a few words of Russian from Natalie Wood, Monroe shook Mr. Khrushchev's hand and whispered in his ear:

"We, the workers of 20th Century Fox, rejoice that you have come to visit our Studio and our Country."

As he flew out of Los Angeles, so the apocryphal story went, Khrushchev looked down and saw all the swimming pools.

"Now I know that Communism has failed," he said.

A year later, John F. Kennedy was elected President because, in a way, he looked like a movie star.

Phil Everly ordered another margarita. The smell of Phil's cigarette was drifting my way and I was dying for a smoke. Shaking out the pack, he offered me one. I confessed I had just given it up. Putting the cigarettes away in his pocket, Phil said, "You're crazy if you go back to it."

I played the scene in my head: "Want a cigarette?" someone would say to me. "No thanks," I'd reply. "Wow. You quit. How

40

did you manage?" In reply, I would cast my eyes down and raise my voice.

"You see," I would say, "it was Phil Everly who got me to quit. Of the Everly Brothers."

Phil was a great flirt. I was having a very good time. The margaritas kept coming. Phil was charming. He was smart. He was articulate. He was witty. He had been in the Marines and was a Republican and listened to right-wing talk radio; it was, in fact, the first time I had ever heard of Rush Limbaugh. I was trying to reconcile just how much I liked him with the way I felt about his politics, which only proved how narrow, snotty, and provincial New York liberals could be.

Leslie Woodhead had always loved Phil's music, too. He loved it in the way that Europeans have always loved America for its seeming glory days, for the open road, the neon and the motels and the diners, for Marilyn Monroe and cars with chrome and tail fins, and, most of all, for the music, the early sounds of rock and roll, Buddy Holly and Chuck Berry, Elvis, and the Everly Brothers. In a way it was the era that produced Dean Reed.

I knew that Phil had visited Dean in East Berlin and I asked what it was like.

"Dean couldn't go out of the house without being mobbed," Phil said. "Man, he was bigger than Elvis."

"Was he any good?"

Phil said, "You can't fool crowds that size, not anywhere."

"Big crowds?"

Phil smiled. "Everywhere he went and he looked great, he was in great shape and he could still walk on his hands. He was the same age as me and still doing that."

41

"So he made out OK over there?" I asked.

"If Dean was doing the same business over here, he'd have been a millionaire many times over," Phil said seriously. "I don't hold with socialism, but, hey, Dean put his money where his mouth was."

Lighting up, Phil exhaled more delicious smoke and sipped his drink. Across the table, Joe, the bass player who sold real estate, was listening hard.

"So who do you guys think killed Dean Reed?" Phil asked, and I realized it was the reason he had agreed to see us, to find out if we knew anything.

Leslie recited the usual litany: the KGB killed Dean because he was wanting to come home to America; the CIA killed Dean Reed because he wanted to come home and they didn't need another commie agitator; it was an accident as the official report said.

Leslie leaned forward. He was always brilliant at what I think John Mortimer once called the "fatal question," the zinger, the one that comes right at the end of an interview.

"Or suicide?" Leslie asked very casually.

Still, Phil wasn't buying it. "There's not a chance in hell that Dean would have committed suicide. A man that can't laugh, that's a man that kills himself," he said for the seond time that day as if saying it again would make us believe it. He had the feeling that, towards the end of his life, Dean did want to come home.

I said, "But he had his passport. He was a US citizen. It was easy. Why didn't Dean just pack up and come back?"

"What about 60 *Minutes*? They are pretty much on the left," Phil said.

"I don't understand. Do you mean *60 Minutes* had something to do with his death?" Leslie asked, but Phil just shook his head and his reticence grew.

"Let's have another drink," I said.

Phil said no thanks, but he added, "Dean was real big over there, though. A big star. You couldn't go into the street without the girls coming up to Dean for an autograph. It was the real thing."

Outside, the sunlight was blinding. Phil had to go back to work. He was making a new album. It was his best album yet, he thought.

In the parking lot, Phil and Joe shook our hands and smiled. We all said, "Keep in touch."

Shading our eyes from the hot California sun, we stood on the asphalt that shimmered with heat and said goodbye. Phil shook our hands again. He looked just like the boy who, with his brother, once upon a time, helped invent rock and roll.

Smiling, Phil Everly put on his sunglasses, climbed into the powder-blue Cadillac and drove away, waving bye-bye.

For a minute I didn't want to go at all, as if staying on in that parking lot with Phil Everly could keep any more time from passing.

5

Dean went south to Chile on a hunch, the way he raced the mule, the way he gave the bum on the road to Hollywood his extra pair of pants. Movement was everything and, like a conjurer's trick, it blurred the reality. Life was a stunt, a gamble, a race to get to the big time, to the finish line, to the party, wherever the party was. Fed up with Hollywood—later he would say it was, for him, "a time of exploitation, a time of fear, a prostitution camp"—he simply left. It was 1962.

He had heard that his record "Our Summer Romance" was a hit in Chile. He was fed up with getting nowhere, as he saw it, and figured he would set out on his own. Or maybe Dean was just plain restless, tired of being cast as a prop at Chasen's.

In February, 1962, when he was still a contract player at Warner's star school in Los Angeles and had a few hits on the provincial charts, he applied for a passport, stating he intended to depart from the US for South America at New York on March 9, 1962. Did he go from New York? Did he catch a plane? Did he, as might have been the case, hop in his Chevrolet Impala and head south, to Mexico first, or had he already been to Mexico?

It didn't really matter. What mattered was that he was on the road now, and though he came home to visit, he never actually lived in the United States again; for the next twenty-four years, Dean kept on moving.

His passport was issued at the beginning of March, and, like all American passports in those days, it was marked: "Not valid for travel in Albania, Cuba and those portions of China, Korea and Vietnam under Communist control."

On his application, Dean listed his hair as brown, although people sometimes referred to him as blond and in some photographs he appeared fair-haired. His eyes were green, it was stated, although they always looked blue; everyone said they were blue. His height, it was stated, was six feet one. This became an important detail in the mystery of his death because there was a discrepancy in his height on various documents, and some people said this meant he was not dead at all. But that came later.

Almost as soon as he got the passport, he left; he didn't tell his agent or his room-mate; he just packed up his bags and left the house. A few years later, he sent a postcard to Johnny Rose, his room-mate, saying Merry Christmas.

Dean arrived that spring in Chile, in Santiago, expecting a modest welcome, perhaps from the local DJs who were playing his tunes on the radio.

Viva Dean Reed! We want Dean!! Viva Dean!!!

The blue-eyed god had come down from the north, and when he opened the shutters of his hotel room that faced the Presidential Plaza in Santiago, he saw a sea of up-turned faces, or so the story went.

We want Dean!

Even when he closed the shutters, he could still hear the roar. There was a DJ at a Santiago radio station; his name was

Ricardo Garcia and although he dutifully plugged "Our Summer Romance" because the kids liked it, he did not think much of Dean's singing.

On the other hand . . . on the other hand, when Garcia saw Dean in the flesh, he knew Dean was hot. The looks were something else, Garcia thought. Dean was very, very sexy, what with the big hair and the big white teeth. His looks were his most important asset. He was as handsome as Robert Redford, and some people thought him a dead ringer for Kurt Russell. He had terrific presence on stage, and warmth, and some ineluctable adhesive compelling quality that drew people to him. You couldn't miss it.

"He was a naive *gringo*, who had come to 'do' Latin America," Garcia said. Like a character from a movie musical, Dean was called *The Magnificent Gringo*.

I pieced most of the story of Dean in South America together from scraps. I never made it to South America. By the time I went looking for Dean Reed in late 1987 and 1988, the obsession, for me, was with the East. The Soviet monolith was breaking up and this was the hottest story of the second half of the century. Cracking like ice in the spring, I thought, but it was the wrong metaphor.

Rather, it seemed as if, beyond the Berlin Wall, for decades Darth Vadar had ruled, evil, unknown, shuttered. Suddenly, you could look. Lift the visor and see inside. Every other feature story coming out of the USSR was about some underground rock band, or a concert, or a club. In the end, for the most part, the Soviets had not wanted to nuke us; they just wanted to listen to our music.

Any drama-documentary about Dean would inevitably focus on the Soviet Union and Berlin, the East, and the Cold War. I was in pursuit, after all, of the man who brought rock and roll to Russia. South America felt like a sideshow.

But there were plenty of people who remembered the South American Dean. By now I was plugged into a weird little network of people who had known Dean and who, energized by news of his death, sprang into life, electric with information or memories.

I must have talked to a dozen of Dean's rememberers around that time, people hoarding their rich titbits of fact, tiny articles of faith, improbable fantasies blurred by memory. All of it added up to a kind of epic South American Dean: the sheer verve of his leaving home and heading south; his sudden coming into stardom; the gilded looks which people recalled; the political awakening, its naiveté, its bravery.

Chilean expatriates in New York remembered Dean's beauty as they mourned their beautiful country; an Argentine woman I encountered in a Los Angeles restaurant thought of Dean as perfectly *raffiné*; Marcello, a New York waiter who had once worked in a Buenos Aires television studio had seen Dean perform. Marcello had contacts in Miami who knew Dean and he gave me their addresses, but nothing much came of this.

Fired up by contact with the star, they all possessed a kind of fatal attraction for one another. Every now and again, as news of our drama-documentary was passed along, the phone would ring and a friend of Dean's, or a relative, or a witness to the life checked in with stories, information, with a covert agenda, a mysterious whisper, a crackle of excitement. The most fabulous witness to the South American years, though, was a Czech countess.

"I knew Dean Reed." A throaty voice inserted itself into my telephone.

It belonged to the Countess Nyta de Val. At the time I met her, in early 1988, the Countess was a *chanteuse* in the nightclub on board the Greek cruise ship *Eugenia Costa*. In the video she sent me of her act she wore a skin-tight beaded gown. She sang in French. She claimed to have known Dean in South America and she wanted to talk. She lived in Florida, but she was on her way to London—to see her publishers, to set up her cabaret act—it wasn't clear, but I was headed for London, too. I was on my way to Moscow and there were still no direct flights from the US.

I met the Countess at the Gallery Rendezvous, a Chinese restaurant in Soho, where there was a picture of Mick Jagger in the window.

The Countess ate spareribs and said she had made Dean Reed a star. She was a cabaret star herself, she said, a well-known *chanteuse*, and her contacts in Hollywood had brought him south. In another version, she met Dean in a hotel lobby in Buenos Aires where he was having trouble making himself understood and she helped him out. She saw he had a guitar and had him play for her and felt that, though he wasn't very good, his looks would make him a star.

About a year after "Our Summer Romance" went to the top of the Chilean charts, the Countess also noted, Dean Reed beat Elvis Presley in the South American Hit Parade poll, 29,330 to 20,805. Nyta de Val was very sure about all this; eventually, I found some newspaper clippings that supported the figures.

An imposing woman of a certain age, the Countess wore a leather skirt as voluminous as a sofa. Her head was tied up in a silk scarf and a hat sat flat on top of it like a pancake on an egg cozy. She wore several pairs of eyelashes and, as she handed me a photograph, she lowered them with the demure moue of a sixteen-year-old coquette. In the picture, she was on a beach in a bikini. She had a great figure. Dean was with her, and his body was great, too: young, lean, and lithe.

"We were lovers," she said. "Women wanted him, but the men were not jealous. He played the nightclubs, he played the stadium. All his singles went to number one. He wore a light-blue . . . how do you call this Italian fabric? I got it made for him, I brought the tailor," she said. "Gabardine! A gabardine suit the color of the sky, very tight pants and he was beautiful," added the Countess, and ate another sparerib.

In South America, Dean also got politics, which made the Countess unhappy. He saw the writing on the wall and it said: YANKEE GO HOME, sometimes literally. He was shocked. Like most Americans, in finding out he was not universally loved, he was hurt. It was his first exposure to what American imperialism had borne in South America.

"I saw poor people crawling on their bellies with their last little bit of something for the church," Dean would say.

He began to read. He wrote to Paton Price and Paton wrote him back, and Dean remembered the things Paton had taught and he set out to dedicate his fame. He wanted to save the world.

"South America changed my life because, of course, there, one can see the great differences of justice and injustice, or poverty and wealth," Dean said in an interview for *American Rebel*, a documentary about his life. "They are so clear to see for anybody that you must take a stand. I was not a capitalist, nor was I blind. And there I became a revolutionary."

In the same film, Cyril Reed said, "He was a normal American boy. And he went to South America. There he saw that ten or fifteen percent of the people were very wealthy, and the great majority of them were at the low end of the totem pole. It was there he began to get, not communistic, but socialistic ideas. There's a difference. Don't ask me what it is. But he can take ten or fifteen minutes and he'll tell you the difference. He did that to me once, but I forgot most of it." Which perhaps told you as much about Cyril's attitude towards his son as what his son felt about the world.

Heady times in South America, with revolution in the air. Already a sex symbol, when Dean acquired a political agenda he was unstoppable.

Within weeks of his arrival in Chile, he took out advertisements in the newspapers, urging Chileans who opposed atomic testing to write to President Kennedy. When he set out for a tour of northern Chile and Peru, the American Embassy told him his actions might be contrary to the best interests of the United States.

Dean also noted that he was an admirer of Mahatma Gandhi, Bertrand Russell, and Linus Pauling, that he was opposed to warfare and military service, and had been a conscientious objector since the age of eighteen. He announced that his friends at home were planning to sue Secretary of State Dean Rusk because of the unconstitutional attempts in Lima to suppress his, Dean's, freedom of speech.

From Hollywood, Dean's friends duly sent a telegram to the State Department, expressing outrage at Dean's treatment, and it was signed by several of Paton Price's students and by David Dellinger, who later became famous as a member of the "Chicago Eight."

Dean did not cancel his tour, of course. Every time he was opposed, whenever he realized that the State Department had taken an interest in him, it charged him up: this wasn't just the movies, this had the smack of real adventure. It was always high noon in Dean's South America.

"He was an idealist," said the Countess. "You could fool Dean easily. But he could get to 5000 workers and tell them how to vote. He was a sincere man. Not like that fat little Allende, who used to wash his hands every time he met the miners." The Countess spat when she mentioned Salvador Allende's name.

South America, for three or four years in the 1960s, was Dean's coming of age. Professionally, it made him a star. He appeared on television in Lima; with a troupe of "Twisters," he performed at the Astral Theatre. Roaming the continent, he gathered a following. Fans adored him for his music and his politics. The times were ripe in Latin America, what with the young Fidel in Cuba and Che only just dead, his handsome death mask imprinted on everyone's brain.

In Chile Dean met the poet Pablo Neruda and the folksinger Victor Jara. They accepted Dean, even though he was a gringo. At last, Dean had found a community.

It was more than a little ironic, because Jara's folk-song movement was intended to fight the tide of American culture that poured down like shit on Chile, as Jara saw it. Chile was a dumping ground for singers who couldn't cut it up north. So long as the pop stars had fair hair and tight pants, the girls went mad for the singing *gringos*.

Dean separated himself from the pack; he cast himself as a political man and he had a genius for the rhetoric probably because he was now a true believer. He picketed embassies and sang for the workers; he went up the Amazon with his Indian comrades.

People went to his concerts even if they didn't agree with his politics. At his concerts he could get away with anything, even the slogans, and people ate it up because he was so handsome, so charming, and because he was an American and a good guy.

For Dean, life had meaning: he saw himself as an emissary, as an ambassador of peace, and he said so to anyone who would listen. Now he was no longer just a dumb pretty boy out of some Hollywood studio; he was a man to reckon with. The South American experience became a theme he played out the whole of his life.

The political limelight did for him what cameras did for other stars: it lit him up; it turned him on; it made him shine. It was the making of Dean, and the more he fought the good fight, the more famous it made him and the fame fed the ambition and there was no stopping him.

And there was Patty, the girl he had met at his agent's office in Hollywood. In 1963, they were married in Mexico City. I saw a picture of her, a very pretty girl in a dress with a big skirt. They had a daughter they named Ramona. Many years later, Dean apparently told a friend that not making the marriage with Patty work was the biggest regret of his life. He always sent money for Ramona when he could. By 1964, Dean and Patty were living in a handsome suburban villa in Buenos Aires, where Dean had his own TV show.

It was a charmed life for a while, but then right-wing gangs shot up the house and someone smeared a hammer and sickle in red paint on his garage door. Dean and Patty got guns. He became increasingly radical.

"Brainwashed," said the Countess, finishing her lunch in the Chinese restaurant in London. She straightened her hat.

"Who brainwashed him?" I was exasperated by now, trying to follow her anecdotes of the years in South America, trying to fit it all together.

"I sent him to Russia," she said. "I was a little bit afraid of how he was going left, left, left, and this scared the wits out of me because being Czechoslovakian, having spent some time in the Soviet paradise, I was not exactly very leftist . . . I admired this beautiful child with all these gorgeous ideas about the world. But I did not like that going left. So I said the only way to prove to him how absolutely wrong he was was to send him to Russia."

The Countess's story rambled. She reported rumors about bank accounts and Porsches that Dean received in exchange for errands he did for the East German Politburo. Chasing Dean Reed, I thought, was like chasing smoke. The Countess was convinced the Communists killed him.

"He knew too much. Over there in the East it is like the Mafia. Once you were in, you could never get out," she said.

As she saw it, Dean was a *Manchurian Candidate*, run, turned, used, a traitor but a victim, too. Having eaten all the spareribs, and turning to the fortune cookies, the Countess started on a tale about an out-of-body experience in which she met her dead father, who told her where the Czech government treasure was buried.

In London, around the same time that I met the Countess, I also met Artemy Troitsky. A friend called and asked if I wanted to meet a rock critic from Moscow. We agreed to meet at Tui, a Thai restaurant in South Kensington.

Troitsky was a Soviet rock critic with half an inch of stubble on his handsome jaw. He was traveling in Britain to help promote *Back in the USSR*, his book about Soviet rock.

Troitsky had a cold. He ate his lemongrass soup and blew his nose. It was his first trip to the West. He was my first real Russian. He said his Western name was Art. Wearing black jeans and sweater, an olive green T-shirt and jacket, and a new pair of sneakers, Troitsky had walked that morning from Bloomsbury to Chelsea. His feet hurt.

In the beginning the two of us made the sort of chitchat that seemed appropriate in those first heady days of *glasnost*. Art's favorite writers were Gogol and Cervantes, although when he was younger he read Kurt Vonnegut and J. D. Salinger. *Catcher in the Rye* was Art's favorite book. In Prague, where he grew up—his father worked there as a journalist—he wore a yellow hat with a peaked brim because he could not get a red hunter's cap like Holden Caulfield's.

In 1963, around the time Dean Reed was already crooning his heart out in Santiago in the pale-blue gabardine suit, Troitsky heard "Surfin' USA." It was the first rock and roll record he ever heard, and because he could not find "surfin" in his English dictionary, he figured it was some kind of dirty word. "Like fucking," he said. "I thought this meant fucking." He was eight years old.

"I only believe in rock and roll and John Lennon," he said now in a way that managed to be both solemn and ironic.

In London, Art spent most of his time going to gigs, sometimes three in one night. Johnny Rotten was fantastic, he said. At the Limelight he heard Pop Will Eat Itself. "They were very good." Art's green eyes shone. "I had a great time. I almost ate myself."

I asked if he had been shopping, but he said that he didn't like shopping much.

"I do have a long list from my wife, Svetlana. She wants a

sunlamp and a riding costume from . . ." He consulted a piece of paper. "Moss Bros. Svetlana is not allowed out of the Soviet Union at the same time as me. She is a hostage," Art said.

There was an uneasy silence while we ate some spicy squid salad and drank more cold Thai beer.

"You know, we have had in Moscow an American singer named Dean Martin," Art said.

Art had very nice manners and this was his first trip to the West, so I supposed he was trying to make an American connection for my sake.

"Dean Martin," I said. "Really?"

"Dean Reed, I mean," he said. "I mean Dean Reed."

"Dean Reed? You knew him? You saw him? Where? Tell me!" I was so excited I knocked a beer into my lap. "Tell me everything!"

But Troitsky just blew his nose again.

"Come to Moscow," he said. "I can introduce you to his interpreter, Oleg. Oleg Smirnoff. Also there is the best friend of Dean's girlfriend. His girlfriend killed herself when Dean Reed died. Big breasts. Very big." Art tugged unsuccessfully at the front of his black pullover.

My head was spinning. There were people in Moscow who had known Dean, people I could meet, a girlfriend, an interpreter.

"Come to Moscow," he repeated.

I said I was coming.

Two

6

February 1, 1988. It was my first night in Moscow. I had followed Dean Reed to the East, to the place that seduced him. As soon as I saw it, saw Red Square, saw the scale, the otherness, I was surprised, excited, elated just being here. Maybe he was, too. Maybe Dean looked at Red Square and thought, Wow!

Off the plane from London we came, Leslie Woodhead and I and our friend Jo Durden-Smith, another journalist. Even years later, looking at my notes, I could absolutely recapture how thrilling it was. All of it seemed exotic: lousy Sheremetyevo Airport with half the lights out; the sudden appearance of an official tourist rep who seemed to know my name but not those of the others; and the ride along the grim endless road into the city with the stark monument to mark how close the Germans had got; the long straight road from the airport that turned into the shabby grandeur of Gorky Street which then exploded into Red Square. And finally, the arrival at the National Hotel where, from the balcony of room 101, Lenin spoke to the masses below.

There was a tingle, a faint sense of danger, which was crazy, of course. I traveled as a tourist with a tourist visa and I had a return ticket, but for me, this had the enticing whiff of the forbidden. I was an American, after all, as Leslie and Jo never failed to point out, joking about how I must be shaking in my capitalist boots. I had grown up with the Soviet Union as the Other, the Evil Empire, the place from which the missiles that would kill us all would be launched. I remembered the Cuban Missile Crisis, I was a kid when my father, terrified, had said he planned to move some money to a bank in some remote rural part of New York State.

Ambivalent, too. I'd also grown up among people in Greenwich Village who, when they were young, idealized the USSR and had been in the Communist Party; many had seen the USSR only through the rosy tint of those ideological glasses. In every way I was astonished to be here, especially that first night.

That first trip to Moscow changed all our lives, one way and another, mine and Leslie's and especially Jo's. That first night late, after we checked into the National Hotel, we sat in the main restaurant of the hotel. From another room came the sounds of a private party, laughter, balalaika music, ice on glasses.

Through the lace curtains in the window, we watched the snow coming down on Menezh Square. The snow mixed with the patterns of the lace. Red Square was just visible, so were the Kremlin walls and the gold onions on St. Basil's, all magical in the snow. Somehow I had envisioned the Kremlin as a grim fortress, not a place where behind brick walls were exquisite yellow stucco walls and ranks of gold domes.

At midnight, we went out and walked, freezing, over to Red Square. It was enormous, vast, eternal, with enough space for whole armies to parade—it was the most satisfying public square I'd ever seen, bigger than you expected and much more beautiful. In front of Lenin's tomb, in front of the massive red granite box where he lay, the guards were on duty, goose-stepping through the night, and, in the distance, pinkish puffs of frozen smoke rose from a power plant near the river.

"Suddenly, in one of the Helsinki parks I see a young man singing, his cowboy hat on the ground. When he finishes, I go up to him and introduce myself. He says that he is Dean Reed. To me that meant nothing."

In Moscow, the day after I arrived, Nikolai Pastoukhov told me how he first met Dean in Helsinki in 1965.

Although the Countess had said she sent Dean to Moscow because she was afraid of his going "Left Left Left," Pastoukhov said it was because he, Pastoukhov, encountered Dean in a Helsinki park during a World Peace Conference in 1965. Everyone had a version, everyone wanted to somehow own Dean Reed.

I had followed Dean to Moscow and now to the offices of the agricultural newspaper *Pravda Selskaya Shizn*, which translates roughly as *Pravda Country Life*, where Nikolai Pastoukhov was the editor. Pastoukhov—he sometimes thought of himself in the third person—had been bored out of his skull at the conference. The conference was dull. The women looked like dogs. The Chinese were contentious and intractable. The speeches were incessant. Which was why Pastoukhov escaped for a smoke.

Strolling in the park, smoking, he ogled the pretty girls in their miniskirts. Right up to their asses, he thought, and tried not to get too excited about this vision of Western pulchritude. Still, it was part of his job, observing life around him; he was a journalist.

Suddenly, Pastoukhov's attention was diverted by the sound of music. A little group had gathered and at its center was a handsome young man with a fine head of thick hair, playing the guitar, his hat on the ground. He was working for money to get a ticket back to Argentina, he said. But he was not an Argentine. He was an American. His name, he said, was Dean Reed.

Stamping out his smoke, Pastoukhov looked the American over. God, he thought, the American had the little group in the park eating out of his hand.

In those days in the mid-1960s, Soviet officials were on the lookout for acceptable entertainers to pacify the Soviet kids and prevent their wholesale defection to the decadent music of the West. (Damn Bittles! Pastoukhov thought, as he often did, for Beatlemania had swept the Soviet Union.) Here was this handsome American with a real cowboy hat, plucking his guitar, singing peace songs. Pastoukhov had a little talk with the young man who, to his wonderment, espoused peace and love and the socialist cause. This was the jackpot! Bingo, he thought, or the Soviet equivalent.

"Come with me, Dean Reed," he said.

That evening at the hall where the peace conference was in progress, Pastoukhov pushed Dean on to the platform and introduced him to the delegates in the packed room.

"Here is new blood come to us with the peace movement from America," Pastoukhov said.

Dean Reed began to play. Pastoukhov stood in the wings and watched, holding his breath. When Dean played the World Peace Congress in Helsinki, things were a mess: the Master of Ceremonies, a doddering old Finn, was hysterical; Bertrand Russell had failed to show; Bertrand Russell's secretary, who was there, took up the Chinese line, which was that you could not talk World Peace until there was World Revolution.

"Bullshit," the Soviets cried.

"Bullshit," thought Pastoukhov, bored to death with this idiotic babble and desiring only a cigarette.

"Stop him! Stop him!" some people yelled at Bertrand Russell's man.

"Let him speak," others shouted.

Pastoukhov said, "There was almost a fistfight starting. And he jumps on to the podium with his guitar and starts singing for us. OK. And I am thinking it would be so good for him to come to us in Moscow."

Maybe Dean looked out into the sea of angry faces, maybe he listened to the contentious voices and escalating fury, and thought: I can make a difference; I can make the difference between war and peace; I can make people touch each other. He was twenty-seven.

He picked up his guitar and sang "Marianna." He sang cowboy songs and he sang something that to Pastoukhov, at least, sounded a lot like rock and roll.

From the podium Dean greeted the delegates—the Westerners in jeans, the chubby Chinese in Mao jackets, the dewlapped Soviets, their chests webbed with war medals, the East Germans in gray leather shoes, and he made them sing. He told them to hold hands. He told them they had to hold hands, even if the girl sitting next to them was lousy looking—this was how Pastoukhov reported it—they had to hold hands and sing.

When that wasn't enough to liven things up, Dean leapt off the stage, climbing over the delegates' legs, striding down the aisles. He made them *hold hands*! The delegates started smiling. They laughed and sang along with the crazy American. Dean roamed the hall some more, then he bounded back on to the stage, picked up his guitar, and, with everyone holding hands,

Soviets, Chinese, Africans in their fancy robes and little caps, they all sang "We Shall Overcome."

In the wings, Nikolai Pastoukhov grinned his delirious grin; he knew a good thing when he saw it.

"Come with me, Dean Reed," he said. And by nightfall, Dean Reed was on the train from Helsinki to Leningrad.

With Pastoukhov, he traveled in a private compartment that belonged to the Deputy Premier of the Soviet Union. Deputy Tikhonov was a celebrated poet and he greeted Dean as a fellow artist. Through the June night, Tikhonov read his poems aloud and Dean played his guitar—you could just hear him singing the "Midnight Special." Pete Seeger had toured the Soviet Union to great acclaim a few years earlier and his American folk music was held in high esteem.

I liked to imagine that they sat in an opulent old-fashioned railway carriage with red plush seats and antimacassars, and a gleaming samovar. Toasts were made. Outside the cornfields sped by forests of white birches. Pastoukhov remembered it like a scene from a Russian novel, from Tolstoy perhaps.

At Leningrad the train pulled into the Finland Station. Pastoukhov took Dean to the Astoria Hotel for lunch. There was a jazz band in the restaurant and he asked Dean to sing. It was a kind of audition and Dean sang his heart out, and the audience fell in love with the young American. Bingo! thought Pastoukhov for the second time.

Dean's final conversion to the East began on that stage at Helsinki. Perhaps he *was* an official delegate from Argentina. Maybe the Countess's version—that she had sent him—was partly true; maybe not. Maybe Pastoukhov's tale of the pick-up in the park was a bit of embroidery. Who could tell?

Finishing his tale, in his Moscow office, Nikolai Pastoukhov leaned back in his chair and puffed on his cigarette. He was past seventy now, but vigorous and canny. Cigarette ash tumbled down the florid, flowered tie that covered half of his dark-purple shirt that was the color of grape juice.

In Pastoukhov's office, there was neither a typewriter nor a note pad, only a bank of plastic telephones with blank faces and a row of Christmas cards on a shelf bereft of books.

Pastoukhov dropped the butt from his cigarette into an ashtray and lit up again, his mouth pulling in smoke between the huge jowls, like a friendly hound enjoying a smoke. Like every Russian I met, he had real narrative talent. Still wrapped up in the tales of his discovery of Dean Reed in a Helsinki park in 1965, he gave those old jowls a good shake.

"*Deanrid!*" He said it as a single word, the way Russians often did, as though it might have been a slogan or a product, the way you might say Kleenex! or Communism!

"*Deanrid!*"

Nikolai Pastoukhov was restless. I asked about the rest of Dean's career, but because he had played no part in it, he was not interested and he waved the question away with an impatient gesture.

"Yes, yes, he traveled a lot," Pastoukhov said. "He left South America and went to live in Italy, then to Berlin. He settled in Berlin because he met a woman."

I asked about the death.

"Officially, he drowned. But he was a very good swimmer. How did it happen? I don't know. Maybe provocation. The American press calls him the "Kremlin agent" or the "notorious Communist." He annoys the Americans."

Glee engulfed Pastoukhov's features. He winked. Then he fixed his face in a somber expression more appropriate to official grief.

"I was shocked when I received the sad news of his death. He was very young, very handsome. He was the first friend from the West. He talked about peace and friendship; we were very much impressed. He visited Siberia; he said his visit recollected his native Colorado in the United States. He liked to make out autographs, to be mixed with girls. But I think he had no time for this sexual business. He is good boy. Look."

Rummaging in his *perhaps bag*—you never knew when there might be a sudden special on bananas or socks in Moscow, so you always needed a bag ready—he pulled out a photograph album. Pastoukhov pushed an old magazine cover with a picture of Dean under my nose. He said, "Dean has written here: 'To my lovely papa from his son, *Deanrid*.' Always he calls me papa, because I gave him birth here in Soviet Union," added Pastoukhov, who leaned back in his chair again and this time rubbed his eyes.

The old eyes filled up, though whether this was from affection, self-pity, or cigarette smoke was hard to tell.

Chasing Dean Reed was like scrambling through tangled webs spun by those who adored him and wanted to protect him, and there were plenty of them: lover, mother, daughter, father, son.

"He called me his second mama," older women said. "I was his second papa," said some of the men, and when I met an American journalist who once interviewed Dean Reed, she said, "I never slept with him, of course. We were just friends." But I hadn't even asked.

They were enchanted because he was so alive, because, if he was always on the make, it was usually in pursuit of love—theirs,

the fans', the world's—it didn't matter. As a result, all these papas
and mamas and lovers wanted nothing to do with the dark side of
Dean Reed, but only to keep his memory intact. For them he was
like a figure in a plastic snow globe from a long ago holiday; you
could take it out and shake it whenever you wanted to remember
how wonderful it all once was.

Pastoukhov's assistant arrived to show me out. A man in a suit
and sneakers, he spoke exquisite French and looked exactly like
Klaus Maria Brandauer. I said so, meaning it as a compliment, but
he looked crestfallen.

"What about Charles Bronson? Everyone says I look just like
Charles Bronson," he said.

As I was pulling on my coat, my mother's ancient mink I'd
brought to Moscow for warmth, Pastoukhov eyed it appreciatively.

He said, "I remember America very fondly. Americans come
here. We go to America. We traveled up and down Mississippi
River."

"What year was that?"

"1978? 1979?" he said. "So, you like this *glasnost*?"

"Oh, yes. Isn't it wonderful?" I said. "Isn't it amazing. Wouldn't
Dean Reed have loved it . . . it's great!"

He shrugged doggily. "1978, that was real *détente*," he said.

For a moment Pastoukhov looked thoughtful. He opened his
mouth as if to reveal something, some fact about Dean Reed,
some hard nugget of evidence, but he shut it; his journalist's heart
no longer stirred and, anyway, the next morning he was starting
a skiing holiday with his girlfriend. We shook hands. We
exchanged addresses.

"So maybe I will visit the United States. I will stay in your
house, OK?" Pastoukhov said and bellowed with laughter so that

his hound-dog jowls shook again and ash from his cigarette toppled on to his tie one more time.

In the lobby of the newspaper building, on a wooden bench, people sat waiting for appointments, their boots dripping snow that turned into puddles on the floor. Over the sound system, Dave Brubeck played "Take Five." On a tiny television propped on a wobbly table, the security guard on duty wearing rough wool mittens watched blurry images of Mikhail Gorbachev talking to people in the street.

7

Dean Reed was twenty-eight when he stepped into the center of the stage at Moscow's Variety Theater in 1966. He sang like crazy for the audience: folk songs, ballads, Latin American songs he learned in Chile, show tunes—"Maria" was a big favorite in Russia—some of his own antiwar songs. He could sing "The Twist," he moved like a rock and roller; he crooned Beethoven's "Ode to Joy" like a pop tune.

Some in the audience had perhaps seen other Americans perform, Pete Seeger, perhaps, or, if they were old enough, Paul Robeson. But no one in Moscow had ever seen anything quite like Dean Reed. It was electric. He was so vital, so handsome, so rock and roll. For an encore, Dean sang "Ghost Riders in the Sky" and it became his signature tune in Russia.

At the end of the concert, the audience cheered, clapped, whistled, and stamped their feet for twenty-five minutes.

In reporting performances, *Pravda* noted that Dean Reed "left his country as a sign of protest against the unjust war in Vietnam." Posters all over Moscow announcing the performances showed that he was gorgeous and played the guitar and hinted at an "exotic" biography. He had a recording contract with Melodiya, the state recording company, which had never before issued a rock and roll record; he got a tour. It was such big news that even the *New York Times* got wind of it, which was pretty rare in those days for a Western newspaper. On page forty-seven of the *New York Times* on November 28, 1966, it was reported that an American singer was loudly cheered at a Moscow theater.

In the Soviet Union, Dean's official minder was Georgy Arbatov, the director of the Institute for Canada and the United States, and an influential player in Soviet–American policy. I went to see Arbatov, who was a pleasant man in a good suit with a benign face and an avuncular manner. His office was elegant, with a long conference table that shone with polish. A picture of Gorbachev hung on the wall. Through a translator, Arbatov spoke about Dean Reed, and how he was for the Soviets like the Beatles, and how important it had been, his coming.

Until Dean came along, though Arbatov did not spell this out, Russian kids mostly had to settle for folksongs celebrating tractor production or maybe for mustachioed pop stars with plastic smiles. Once in a while a foreign folkie like Pete Seeger might show up. There had been a time when Soviet bureaucrats had tried to offer a bit of modern culture to the kids; somewhere along the line, apparatchiks tried to replace the Twist with new dances for socialist youth. The *Moskvich*, the *Terrikon*, and the *Herringbon* were not a success.

Georgy Arbatov told me that he was convinced the KGB had not killed Dean Reed.

"I know that the KGB had already decided a long time before Dean's death not to interfere in this way, not to practice any terrorist activities," he said. An accident, Arbatov suggested, perhaps Dean's death had been an accident.

What he was saying hit me only after I'd left Arbatov's office, a kind of delayed shock. I wasn't exactly tuned into the activities of the world of covert activity, so only when I was walking through the snow in Moscow did I realize that "terrorist activities" meant state assassination. No longer practiced at this time, Arbatov had said, meaning, of course, it had been practiced and perhaps not so long ago; Arbatov could refer to it casually in the middle of a conversation about Dean Reed and the Beatles and rock and roll. I shivered. My feet were wet. It was freezing out.

No one in Russia had cared who was in charge of Dean, of course, not when he arrived. The lust for Western culture was huge but undiscriminating, and nobody cared if Dean Reed was run, as someone said, by the Communist Party or the Soviet cosmonauts, or a monkey.

Dean's arrival in the Soviet Union had the verve, the heroics, the aspirations of his conquest of South America all over again. Although he would continue to live with Patty in Argentina for a while, then move on to Madrid and to Rome, he went back to the USSR again and again, tempted by the adoration the Russians gave him, seduced by the feeling that he mattered so much.

On his first tour of the Soviet Union, Dean played twenty-eight cities and he sang "Yiddishe Momma" to a little old lady with a round face. Again and again, he went to Russia to record, for concerts, as a peace delegate. He made rock videos, after a fashion: Dean riding his motorbike; Dean clowning in parks, on riverboats, singing "Yesterday" and "Heartbreak Hotel." Everyone I ever met in the Soviet Union remembered Dean. He was as big as Frank Sinatra, people said.

On *Go for It, Boys*, a televised competition in which young men vied in several categories for the title of "Most Macho Male," Dean appeared as the celebrity host.

And Dean Reed was impressed with what he saw in the Soviet Union. He spoke with the comrades on long plane trips across the country—pictures show his face wreathed in smiles under the big fur hat. He studied Marxism-Leninism. A little boy gave Dean his Pioneer's badge.

There were people everywhere who had met Dean and kept his autograph or his pictures. One of them was named Sasha Gurman. He was from Tblisi and I met him about a year after I went to Moscow, met him in Beverly Hills of all places, on a balmy winter night. He had thick wavy hair and impish eyes, and he was sexy, like a magician, which in a way he was. He was an interpreter, the sort who gets not just the words, but the subtle magic of language. *Glasnost* had come to Hollywood in the form of Elem Kilmov, the Soviet film director, and Roland Joffé was giving a dinner for him. Sasha had come to translate.

The sky was a rich tuxedo blue that night, the stars were out, and Beverly Hills was sleek and lush. Drinking it all in, Sasha inspected the crowd on the patio at Roland Joffé's house, where he, a kind of vigorous human sputnik spun off by *Glasnost*, had put down for the evening.

Ah, *Glasnost*! It was the fashion in the late 1980s, even in Hollywood. Elem Klimov gave me a button with Gorbachev's face on it. Roland raised his glass.

"We may not share our politics, but we have to share our planet," Roland Joffé said. (A Russian taxi driver in Los Angeles was more skeptical and when I asked what he thought about Gorby, he shrugged and said, "Same studio, different head.")

Anyway, I cornered Sasha Gurman and said, as I did to every Soviet I met, "Did you hear of Dean Reed?"

"Ah, Dean Reed," Sasha said, and he told me a story.

When he was seven, Sasha's mother asked what he wanted for his birthday. I want to see Dean Reed, he said, and his mother took him to a concert in Tblisi.

The American singing star, was particularly big in Georgia, where his picture was sold alongside that of Joseph Stalin. At the concert, Sasha was taken up on the stage to meet Dean; the singer shook hands with the little boy and then he did one of his stunts: the big, handsome blue-eyed American flipped the child head over heels. He laughed. Then he kissed Sasha and gave him an autographed picture.

For years, Sasha kept the picture of Dean Reed in his school notebook next to a picture of Lenin. By the time Sasha was a teenager, the notebook had come apart but he kept it, the photograph.

In the late 1970s, his mother took him to East Berlin for a holiday. They climbed the television tower at the Alexanderplatz. Sasha looked out. He craned his neck so that he could see over the Wall into West Berlin, where he noted there was enough electricity to fuel a small African nation, enough neon lights to power up his dreams.

He imagined a world populated by tall, blue-eyed American cowboys like Dean Reed who gave little kids a hug and sang them rock and roll.

"That's for me," Sasha said.

8

Back at the National Hotel, after my meetings with Pastoukhov and Arbatov, I looked out the window of my room at a drainpipe. I then went downstairs to the front desk, where a woman who wore two cardigans and spoke soft, old-fashioned English did not smile at me. I asked her for a different room. She told me that, as I was not a head of delegation, I was not entitled to a Class A room. Leslie Woodhead had somehow been anointed as head of our delegation and he had a suite with a view and cranberry-colored velvet drapes.

"But, you see, this is my first trip to your country," I said. "I really want a room with a view of RED SQUARE!"

All around me in the lobby of Moscow's best hotel, tourists shuffled across an expanse of turd-colored linoleum, looking for something to buy. There was nothing in the souvenir shop except wooden dollies, vodka, and crappy fur hats. At the front door, men who resembled Leonid Brezhnev barred the way to Soviet citizens, admitting only foreigners who showed the slab of cardboard that served for a passport to the National.

"Here you may want," said the woman in the two cardigans, "but here you may not necessarily get."

"They have a plan for you," said Art Troitsky, who turned up to meet us at the hotel with his wife Svetlana. Art was chic in the casual black clothing he purchased in Tallinn's street markets, where you could get Western goods. Svetlana was over six feet tall and wore elegant Italian boots. They were so stylish, so foreign-looking that the doorman at the National simply let them in most of the time. Once, though, they had to wait for me to come and get them and they hated it.

Svetlana Kunetsina was twenty-eight and you could just still see where the tall, gawky teenager had evolved into this butterfly. She had beautiful manners, she was a passionate feminist, itself a rebellion in a country so brutal towards its women it was enough just to survive; and she was systemically incapable of being on the take, which amounted to a kind of dysfunction in Moscow.

This made her different from everyone else. To some it made her seem haughty. Westerners loved her. Every Westerner who met Svetlana fell for her, perhaps because she was so un-Russian. Or maybe it was just her legs.

In the hotel, she removed her coat and gave it to the woman in the cloakroom. Svetlana was wearing a shocking pink Gianfranco Ferre suit with a miniskirt and the thigh-high boots. Because she was a fashion journalist, she knew how to get designer clothes in various markets, or how to have them copied; sometimes she found vintage couture clothes and remade them.

We went to the ground-floor restaurant, where most of the things on the menu were unavailable; Svetlana, who knew her way around these problems, suggested borscht and baked sturgeon. She was pleased that there was white bread available because she liked it better than the usual coarse black stuff.

"You may want, but you may not get," I had been told and I

quickly learned that it was a lifetime of not getting, in a country where almost nobody got. This big, rich country that stretched across eleven time zones was reduced for most people to a tiny plan, to twenty square meters in a shoddy apartment block, to a school where everyone wore the same clothing and a job where everyone did the same chores.

"We pretend to work, they pretend to pay us," the saying went.

We ordered another bottle of red wine—young people like Art and Svetlana drank wine much more often than vodka if they could get it and they did it because they liked the wine but also as a statement. It said we are different, more sophisticated, more European. But everything different, unconventional, rebellious was always a statement in the Soviet Union, nothing more so than rock and roll.

No one understood rock in the USSR better than Troitsky; he had just published a terrific book on it called, naturally enough, *Back in the USSR*. From Art and from his book, I learned about pop culture and its roots in the USSR, and what made the country so ripe for Dean Reed when he arrived, when he seemed to fill a void. The longing for rock and roll and the West were a kind of mute rebellion among young people. This was Art's territory: he had invented it, and he talked about it fluently.

"In the Soviet Union, even the rednecks, I mean, you know, the peasants, were obsessed with America. Because of that, Dean Reed was no ordinary foreign musical visitor to their country. He was American. He had this image of being a rock and roll singer. He had moderately long hair, flared jeans, and all those things. So it's quite natural that the unsophisticated part of the young audience really fell for Dean Reed." Art finished his glass of wine and added, "No living Western performer of rock and roll ever

came to the Soviet Union. Dean Reed was young. He played
guitar. He was American. We believed."

In the 1950s, the Soviet Union's passion for America began with
the movies and the records that the Red Army had captured in
Berlin after the War. Johnny Weissmuller, the first and the best
Tarzan, and the ice-skating star Sonja Henie captured the hearts
of postwar Moscow. Among the films the army brought home was
Sun Valley Serenade, a kitsch caper that featured Sonja in an
ermine cap doing sit-spins on an ice-rink in the Idaho resort. But
it was because the picture had a soundtrack by Glenn Miller—
Miller debuted "Chattanooga Choo Choo" in it—that the *stilyagi*
adored it.

The *stilyagi*—the style hunters—ruled Moscow's street
corners in those days and they only cared for clothes and for
dancing. In platform shoes, zoot suits, and fat ties painted with
Hawaiian palms, they wore their hair in duck's asses, slicked
back with loads of grease. Officials who caught them, shoved
them up against the wall and cut their hair off, but the *stilyagi*
persevered and they held cocktail hours and listened to jazz.
Louis Armstrong and Duke Ellington were heroes, but, above all,
they adored Glenn Miller. "Chattanooga Choo Choo" was their
anthem.

The *stilyagi* were Art's nostalgia heroes. For his mother, who
had been at Moscow University in the 1950s, they had had no
charm at all. She despised them because they had no spiritual
values. They were empty, stupid, and superficial. They only
wanted to dance the *bugiwugi*.

Interestingly, this was exactly how American folkies, usually
left-wing kids, had felt about the blue-collar rockers like Elvis and

at almost exactly the same time. How the old folkies had despised rock and roll!

"I've heard rumors that the KGB house-band's favorite tune these days is 'In the Mood'," said Art suddenly at the National Hotel, where we were finishing lunch.

For Art, the 1950s in the USSR and its nascent youth subculture had the charm of kitsch. The taste for kitsch went deep with Art. On that trip in February, 1988, I realised that kitsch was a rebellion. If you couldn't get anything good—and there wasn't much that was good to get—you settled for what was lousy and made it into a style. Kitsch was a put-on, a parody, a form of survival. "Up yours," it said to conventional taste and the clothes and furniture of officialdom. Moscow humor was tough, urban, and seditious. The more freedom there was in Moscow in the late 1980s, the more inclined its rock bands were to dress up in old KGB uniforms.

Pouring himself another drink, Art talked some more about the 1950s, in America, in the USSR, about the music and cars, the big pastel Harley Earl cars with acres of chrome and tail fins poised for flight.

Many Muscovites remembered those cars from the brochures they took home from the American exhibition in 1959.

At the exhibition, where Nixon and Khrushchev faced off in an American model kitchen among the Frigidaires and the Mix-o-Matics, Coca Cola was served in plastic glasses by pretty girls who smiled at you.

Lining up to sample the drink, many people said it tasted like shoe polish, then, still sneering, lined up for another glass. And the plastic glasses! And the smiling girls! Who had ever heard of or imagined such a wonderful thing? And the cars, of course.

Lovely cars, in many pretty colors, with musical names. Cars that went with rock and roll music. Carrying away the brochures with the pictures of those cars, people studied them in secret, for years, as if they were art.

With these glimpses of the magical West, the taste for rock and roll grew. Paul Anka and Pat Boone were hot in Moscow, so was "Love Potion Number Nine." Electric guitars came in through Czechoslovakia and a group called the Revengers played Little Richard covers. It was all unofficial, of course. Kids strung telephone wires across a table and called it a guitar; they made themselves into bands through sheer willpower, ripping off telephones for the wires whenever they could, so that, in one period, not a single public telephone in Moscow worked.

The production of records required similar ingenuity, which was how *Records on Ribs* were invented. You stole X-ray plates, which were made of a thick plastic material, rounded out the edges with a pair of scissors, cut a hole in the middle, and recorded on top of them. In the underground, rock music was produced on pictures of somebody's lungs. I saw them, these incredible artifacts, and you could actually see the ribs while the needle went around and around. Young hustlers who sold them on the street secreted the records in their coat sleeves because the X-ray material was pliable and you could fold it over.

Tolya Shevshenko, a translator I got to know in Moscow, remembered how as a kid he got hold of some *Records on Ribs*.

"I remember it quite vividly," said Tolya. "It was a winter's day. I was wearing a heavy coat and looked like a young old man. I went to the GUM store to buy myself something. And, in front of this store, a man, maybe twenty years old, approached me and asked what I was looking for. I said that I was looking for some rock records. These are not available in the official state store. And he said, 'Well, I've got some.' I asked him what was on the records, and he said, 'Rock and roll. Chubby Checker.' I said, 'OK, I'll take one.' It was really Chubby Checker, very badly recorded with a lot of noise. But anyway it was Chubby Checker. It was rock and roll!"

For a few years in the early 1960s things changed, Art said; decadence and disaffection went out of style. Soviet youth was full of enthusiasm over Yuri Gagarin, the Cuban Revolution, and the 22nd Party Congress.

"For the Russians, these were the gung-ho years of the hero astronaut, and Soviet culture could even withstand the Twist," Art added. The bureaucrats said, "Of course, it is all nonsense, this 'tweest', the music is for idiots, but let them fool around, it is nothing terrible."

By the late 1960s, though, the years of stagnation had ground into play. For almost twenty years under Brezhnev, nothing much had seemed to happen. Gray times. Only the distant sounds of the Beatles singing through the crackle of static on illicit radios sounded like life to Art's generation.

Beatlemania swept Russia. Beatles bands were formed. Singing "They say it's your birthday," at birthday parties was a ritual. People learned English to understand the Beatles. Kids took terrible risks to get a look at a poster, and at least one man claimed he had been the first Russian to identify the individual members of the Fab Four from a torn newspaper cutting. Here is John, he said, and George, and Paul, and Ringo.

A Beatles album was an almost undreamed-of treasure, but for half a ruble you could rent a Beatles poster for a day. Fans wore jackets without lapels called *bitlovka*.

"Elvis was nice," Art mused now. "But the Beatles had melodies. The Beatles were wonderful. The Beatles came knocking at our hearts."

Still, the Beatles were not official and had never been to the Soviet Union, unless you counted the legendary stopover at the Moscow airport their plane once made en route home from Japan. That stopover became the subject of endless conjecture.

Had they really been in Russia? Had they actually disembarked from the plane, and did they play a secret concert, or had it all been one of Moscow's great urban myths?

"Rock and roll meant something extremely exotic," Art said. "It was the most exotic of all Western forbidden fruits, you know, like Salvador Dalí, or striptease, or something. I mean, you know, it was always totally obscene because the articles in the local press said that rock and roll performers make pornographic movements while they sing. And that they make the cries of agony or ecstasy, into the microphone before the public. So, yes, it was like, like a very, very attractive, but at the same time, a very distant thing."

I sipped some wine, so did Art, and then he said, "Rock was a concentration of all the good things in life."

"Rock and roll meant a lot to absolutely every Soviet kid, even if they lived in a village. Because this was the music that made them feel free, that made them feel slightly different from their parents, you know, who, of course, didn't understand this music." Art paused. "And, for us, more than that, it also meant, you know, it was like a door into another culture, a door into another way of life, which we all fancied, of course.

"We really hated what was going on around us," Art said. "We didn't care about politics. We didn't care about Communist ideology. But we did care about how badly people were dressed in this country, about what an awful thing is official Soviet pop music. What was going on at this official level of culture was absolutely disgusting," Art added, referring to folk music and men in fake Cossack shirts and women in nylon frocks with trilling voices, and choirs of Young Pioneers with reverent faces and zealous eyes singing patriotic songs. "Not exactly for political reasons," Art mused. "But for the reason that this was ugly, unstylish, unlike the West."

Even Art, even this stylish, sophisticated, traveled Muscovite, when he recalled what the West had meant, came alive. His handsome face just lit up like a bulb and he seemed to purr with pleasure when he said the word "West." It was the most potent insight into how ripe the Soviet Union was for Dean Reed when he arrived.

Then he said, "The West was something good. I mean, everything Western, was right. And Dean Reed came and he wore cowboy boots and he came from the land of the free and the home of the brave. And Chuck Berry," Art continued. "He meant everything."

"Come for dinner on Friday," Svetlana said, as she got up to leave. "We will introduce you to this girl who had a friend who loved Dean Reed," she added, while Art tugged at the front of his sweater to remind me it was the girl with the big breasts.

I got a room with a view in the end. Outside my window, in the distance, beyond the Lenin Museum, was Red Square, and at night, from this angle, it somehow resembled the landing pad in *Close Encounters*. Suspended by day in frozen sunlight, at night it was backlit by those clouds that drifted in from a power station. The red neon star—5000 watts of it—on top of the Kremlin's Borovitsky tower, blazed among the real winter stars.

I couldn't get enough. I couldn't spend enough time looking or walking across it or thinking up metaphors for this—I didn't know what to call it—awesome place. Across Red Square, St. Basil's looked rich and whimsical, a Spielbergian starship just touching down after a trip to the Arabian Nights, a pile of red and green striped pineapples, of squashed onion domes and spires, and gold, all filigree and inlay. My metaphors collided and crashed, none of them any good. I just looked at St. Basil's and thought: such a pretty thing!

Make me something unique, Ivan the Terrible said to his architects, and they made him St. Basil's, and he asked if they could they make him another. Yes, they said, and thought about a new arrangement of striped pineapples and golden onions. Yes, we can, they said, and Ivan had their eyes put out because he didn't want anyone else to have one.

I liked Moscow best at night. I liked it in the snow, winter obviously its natural element, its grandeur underscored by the sweep of empty squares, vast plazas as burnished and forsaken as the uninhabited ballroom of a tsar's palace. Night hid the cracks in the buildings. The hard-currency hustlers stamped their feet in the snow outside the hotel and in the shadows of the Bolshoi Theater.

Fur hats? Rubles? Sex?

I sat in my window at the National Hotel and somehow it all seemed oddly familiar. The American Revolution always appeared in my mind as a remote woodcut of tiny eighteenth-century figures in wigs in a formal landscape. The Russian Revolution was always a movie. Sergei Eisenstein's fictional footage had shown up so often as documentary evidence of the events that finally everyone just believed his version was fact.

* * *

There was a knock on my door. It was Martin Walker. He was wearing very tight jeans and a fur hat a foot high. It had been awarded to him for extraordinary feats of macho fishing by some Siberian tribe.

Martin was the *Guardian*'s correspondent in Moscow and he had written brilliantly about the coming of Gorbachev and *Perestroika* and *Glasnost*, rediscovering the Soviet Union for his readers as a place where people had sex and permanent waves, listened to rock and roll, ate Chinese food, and did not have Tampax. There were no sanitary napkins anywhere in the country.

Art Troitsky was Martin's best friend in Moscow, which was not surprising. It was a very tight circle, the foreign journalists who were loving it because the stories just exploded, dozens every day, the Muscovites telling it, stuff pouring out of them, stuff they'd been saving up to tell for years, even decades. Martin and I went down to the hotel bar to meet Leslie Woodhead and Jo Durden-Smith.

The second-floor bar at the National drew the gossips and the high rollers and it had a chancy edge-of-the-world feel. At night it throbbed with possibility. I sat with Martin and we gossiped and Jo and Leslie joined us. East German businessmen in green loden coats and gray leather shoes exchanged business cards. There was a chatty textile man from Atlanta, and a "professor" from Bloomington, Indiana, with a wispy chin beard. Professor of what? I asked, and he turned away, no longer garrulous.

Behind the bar, a pair of young waiters with the sullen, smooth, empty faces the Soviets sometimes had, played an interminable game of chess. Near them was a glass case, which held two chocolate buns and a pyramid of Pepsi Cola cans and next to it an ancient *babushka*, her head encased in a cotton scarf, her body draped in a dress or coat—it was hard to tell which—her broom in her hand, frozen in time.

At a table in the corner was a pair of hookers, one in a red satin top, the other in a yellow angora sweater with glitter on the shoulders, which were padded out like a quarterback's. Ignoring the East Germans, waiting for customers with hard currency, the women ate chocolate-covered cherries from a large box on the table, reaching into the frilly papers with a steady rhythm and popping the candies whole into their big, red mouths.

Martin, who was taking it all in—you could tell that the bar at the National would be a column in the *Guardian* by the following week—scribbled a list of people for us to see. His contacts were astonishing. Then we all went out to eat Chinese food at the Mei Hua, where we met up with Julia Watson, who was married to Martin. Art and Svetlana joined us.

At night, a minor form of tourism in early *Glasnost* was making the rounds of the cooperative restaurants. We ate Indian food at the Delhi, where Mr. Rajneesh Kumar Verma had the spices and the rice flown in regularly. A Russian band played eerie covers of Dire Straits and a fat bride shook her bosoms to the impeccably mimicked lyrics of "Money for Nothing."

With Art and Svetlana one night, we went to the Skazka, a club for tourists and *apparatchiks*, where there was a floorshow and a gypsy fiddler.

He played everything, he played "Hava Nagila," he played the "Mull of Kintyre." Afterwards, a male exotic dancer, his pectorals oiled to a shine, began his routine. He jumped around, then posed on a bed of nails.

"A representative of the Soviet Socialist Sado-Masochistic Republic," Art said sarcastically, but the audience was wild for it.

A magician coaxed golden coins from behind Art's ears, and then stole his watch. Svetlana and I shared a pear the size of a melon. I hadn't seen much fresh fruit in Moscow, but as the juice ran down our chins, I understood that, for a price, you could get almost anything in the Soviet Union.

The Skazka would have been a perfect venue for one of Dean's impromptu concerts. He would have held Svetlana's hand, looked into her eyes and sung "Yiddishe Momma" to her, then treated the tourists to one of his comic songs. "Old Cowboys Never Die (They Just Smell That Way)," he would have sung. I was suddenly so sorry that Dean Reed was dead.

Like Dean, in my first week in Moscow, I was a tourist. I went to the museums. I went to the public parts of the Kremlin. I went to the Ukraina Hotel, a Stalinist wedding-cake of a building that towered over the river. In the lobby, where tourists stomped their feet in brown puddles of slush. Here Dean encountered a black Ukrainian girl singer who appeared later on his television specials. While the astonished tourists watched, he grabbed her hand and on the spot they did a rendition of "La Bamba."

I also went to GUM, where, astride the rococo fountains, among the beautiful galleries made of glass, Dean had once played his guitar. There was nothing much to buy at Moscow's biggest department store except ugly underwear and plastic gilt models of the *Kremlin*. At the Museum of Musical Instruments, on Fadeyev Street, I saw Dean's guitar. It had a little yellow smiley face pasted on to it and it was signed.

"Dean was very popular; he had a beautiful voice," said Anatoly D. Paniushkin, the director of the museum. "He gave a concert for us here in the museum. It was so sad he could not go to America, where they rejected him."

Later, in Red Square, I waited in the snow in the long line for Lenin's tomb. Some of the comrades, their ears bare—for only tourists and wimps turned down the earflaps on their square fur hats—ate ice cream.

Alongside gruff Bulgarians and impenetrable Albanians, were a group of smiling Cubans, who spoke lilting Spanish. As the line was halted in its progress at regular intervals by the arrival of official delegations, the Cubans chatted happily, although their shoes were very thin and they must have been very cold.

Inside the red granite mausoleum in the very center of Red Square, Lenin, stuffed, lay in a plastic box. The small, shriveled man, with a bald head and the familiar pubic beard, wore an utterly bourgeois black suit. His was a face completely without humanity or humor. Backlit, he resembled a plastic doll. His skin had a curiously orange cast and his hands were twisted, like an arthritic's.

A brain surgeon I met in Moscow was obsessed with the idea that Lenin had had a peculiar malformation of the cerebellum—for years, slices of his brain were kept in jars in scientific labs and studied—that resulted in the deformation of his hands. It also killed him, although for years his enemies gleefully circulated the rumors that syphilis killed Lenin.

In his airless tomb, the crowds shuffled past, prodded on by men in uniforms. Some years earlier, a tourist observing the mummified man in the plastic box, drew back, startled by something he saw.

"My God, Lenin's lost an ear," he shouted.

Lenin's ear had fallen off. The tomb had to be shut up for days while officials searched for it.

"Have you ever been to Lenin's tomb?" I asked Art that evening over dinner at his apartment. He barely raised his urbane eyebrow as he said, "Have you ever been to the Statue of Liberty?"

9

"Rada set out her stall to get Dean Reed," said Alla and blew her nose. She accepted a beer and a cigarette and sat down, cross-legged, on the floor of the Troitskys' flat on the Horoshovskoje Chausee near the Begovaya subway station.

"Alla's best friend, Rada, was a friend of Dean's," Svetlana explained, translating for Alla, who spoke a sexy, cooing Russian. "A close friend," she said, gravely.

Across the room, Art pulled at the front of his pullover to remind me we were talking of the page-three girl with big breasts. "Very big." Art mouthed it.

"She set out her stall to get him," repeated Alla.

Alla wore a little Lenin badge, tight jeans, and a homemade pinafore. Red lips, big dark eyes, and frizzy hair, she was a gypsy girl from Moldavia, half Hungarian, half Romanian. Her husband was a filmmaker. He was away in Sweden.

She wept for her dead friend for a while that night at Art and Svetlana's place, the friend who had loved Dean Reed. Then she lit up a Marlboro.

Svetlana whispered, "She is very emotional about this."

Alla rearranged herself, blew some smoke into the air, sipped her beer and launched eagerly into her friend's unhappy story, stopping only to wipe away the tears that brimmed up in her big eyes and ran down her pink cheeks. All it needed was the violinist from the Skazka.

"Rada loved Dean from the age of thirteen," Alla said. "Rada was a big girl [Art pulled his sweater again] whose ambition was to become famous or to meet famous people, and when she saw Dean on television, she loved him to death, even from afar, even when she was only thirteen years old." Alla drew breath.

Years and years passed. Rada collected all of Dean's records, went to his concerts, watched him on television, bought pictures of him, daydreamed about his slim waist and the way he moved. All the other girls she knew felt the same way. Unlike the others, Rada had a plan.

When Rada was sixteen, she went to work as a model for the painter Victor Kropotkin. She heard that Dean Reed was in Moscow, and she borrowed a nude portrait of herself from Kropotkin's studio. She hired a taxi and tied the big canvas on to the roof. She went with the taxi to the airport to greet Dean. Huge crowds were waiting to meet Dean and, with them, was Rada with her taxi and the picture of herself, naked, on the roof.

After the incident with the picture, according to Alla, Rada and Dean were inseparable. Or so she thought, because Rada was a very unstable sort of girl and everyone knew Dean had lots of women. Rada thought Dean would leave his wife and marry her, even though, during some years, they only saw each other once or twice, if Dean was in Moscow and had the time. She covered her ears when people told rumors about Dean. Rumors that he had an illegitimate child in Moscow, for instance. The truth was even worse. The truth was he loved his wife.

Maybe Dean did see other girls, but he told Rada that he could give himself entirely to two or three women a day. That's how it was for him. He could give that much. Rada was sure Dean loved her best. She was sure that he would marry her.

Then Dean died. There was hardly anything in the official press, but the news was known in Moscow. Rada took many pills. She drank a lot. She ended up in a mental hospital, where she had been before.

"The hospital was on the outskirts of Moscow, but Rada managed to escape." Here, Alla paused for effect and added: "Rada had her pockets full of pills! Next day," she whispered, "Rada's body was found, sprawled on a garbage dump on the edge of town. All that she left behind were her diaries."

Alla drank the vodkas that Svetlana handed her for comfort. She implored us to help her: Rada's mother wanted to sell her daughter's diaries, Alla said. Could I not help?

Art said: "Alla says Rada kept very good diaries. Her mother wants to get them published, not for the money, but because her daughter was the friend of a big star, which was almost like being a star."

"Rada was in love with Dean," said Alla.

"But he treated her so badly," I said.

Alla said, "He was a big star. He was a man. He had the right," said Alla.

Quietly now, Alla sat, crying. I wondered how many other girls he had left behind him, bruised, in Moscow, convinced that he had the right because he was a star. I wondered how much the diaries would, in the end, cost me.

After Alla finished her sad tale and had another good cry, she went home and we sat down to dinner. There was chicken and pickled garlic, cucumbers and cheese, chocolate cake and red wine.

"Stalin's favorite vintage," Art said examining the label.

At the end of the meal we had tea; Svetlana put cherry jam in hers and it was the only time in Russia I ever had what could pass for a race memory: my father liked to eat cherry jam with his tea. He said it was a Russian custom. Otherwise, I had never once felt Russian, never.

My grandparents had been among the Jews of the Pale of Settlement, an area of parts of what are now Belarus and Ukraine. From 1791, it was a kind of vast ghetto. Peasants and villagers like my own grandparents often did not speak Russian, only Yiddish. They were obviously not baptized, so there were no church records. They were barred from going to university and there were restrictions on what trades they could enter. Then came the murderous pogroms of the late nineteenth and early twentieth centuries. Those who could fled to avoid being killed by the Cossacks.

What was there for me to feel? When people asked where my ancestors came from, I would say, "*Fiddler on the Roof* without the music." I felt nothing. But I knew that for my great-grandparents it had been much, much worse than I could imagine and even the jokes were often bitter.

Svetlana, long legs stretched out in front of her, was pre-occupied. We were all delighted by the onset of *Glasnost* and *Perestroika*: the restaurants that had suddenly opened, the way people talked with increasing candor about the system. In Moscow there was real excitement, a sense of drama, a lot of intellectualizing about the new revolution and its possibilities. The nascent free press, the sheer exuberance of free speech.

Svetlana wanted action. Her vision of a better life was born in long lines at the butcher and waiting rooms at the doctor's office. If it was tough for her, for a well educated, urban, sophisticated Muscovite, what was it like for ordinary people?

"Did you ever believe in Communism?" I asked.

"Not for one single day in my entire life," she said. "When I was a little girl, I drew wigs on Lenin in my schoolbooks and my mother had to be called in to discuss the problem."

She did not believe in any of it, not even now. In the Soviet Union things would deteriorate, Svetlana believed. The lines would get longer. The meat would get scarcer. Everyone would get meaner, more vicious. And the men would keep on talking.

Maybe it was OK for the men, who sat around Moscow's restaurants with their Western pals, arguing, drinking, laughing. Boy, did they talk. Sometimes you felt Moscow's intellectuals would talk the whole enterprise to death. Maybe glorious *Glasnost* was OK for them, Svetlana said, but she saw no reason to stick around just to stand in food lines. If she could get out, if she could go to the West, she would go and happily.

"What good is this *Glasnost* if I have to wait in line for a chicken four hours?" she said.

"Why do we need a chicken?" asked Art.

"I don't care about a chicken. But you would care if our friends had nothing to eat. I don't want to wait for a chicken. I want to be doing my work," she said.

Svetlana turned to me. "Can I say this in Russian and Art will translate?"

"Yes, of course."

Eyes blazing, fists clenched, Svetlana suddenly let out a torrent of Russian.

"Well, the first thing I must say is that Svetlana is absolutely wrong, now I will translate what she says," said Art.

Svetlana turned away. She wanted to leave the country and her husband didn't get it.

Art, of course, did not want to leave. It was his moment. He was much in demand by visiting Westerners and anyhow things in the music business were jumping. He told me about his conceptual punk band. It was called Vladimir Illych.

"We wore *Komsomol* outfits and we had several big hits such as 'Lenin is Alive' and 'Lenin, Come Back', after *Lassie Come Home*. There was also 'Brezhnev is Knocking at Your Door'." Art picked up his glass of Advocaat liqueur. "Of course, the band only exist in our heads," he added. Then he looked at Svetlana and said, suddenly, "I think I will send Svetlana to the West."

"What? Like a parcel?" Svetlana banged her fists on the table; the plates jumped. "You don't understand," she said. This was addressed to Art. He looked bemused.

In her way she was much less sentimental and more astute about the world than Art. A year or so later, when they came to New York for the first time, I took her to Macy's. I asked if she was surprised.

"No," she said. "I think this is the normal way to live."

It was tough times in New York, plenty of homeless all over the city, crime, crack, poverty.

"I understand," she said. "But at least there is the possibility to live a better life. In the Soviet Union there was none. Everything was arranged for you: where to live, how to live, what job to do. Nothing. No chance."

There was a New York City subway map on the wall of Art and Svetlana's flat and, in the living room where we ate, a large Sony

Trinitron monitor. It didn't work as a television set, of course, because the broadcast standards were different in Moscow. But it was the only set Art found stylistically interesting, so he used it as a monitor for his video player.

"You know," he said, "when Dean Reed first arrived, he did numbers like 'Blue Suede Shoes'. This meant something to us. There was nothing in Soviet culture that reminded me of my dreams, and rock was a concentration of all good things." He polished off his Advocaat. It was late. I asked what records he wanted from New York when I got back.

"Cab Calloway," he said and grinned sardonically. "And early Louis Prima."

10

On the night I was to meet Dean Reed's Soviet translator, we—Leslie, Jo, and I—went to a bar on the third floor of the National Hotel.

The hotel was like a little city, with many restaurants, bars, meeting rooms. I thought of the third floor bar as the Carpet Bar because it had what resembled old carpet on the wall. There was a friendly bartender and you could get plates of smoked fish and hard-boiled eggs and caviar. The bartender would also sell you jars of caviar, for about seven bucks. It was the blue and white china, though, that I was obsessed with.

The bar had a set of china on which it served snacks and which was also decorative, propped up on shelves among the vodka bottles. Somehow I got it into my head that this was the original National Hotel china, that it dated from the 1920s, a wonderful period in Soviet decorative arts, and that, in the course of history, Lenin had probably eaten his sandwiches off it.

Everything in the Soviet Union on that first trip was interesting, everything had an exotic glitter for me, and if there were few souvenirs, there was, nonetheless, the history.

I began to barter with the bartender for the plates. Pantyhose changed hands, and so did ballpoint pens, but the thing he seemed to desire most were music cassettes. He was willing, for instance, to trade a blue and white teapot for a James Taylor, a large serving plate for Paul Simon, and for the Rolling Stones I was able to acquire four nice soup bowls.

And so it went, not just then, but for the several trips to Moscow that followed. I carried the blue and white china wrapped in newspaper, smuggled along with the seven dollar caviar, out of Moscow, convinced the china was more or less national treasure. And then once, on a TV program, I saw a reporter interview some very poor people in a remote region of the USSR; they lived in what appeared to be a hut. But in the hut, when they invited the reporter in for tea, was a set of blue and white china. The same blue and white china. It didn't matter though; the dishes I bartered in the Carpet Bar of the National never lost their luster.

After a snack and a drink, we took the subway to meet Art and Svetlana at the appointed station. In the subway train, the Muscovites stood and sat, behind books and newspapers, secret and unsmiling and blank. One beanbag of a woman, who seemed to have been stitched permanently into her overcoat, clutched a string bag triumphantly. It held a rush of yellow oranges. Fruit was more precious than gold in a Moscow winter and there must have been a special on somewhere. All over town that day I had seen oranges spilling from suitcases or stuffed into net bags, bright yellow and orange balls of fruit, like jewels caught in nets.

The Moscow subway stations were everything that had been promised. The walls were marble and granite; there were chandeliers and stained-glass windows; there were stations like Las Vegas hotels and stations as streamlined as Rockefeller

Center, where the Art Deco bronzes glittered just for the pleasure of the strap-hangers. In the subways, the imperial ambitions of Mother Russia had been passed on to the working classes and I would not have been surprised to find walls made of solid silver. For five kopeks, you could ride forever.

Warm, efficient, safe, the subway was one of the few institutions in Moscow that worked. Above ground things were changing every five minutes. Here, amid the subterranean splendors, was the only place that Art Troitsky felt on firm ground.

At the Gorky Park Station, Art was waiting with Svetlana. Outside, a light snow was falling. The black iron gates to Gorky Park glittered with gold filigree. Inside the park was a silvery, moon-shaped ice-rink on which skaters raced, twirled, stumbled. From the loudspeaker system came the insistent strains of "Volare."

"Nel blu di pinto di blu," Domenico Modugno warbled. The skaters circled. The music changed to the "Skater's Waltz" and the show-offs spun on to the rink, dancing, spinning, jumping. Millions of distant little stars twinkled coldly overhead, and we trudged off into the park, Leslie in a Russian-style hat made of monkey fur, the earflaps down, Jo in a newly acquired caracal, his huge leather bag over his shoulder, Svetlana graceful and sure-footed. The ground was frozen and occasionally skaters suddenly sped out from among the stands of trees. I thought as we walked, alone, silent, in the empty frozen park, even the music fading and distant, about *Gorky Park*, the novel, and the dead man left in the park, his face flayed.

In a clearing, near the embankment of the Moskva River, was a building painted the same blue as the café in East Berlin, and I wondered if there was an oversupply of duck-egg blue paint in the

Eastern Bloc. An old man without any teeth was its gatekeeper. He pulled open the door andfollowed us in.

Waving a filthy handkerchief at us, he blew his nose on it and stuffed it up his coat sleeve. He did a little Charlie Chaplin dance and snatched our coats, locking them away in a sealed cupboard.

It was useless to try to hang on to your coat in Moscow— perhaps it was bad manners, or bad luck. Perhaps the doormen were afraid the pockets concealed something dangerous, maybe it was only for the tips.

I was hungry. On Mondays, Moscow's restaurants closed for cleaning and I'd had only a minuscule portion of bootleg caviar to eat since early morning when, with the take-it-or-leave-it look that came with the breakfast, a sullen waiter in the hotel dining room tossed a couple of limp hot-dogs on my plate. Art had promised dinner, and somewhere, from the bowels of the building, came the delicious meaty smell of lamb cooking.

We followed Art down a long corridor and I heard music from behind closed doors. In the hidden maze of ramshackle rehearsal rooms, Moscow's rock bands practiced their liberation. In the basement was a cooperative restaurant. It was very dark.

The building belonged to Stas Namin. A rock star, he was also the grandson of Anastas Mikoyan, a former premier of the Soviet Union, and politics ran in Stas's blood; so did commerce.

He was the quintessential promoter—wily, political, charming. As a young cadet at the Military Academy, he had formed his first band and, curiously, no one seemed to mind. Stas used his talents and connections so cunningly that, long before *Glasnost*, he was recording for Melodiya in Russian. Stas even had a line on foreign equipment; once, apparently, Cat Stevens had given him a synthesizer, presumably before Cat became a devout Muslim.

Now, Stas was Mr. Rock and Roll and he presided over the building in Gorky Park, where there was an outdoor theater at the back and this restaurant in the basement.

Pictures by local artists were just visible in the faint glow from the candles in the Chianti bottles; in one of them, Stas was depicted as a fat, naked woman. Loudspeakers were stacked up like cubist sculptures. The music was by Stas's own band, the Gorky Park. Stas's sister did the cooking.

We all shook hands, made rock and roll small talk and sat down at a table in the corner. I felt like crying, because on the table was more good food than I'd seen in all of Moscow: tomatoes, cucumbers, stuffed vine leaves, fish salad, hot meat pies. We stuffed ourselves while Stas Namin asked our advice about a name for this new venture.

"What would sell it to foreign visitors?" he asked.

Inevitably, it became the Hard Rock Café.

We began to eat and Art Troitsky drifted away, as Russian men always did. In the smoky distance, at a table where there were only men, he sat and talked with them. They formed a circle. They crouched over their cigarettes and vodkas and beers. As far as I could tell, they were rock musicians: they were young, hip, and thin, and they dressed in black, what I always thought of as the international brotherhood of black clothing. Somehow they resembled all other Russian men I'd seen in the way they formed a closed circle. Dissidents, miners, musicians, it didn't matter; the circle was closed. I watched as they whispered among themselves and smoked the cigarettes as if they wanted to eat them.

After a while, Art returned. With him was a young man in glasses.

"This is great!" Art said in English. "The guy I wanted you to meet happens to be here, tonight. Surprise. We have had good luck. This," he added, "is Oleg Smirnoff."

"What do you mean, 'happens to be here'? I thought that's why we came," I said.

Looking at me gravely, Svetlana shook her head. I kept on talking. She seemed to want me to shut up, but why? Hadn't we come to meet Oleg, the interpreter? Why the secrecy? Still, it was clear that for whatever reason the meeting was supposed to be accidental. This really was a foreign country.

Oleg Smirnoff, who wore round rimless glasses, had a row of ballpoint pens in the breast pocket of his plaid button-down shirt. He wore a blue pullover. He spoke nearly perfect English.

"So. Dean Reed," he said after sitting down next to me. "Dean was a great guy. He was as American as an apple pie."

"How did you meet Dean Reed?' I asked.

"Dean Reed is the first singer for my generation. First time, I am sixteen, in front row at concert. Dean Reed jumps down and together we sing 'When The Saints Go Marching In'. It was great."

"Great," I said.

Oleg was not listening. "Ten years ago—1978?—I was a student translator. I got a call to work for Dean, but I said, No thanks. Who is this guy who's telling us how to run our lives? Dean did that. But I was wrong. He was an emotional Democrat. What I didn't see for a while was that he was an idealist in a wilderness. He taught kids here to believe in the possibility of idealism even when it was impossible."

Oleg talked fluently about Dean Reed, eager to get the story out.

"Dean's words were important. That's why he needed an

interpreter. I would sit on a stool on stage, just next to him. Talking to the audience was as important as the songs. We each had our own spotlight," Oleg said.

"Every song was a page from Dean's book of life," he added. "He wasn't complicated or well read, but he believed. He was an innocent. He had a minder in the East German Politburo who was responsible for him there; here Mr. Arbatov was Dean's Godfather. Dean wrote about socialism. He made one big mistake, though, and he regretted it. He criticized Solzhenitsyn and then wanted to apologize, but he would have to acknowledge he had been used. He knew it, though. Anyhow, you couldn't apologize."

In 1971, Dean wrote to Alexander Solzhenitsyn:

Dear Colleague in Art Solzhenitsyn:

Mr. Solzhenitsyn, the society of my country, not yours, is sick. The principles on which your union relies are healthy, pure, and just, at a time when the principles on which our union are built are cruel, selfish, and unjust.

That night in the café in Gorky Park, his elbows on the table, Oleg Smirnoff talked and talked. For ten years, he said, he and Dean had worked together. They had worked together in Siberia, where Dean sang "Tutti Frutti" for a handful of loggers and in Kiev; in Minsk, Mongolia, Tashkent, and Moscow, Oleg translated for Dean. "I believe in music," Dean sang and everyone adored him, Oleg reported.

Girls followed Dean everywhere. Girls tried to rip his clothes off. The stage-door *Ninas* pursued him relentlessly. Dean could have any woman he wanted in the Soviet Union, said Oleg, savoring the memory. Everyone wanted to possess a little piece of Dean.

"But he was a very shy guy," Oleg said, pleased with the little rhyme he'd made and he repeated it. "A shy guy," he said again.

"Did Dean speak Russian?" I asked.

"Not much. A few words only," said Oleg.

Then, unaccountably, Oleg went silent. He sucked his drink from the bottom of the glass and averted his eyes. For half an hour, I'd been drawn in: we were in a club in a basement which, if it smelled of burned lamb, nonetheless had the black walls, the loud music, the lank-haired kids that were the universals of rock clubs. But in Moscow this was still a half-secret venue. An underground club in a still secret country where a million half-facts made up a forgotten history as hidden as the little wooden dollies you bought in the souvenir shops.

I wanted more from Oleg. I wanted everything he knew about Dean Reed. I sensed he had been as close to Dean for a decade as anyone in the Soviet Union. I wanted it and I thought of the woman at the front desk in the National Hotel and how she tried to help and then drew back. I wanted but I didn't necessarily get, not right away, not the room with a view or secret things that Oleg knew about Dean Reed.

Intellectually, I got it, but it was still hard for me to grasp in my gut that one way or another pretty much everything in this enormous country was a function of officialdom. An American I met later said of a guide who helped her in Moscow, "Well, who does she work for?" And by then I had learned enough to say, "For the state, of course. Everyone works for the state. There isn't anything else."

Now, in the restaurant in Gorky Park, his face suddenly seizing up in anger, Oleg removed his glasses and put his twisted features close to mine.

"How do I know who you really are?" Oleg said.

"I've told you, we're planning a drama-documentary about Dean," I began patiently, looking at Leslie, who was deep in conversation with Jo and Svetlana at the other side of the table. He turned around and confirmed what I'd said. Oleg was not convinced.

"Oh yeah? Yeah? How do I know? How do I know you're going to preserve the memory of Dean properly?" Oleg asked.

Christ! I thought, he's going to leave. He had videotapes of Dean's concerts and I wanted to see them. I looked around for Art, but Art had gone with Stas and the boys into the maze of little rooms at the back of the Gorky Park Hard Rock Café.

I tried to suck up to Oleg. "So, did you play an instrument as well?"

"It wasn't my job."

"No, of course not. I mean, why should you? So when did you last see Dean?"

"I can't remember," he said. "I stayed in his house the last Christmas. Dean took Renate to London, and I stayed in the house in East Berlin to look after the dog and have a holiday. Germans! In Germany, when you went for a walk, people said hello to the dog but never to you. I don't know how Dean stood it," Oleg said.

"If you took down the Berlin Wall, half of the people would fight for the system; the other half would rush to the other side. Here, everyone would fight for the Fatherland," Oleg added.

"Who do you think killed Dean?" I said, exhausted finally, not much caring if Oleg defected from the conversation or not.

He drew himself up and fingered the row of pens in his pocket.

"He was killed by the forces of evil," Oleg said.

"Which forces?" I asked.

"You decide," he said, and the evening was over. We paid and got up and went upstairs and out into the black, cold night.

It was after one and the subway was shut up. There were no taxis in Gorky Park. The only way back to town was in Oleg's car, and we piled in. Looking straight ahead, he drove silently until he pulled his car up to the front door of the National Hotel.

The next morning, I was going down in the elevator at the National to meet Art and Svetlana, when a couple of Romanians—they looked like father and son—got in on the second floor. They wore Sergio Valente jeans and they spoke English quite well. They smiled delightfully.

"First floor?" I asked.

"Ground floor, please," they said.

"Where are you from?" I asked.

"Romania. Maybe you have heard of it. Bucharest?"

I had heard of it, all right. Ceauşescu and his wife had turned the country into a Stalinist nightmare—this was long before the crowds rooted them out and shot them. What could I say about Romania? It was home to the men in the elevator. Dean Reed had made movies in Romania and he claimed to know the Ceauşescus. These men in their fancy jeans were probably officials, but they smiled nicely and I was a sucker. Romania, Romania . . . I had it.

"Yes, of course, I've heard of it. Very good food," I beamed back. "Pastrami!"

They beamed back.

"You speak very good English," I said, and they smiled some more.

"Where are you from?" asked the younger Romanian.

"New York City."

Oz! You could see it written on their faces: that they knew I had come from a magical planet. Oz or Shangri-La or Eden, it didn't matter. Satisfied, the Romanians nodded at one another, and I knew I had become a postcard from the trip to Moscow—a real New Yorker in an elevator in the National Hotel. For a minute, I was their American. For a moment, I was their Dean Reed.

As I got out of the elevator, I saw Oleg Smirnoff. In a nice gray suit, he was coming through the revolving door of the hotel. The front hall porter, the one who looked like Leonid Brezhnev, did not challenge him.

I got out of the elevator. Oleg got in. I really wanted his videotapes. I held the door open.

"Hi, Oleg," I said. "How's business?"

He grunted.

I said, "What are you doing here?"

"I am working," he said.

"Can I have those videotapes of Dean Reed's concerts? Can I have a look?"

"Maybe."

Suddenly, I was weary of his games. "Working?" I said. "What as?"

"I am working on cementing international relations," said Oleg, and the elevator doors shut.

11

There was something suspicious about this man supposedly having been killed. And I wondered, "Why would anyone want to kill Dean Reed?" Vladimir Pozner stood in the doorway of his apartment in the center of Moscow. He smiled and invited me in.

"You'll have to forgive me, but I thought Dean Reed was a terrible phony," he added. "I'm a folk music man myself. The music teacher at my school in New York was Pete Seeger."

"What school was that?" I asked.

"City and Country," he said.

"Really," I said. "Where did you grow up?"

"24 East 10th Street, in Greenwich Village," he said, "I don't know if you know it."

I knew.

We had grown up on the same block. We had gone to the same school. Although we were fifteen years apart in age, the particulars of our childhoods were identical. We reminisced about Bluie, the librarian, and Ottilie, the cook, and Al in Shop; City and Country was a school so progressive you could practically major in Shop.

Vladimir Pozner remembered Sam, the newspaper man on University Place, and Wannamakers Department Store, where he bought his first bike, and hootenannies with Pete Seeger. I had come 5000 miles to the heart of the formerly Evil Empire to find myself with a man who had . . . Bluie for library!

What's more, Pozner had mimeographed copies of the school newspaper from the 1940s. There we suddenly were, on the floor of Pozner's study, reading through the exploits of the "Eights" or "Nines" (no grades at City and Country, only "groups") in the school printing shop or on a trip to the country to try out milking cows or making parchment paper by hand.

My first week in the Soviet Union and I'd met a man who grew up on my block and went to my school and, more astonishing, spoke not just American, but in my exact accent, though his English was just slightly more New York than mine. He was a Greenwich Village boy. In his study, there was a glass model of the Empire State Building on his desk, and an American quilt on the wall.

The face was utterly familiar, of course; Pozner had appeared so often on television in America that he was the most famous Communist in the country, with the exception of Mikhail Gorbachev. Our commie, polished, witty, urbane, a man who knew his way around a soundbite.

When Pozner began turning up on TV in the early 1980s, in the middle of the Cold War, people were perplexed and intrigued by the anomalous Russian who spoke colloquial English, who rarely used the conventional dreary rhetoric of the Soviet hack, and who was very charming, very slick, very enigmatic.

He looked like one of us, but he was one of them, a member of the Soviet Communist Party, a man who had, for a time, at least, been a true believer. He understood the system and the culture and he could talk about it in a language I understood.

Like Art Troitsky, Pozner could talk about Dean Reed's dazzling career as a superstar in the USSR in terms of the country's obsession with everything American. It had started around the time JFK was shot, Pozner said, and affably poured out Scotch and settled onto a leather sofa. I took a chair.

In the early 1960s, Pozner said, people began to see America in a way that was different from that dictated by the Communist Party.

"The picture furnished by the media, by propaganda about America was false," Pozner said. When people began to understand the truth, really, what happened was that they did a 180 degree turn. Everything about America was great from that point on."

Pozner had been a young reporter when JFK was shot in November, 1963. That night he went door to door in Moscow to get a feel for what people thought about the American President's death. He found almost everyone in tears; they had adored the handsome young President and now he was dead.

When Soviet propaganda films about the horrors of the West were shown on TV—race riots, segregation, guns—teenagers simply turned off the sound and read these details: the clothes in shop windows, the shoes worn by people in the street, the names of movies playing at the cinemas, background details that gave them the information they craved about the West.

Pozner went on, "Dean represented the American man for most Soviet kids. And that was very attractive at a time when anything American was so much desired by most people, especially young people. He was a real living, breathing American."

Pozner held up the bottle, but I refused the Scotch; I was too busy scribbling down what he said.

"Also," Pozner added, "let's keep in mind that it wasn't just the Soviet authorities that gave Dean a big hello, but the so-called Socialist camp."

True enough, not only the Soviets and the Eastern Bloc embraced Dean. He went on playing in Latin America. He went to Chile and played for Salvador Allende and in Nicaragua he played for Daniel Ortega. He even played for Yasser Arafat.

There's a piece of film I found later, after I met Pozner, that showed Dean Reed, a checkered headscarf on his head, jogging with what I assumed were Palestinian troops, all carrying small missiles or AK-47s. And then it cut to Dean Reed, guitar on his knee, singing "Ghost Riders in the Sky" and when the camera pulled back, you saw he was singing it to Yasser Arafat, with Arafat tapping his fingers merrily on a table, and smiling and clapping for Dean Reed.

Pozner said, "So you see, Here's an American who's saying everything that we want him to say. And he's doing it in an American way. And that's very effective."

I asked, "Do you still have an American passport?"

"I never did," he said.

Vladimir Pozner's cultural coding was quintessentially cosmopolitan. Survival was bred in the bone. His father's family were originally Spanish Jews who migrated to Poznań in Poland, and then to St. Petersburg. In order to enter a university, which was forbidden to Jews, they converted to the Russian Orthodox Church. In 1922, Pozner's grandfather left St. Petersburg in the wake of the Revolution; in 1940, his father fled Paris as the Nazis marched in.

The family settled in Greenwich Village. Vladimir was six, and sometimes kids at school called him Bill because William was the nearest equivalent of Vladimir in English. He grew up during World War II, when America and Russia were allies, and his two heroes, he said, were Joseph Stalin and Joe Di Maggio. All his life, Pozner's father nurtured dreams about the romantic Revolution of his youth and the importance of the socialist enterprise, and he instilled them in his sons, Vladimir and his brother, Paul, too.

Pozner's father worked in the movie business. With the onset of the anti-Communist frenzy that began in the late 1940s, his boss offered to obtain US citizenship for him. Otherwise, he was told, he would be fired. The father refused. He took the family East, first to East Berlin, where his job was to restore the film industry.

Vladimir, aged fifteen, hated Germany. It was gray and oppressive. In 1952 the family moved on to Moscow. Under Stalin, the Pozner family, part Jewish, part foreign, would almost certainly have been labeled *Enemies of the State* and sent to a gulag. But, in 1953, Stalin died.

Vladimir settled down with his family, but after a while he grew homesick for New York. A group of young Americans came to Moscow in 1959, when under Khrushchev things opened up a little, Pozner remembered.

He remembered how it had been in New York, how free and friendly and easy, and he said to his father: I'm going to leave. I'm going back. His father said to him: If you try to defect, I'll report you to the KGB.

Pozner adapted to life in Moscow. He passed his exams. He became a journalist. He joined the Communist Party.

"It is easier to believe if you are ideologically motivated. I've always been very political," he said now in his apartment in Moscow.

In 1979, Pozner first appeared on American television, and he was cool. Cool for a cool medium. In a perverse way, ordinary Americans admired him because he was loyal. He was also very good-looking.

The mistake, I realized after I got to know Pozner better and he became a friend, was to think of him out of context. Just because he looked like a Western journalist didn't make him one. It didn't make him a Soviet dissident, either. He was a man doing his job. He was a survivor. And what I also realized was he was the kind of true believer I'd known all my life, a New Yorker, a man of the left but for whom the true tune, more than that of Marx or Lenin, was that of Pete Seeger, who had been the music teacher at his school—and mine—in Greenwich Village.

Vladimir Pozner was fifty-four and he had the perfect face for a messenger between cultures: the good cheekbones, which the cameras loved, gave the face a Slavic cast; the fast-breaking all-American smile warmed it up; the receding hairline made it accessible. Like all of the great TV performers, Pozner was both aloof—as befitted a media royal—yet so knowable that people in the street thought he was their cousin.

In the 1980s, Pozner set up a television "Spacebridge" with Phil Donahue in the US. This allowed citizens in both countries to talk to one another on camera. Pozner and Donahue became friends and Donahue invited Pozner to New York City.

In 1986, Pozner went back to New York for the first time after thirty-eight years. Although he had been a good Soviet citizen, a faithful and loyal Party man, he had never quite been trusted. He had not been allowed to travel to the West, and it had eaten at him for decades. It was the worm in the whole of his life. Doors had opened and shut, permission given and withdrawn, and for a while he drank too much because of it. But now he was back. He was home. New York City.

On the 59th Street Bridge in the taxi coming in from the airport, he suddenly saw the city.

He said, "In the distance, I saw New York. And my heart stopped." In the streets, he stared at people and he knew them all, knew how they felt, who they were; he was one of them.

"I wanted to cry out, Hey, you, all of you, look, it's me, I'm back . . . I love you."

I could never shake the feeling that Pozner was an American.

"Of course I am," he said. "I got my idealism there. Tom Paine was my hero."

And like Art Troitsky, Pozner identified with Holden Caulfield in *Catcher in the Rye*.

"When I read *Catcher in the Rye*," he said, "I thought: Holden Caulfield is about me."

As he headed down Fifth Avenue on his first day in New York, he looked around him with the possessive ease of a man who had come home. "This is my town!" he thought. Eventually, he got a US passport, though subsequently he went back to Moscow and became a TV star in the post-Communist era.

On that winter's day in Moscow, though, putting away the school newspapers, purple with the ink from the ancient mimeograph machine that I knew too well, Pozner drank his Scotch thoughtfully.

"To be honest," he said, "I thought Dean Reed's music was junk. I thought he was plastic Hollywood beefcake. The first time

I saw him, to tell you the truth, my hair rose up at the sight of that hustler. He wasn't stupid. But he wasn't politically sophisticated either. Who else have you seen in Moscow?"

I said that I had seen Nikolai Pastoukhov.

"No shit. How is the old hack?" Pozner asked.

"He's editing *Pravda Country Life*."

"How the mighty have fallen."

I said, "He says he discovered Dean Reed when he was walking in a park in Helsinki."

"Pastoukhov, never took a walk in his life," Pozner laughed. "I'll tell you something. Dean Reed lived here for a short while. He couldn't be a star anywhere else. Nothing really worked for him. He went from Hollywood to South America, to Italy, where I think he even made Spaghetti Westerns with Yul Brynner, and finally to the Soviet Union. He came here to milk a very naive cow. Drink?"

I nodded. Pozner poured.

"I couldn't stand him," he said again. "You think of Paul Robeson, or Vysotsky, or Pete Seeger, for that matter, who stood up for their beliefs . . . Dean Reed just took it where he got it. He was very good-looking, that's true, so he was a big star with women, and he also fulfilled the image·of people who knew America from films we grew up on. Dean was certainly used by the Soviet regime."

"Who do you think killed him?"

"Frankly, as I said, I don't think he was important enough for anyone to bump off," said Pozner. "Unless he knew something important by chance. But the US Embassy wasn't interested. A lot of people said there was a woman involved. Well, *cherchez la femme*," Pozner said.

"Didn't he sort of bring rock and roll to the Soviet Union?" I said.

"He had no talent: that's why no one has heard of him in America. And he didn't bring rock and roll to the Soviet Union. The Beatles brought rock and roll. When Pastoukhov and his sort discovered Dean Reed, they thought they were giving the kids something." Pozner shrugged contemptuously. "They thought they bought the Beatles and they didn't even buy Pat Boone."

It was Friday evening and, as I walked away from Pozner's house and into the Arbat district, I felt I could hear a million voices chattering, gossiping. Moscow felt like a huge café where everyone knew everyone and everyone chattered all the time. Everyone had a story to tell. Information was like cash in Moscow; it was often the only commodity worth having. Information was still so carefully controlled by the state even in 1988 that, although the telephones were free, there were no telephone books at all.

Before I got to Moscow, I thought I'd begun to know Dean Reed. Now I realized I'd barely cracked the surface. I thought of Pastoukhov, who said Dean Reed was a fine young man who didn't have time for sexual stuff, and of Alla who said he had two or three women a day. Oleg Smirnoff said he taught the Russian kids democracy but criticized Solzhenitsyn. Millions of kids had believed in Dean Reed. And Vladimir Pozner thought he was just a fake, a two-bit hustler who could whack a guitar and swivel his hips.

The rest of the day I thought about Pozner. I thought about his love for American folk music and jazz and the blues, and his life as a kid in Greenwich Village, where I had grow up too. I thought about the rhetoric, too, of the American Left. I knew it by heart. My mother, the Commie, I thought.

My mother who, during the Depression, had attended Workers College, who went on bread marches wearing the Persian lamb coat her father gave her. My mother, who had gone to Moscow with a friend on a package tour in the 1960s and danced in her nightgown with a Soviet naval officer at the hotel nightclub. "I didn't have any evening clothes and anyhow it looked better than anything they had," she said. In Moscow, I missed my mother.

In the Kalinin Prospekt, after I left Pozner's apartment, a little crowd had formed. At its heart was an old crone with a crate beside her. The crowd pushed forward.

"Pineapples," she said. "Pineapples."

The crowd looked skeptical.

The old woman tore open the crate and extracted from it tiny white boxes. The crowd moved in. Showing her toothless gums in a triumphant smile, the woman tore the cardboard away and held up her proof: a slice of frozen yellow fruit. It was not unlike a slice from the pineapples that grew on the plantations near Mrs. Brown's condo in Hawaii, except the Moscow pineapple had no smell at all.

Inside the record store nearby, I looked for Dean Reed's records. I ran into Tolya, the rock fan who had once bought *Records on Ribs*. He said that he remembered Dean Reed. "I remember him very well," Tolya said. "He was a young, tall, lean guy, with a mane of hair. He was completely different by comparison with Soviet singers."

But I looked now for the records in vain. I wondered if they were out of print or out of stock. I found a Pat Boone album, though, and on it was a picture of Pat in white buck shoes. I bought it for Art Troitsky. He was in heaven.

Walking through Moscow, thinking of how Dean Reed had

loved it when he arrived, I remembered what the Countess in the Chinese restaurant in London had said.

"Dean went to Russia. Now if you have a person that is kind and lovable, the entire world should not be punished; it should be loved. But he comes back after a couple of months of Russia, telling you he's got to murder half of the real world. The only way to teach people how to live is to kill them."

She said, "And then he told me that he had been in a car accident and had to spend many weeks in a Russian hospital. Now, as I have lived under the two worst regimes in the world, Communism and Nazism, both with the capacity even in those days to brainwash people, the more I heard him speak, the more I became totally convinced that in the hospital they had brainwashed him."

In a sense, Dean had been brainwashed, but not in the way the Countess meant. It was the romance of revolution that seduced him and the way the fans made him an idol.

At the Lenin Museum later that day, I looked at the Soviet Realist paintings, many of Lenin himself, the most famous with him pointing to the future. Lenin's Rolls-Royce was also on display. And there was something touching and funny about the wig Lenin wore—it was there in a glass case—when he smuggled himself into Russia to start the Revolution he starred in. I thought that, somehow, for Dean, too, this country offered him a future and provided a perfect starring role. Within a few years, the museum would be shut.

12

After his first trip to Moscow in 1965, Dean Reed returned to South America. Back in Buenos Aires, where he was then living, Dean was questioned by the police about his visit to the USSR, and as the military began to crack down on the country, he was expelled.

For the next half dozen years, Dean commuted between South America, Europe, and the Soviet Union. Deported from Argentina, threatened by the Right, he tried to get in again by traveling to Uruguay. He was arrested. To the world that knew him, he had the glamour of a political cowboy, moving faster and faster. By now the FBI and the US State Department were on his case.

When I returned from the Soviet Union, I applied for Dean's file courtesy of the Freedom of Information Act, but it didn't arrive on my desk until about 1990. Much of it was blacked out, as was usually the case with FBI files. What I could read, as far as his exploits in South America went, seemed pretty accurate.

Anyway, after the illegal entry into Uruguay, a policeman who had previously arranged Dean's deportation recognized him.

"Hello, Dean," the file recorded him saying, "I always suspected we would meet again."

In 1966, Dean went to Madrid; the following year he moved on to Rome, where he made some Spaghetti Westerns. (This wasn't a life, I began to think; it was a mini-series!) He made eight movies altogether: in 1967, *Buckaroo*; in 1968, *20 Steps to Death*, *The Three Flowers*, and *Adios Sabata*; in 1969, *Death Knocks Twice*, *Pirates of Green Island*, and—my favorite title—*Machine Gun Baby Face*. Sometimes, late at night, you could still catch *Adios Sabata* on TV. In it, Dean worked with Yul Brynner. Dean was taller than Yul, but Yul was the star, so Dean played their scenes standing in a hole on the beach that had been specially dug for him. Dean told the story for laughs, but it clearly got up his nose that he was less important than Yul.

Around that time Dean got divorced from Patty and said Jane Fonda had told him Santo Domingo was a good place to get a divorce. When he arrived there, he laughingly told the press about how he was taller than Yul. Next thing he knew, he saw a story in the paper that Yul Brynner had arrived in Santo Domingo. He hinted at scary reprisals from Brynner.

In 1970, when Dean applied for a new passport—his old one had expired—his height was listed not as six feet one, as it had been in his original document, but as six feet four, and this became a tiny fact in the confusion over his death. Or maybe by 1970 Dean just felt he had grown taller.

In 1972 he washed an American flag out in public. It was the year of the Miami Convention, when Richard Nixon was already deep in his own paranoia and lies, and in Vietnam and Cambodia more and more people were dying. Washing the flag became Dean's emblem. He proclaimed that he was cleansing it of the blood of North Vietnam, making it clean of American guilt. Making it clean, clean for Dean.

He loved stirring things up and getting arrested; in a way he loved going to jail. Except maybe for the time the gay guys got after him. There were plenty of gay guys in South American jails because homosexuality was a crime. "Give us Dean! Give us Dean!" they cried merrily, and banged their tin mugs on the bars of their cells. As Dean told it, these men had faces so painted up, you would not believe it.

"I was never so frightened in all my life," Dean admitted.

"You be good, Dean, or we will give you to them," a guard and prisoners said on one occasion.

Instead, the guards gave them Dean's washing—the gays did laundry for a price—and it never came back.

"They tore it up into little strips for souvenirs," Dean said, whenever he told the story.

The South American stories, which reminded him of some of his most heroic days, were threaded through his life. He loved telling them. Dean courted trouble in foreign places and he said it was for honor's sake, for the cause, for the righteous position he took on things, for the revolution. Part true believer, part bad boy, he played politics because it was subversive and sexy and it got him in the news and it was loads of fun. He was a star. And he was everywhere.

During his time in Rome he became, briefly, a Maoist. I learned this from Georgy Arbatov, his Soviet minder; Arbatov told me he wrote to Dean about the Maoist business, but you couldn't really persuade him.

He also joined antiwar speakers in Rome, at the Piazza Navona. Wearing a suit, flashing his American passport, he talked his way into the US Embassy. From the steps, he turned to the crowd of protestors who stood outside the gates and he raised his fist.

"Ho Ho Ho Chi Minh!" Dean shouted.

* * *

Many of Dean's adventures during the late Sixties and early Seventies were recounted to me by his second wife, the East German Wiebke Reed. They met in 1971 in Leipzig, at the international film festival. Over lunch in East Berlin seventeen years later, in 1988, Wiebke told me she could remember her first words to him.

"You are the best-looking man in the world." It was a line she got off a Little Richard record.

Earlier that day, I'd met Leslie Woodhead in West Berlin, and we took the subway to the Friedrichstrasse station to meet Wiebke. Friedrichstrasse station in East Berlin was three stops from the Zoo station in the West, and it was a much more surreal way to come across the Wall than through Checkpoint Charlie. It was banal and had no melodrama. You got into a subway car; the train juddered across no-man's-land; the passengers read their paperbacks, didn't talk to each other, and got out.

When you traveled by train, you barely saw the Wall. But at the turnstile in the station there were border guards with guns, the requisite exchange of hard currency for visas and the worthless East German money.

It was raining. Outside the subway, alone and in small groups, people scanned the crowd anxiously, waiting for relatives from the West. The hard-currency hustlers turned up the collars of their leather jackets against the weather and scanned the crowd for the suckers.

Wiebke was in her late forties, but looked a decade younger. Small-boned, pretty, and tough, she had a blonde ponytail and wore good leather boots and a cheerful expression. She was chatty by any standards; for an East German, she was gregarious. Her

English was very fine—fluent, full of nuance and detail. She had learned it as a result of her marriage to Dean, and she worked as an interpreter.

We got into the tinny orange car of which she was dutifully proud and she pointed out the opera house that had been restored to its prewar grandeur.

I asked about the Wall and she produced a pro forma, but quite spirited, defense. I had heard it all before: the calm conviction that the system, if not perfect, was better than most. As we drove, she talked of the hemorrhage of talent, which had made life impossible in the East before the Wall was built; she described how the East had suffered during World War II; she recounted how the GDR was steadfast in its anti-Nazi stance. She wasn't at all aggressive about it; she simply believed.

At the Stadt Hotel, where, a few months earlier, a sullen doorman had turned us away, Wiebke had things in hand. A table had been booked. The waiter smiled at Wiebke as we sat down and she began her story of her first meeting with Dean.

At the film festival in Liepzig, when she saw Dean across the room, she was determined to meet him.

The room was full of filmmakers, but all she could see was the gorgeous man with the blue eyes in a white turtleneck sweater. Every other woman in the room was staring at him, too.

A clever, curious girl, she was thirty, worked part-time as a model, and had trained as a teacher. She adored music and art: she was especially into Simon and Garfunkel, the Beatles, the Mamas and the Papas, and Leonard Cohen. Their records were not always easy to come by in East Berlin, but there were ways, and Wiebke was hip. She was standing with a friend who followed her gaze.

"What an astonishing-looking man," said Wiebke's friend.

Wiebke had an idea and she ran out of the room. She found a friend who was a photographer and she whispered in his ear.

"OK," he said.

He let Wiebke carry his light meter back into the reception, where she saw Dean again. She knew he was Dean Reed. Everyone knew.

Already Dean had a reputation in the East, he was big in the Soviet Union and word had filtered through. He was the center of attention. He was dazzling. From the second he set foot in East Germany, he was a star. He had no idea, of course, but Berlin would become his home for the rest of his life.

At the film festival, Dean had serious things on his mind. He was talking earnestly about his plans for a gesture of solidarity with the North Vietnamese. A group of Americans had gathered and was trying to decide what to do about Vietnam. Give blood? What were the alternatives?

Everyone from the Left was there at the festival. It was an annual event on the Leftie circuit. The room bulged and throbbed with people drinking, talking, making deals. There were a couple of elderly Americans, two members of the Hollywood Ten, who, persecuted by Joe McCarthy, had lived in exile in Europe ever since. Old men now, they talked a lot and cracked cynical jokes, and who could blame them?

The two blacklisted writers cracked up because Dean wanted to send white doves to Vietnam.

"Why don't you send the blood of the doves, Dean?" said one of them.

"How about we drink the blood of a couple of white doves, Dean?" said the other.

Dean didn't mind. He went on talking; he had seen news

footage where some pretty North Vietnamese girls pushed bicycles loaded with provisions and ammunition up the Ho Chi Minh Trail. He wanted the delegates to load up bikes and push them into the market square at Leipzig as a gesture of solidarity. The Americans he was talking to at the festival thought this was a hoot.

"That's a good one, Dean," said one of them. "That's wonderful."

On the other side of the room, Wiebke tossed down a few vodkas; she hardly ever drank, but she was nervous. She made her way over to Dean.

"You are the best-looking man in the world," she said. She blushed horribly. Dean laughed and said something back to her in English, but she didn't understand. She had used up all her English with the one sentence "You are the best-looking man in the world."

"Let's get away from all this," Dean said to Wiebke. "Come up to my hotel room." He talked through a translator named Victor Grossman.

"I'm not going to do something as sleazy as that. I don't want to compromise my husband, who's quite well known here," Wiebke said. Victor translated this, too.

Not long after the festival, Dean left for Moscow. One day Wiebke was curled up in a chair and the phone rang. A girlfriend picked it up.

"It's your Dean. From Moscow, I think," she said.

"Hello? Who are you?" said Wiebke, trying to locate some English. She wanted to say "Where are you?" but it came out wrong.

"Who are you?" she said again.

"Dean Reed," the voice answered.

"I know it's Dean Reed. Who are you?"

"Dean Reed! This is Dean Reed."

It was a terrible mess.

Wiebke hired a Fräulein Schultz to teach her some English. She worked hard at it. The fräulein was seventy-five and proud that she was still a fräulein. They worked on English with "Cecilia," a Simon and Garfunkel track.

Wiebke persevered, and when Dean returned to East Berlin a few months later to begin work on a film, her English had improved. The relationship blossomed. Dean was some catch. He had his own minder, who was a member of the Politburo. He experienced the privilege that artists enjoyed—nice housing, good medical care. He always wore that white turtleneck. Rock and roll in East Berlin had had its ups and downs, as often as not, the state took its cues from the USSR.

In 1972, Dean made his first German film. In *The Good for Nothing*, an adaptation of a nineteenth-century novel, Dean was deliciously miscast. His German was lousy, but it didn't matter. In a long pageboy and a ruffled shirt with puffy sleeves, he looked gorgeous.

Wiebke and Dean began seeing each other and he took her to Moscow with him. In those days he could draw 60,000 people for a concert. Women followed him openly in the street.

Wiebke was astonished. After a performance one night, a girl tried to rip his cowboy shirt from his back when he came offstage. A bit of cloth came off in the girl's hand and she stood there, looking at it and weeping. Another slipped him a note that read, "I'll meet you at midnight."

Before a performance, he whistled from anxiety. When Dean began whistling, Wiebke knew he was worried. He had enormous energy. He lived off big rushes of adrenalin, and then, at the end of a day's work or after a concert, as it drained away, he was exhausted. He fell into a chair one night at the Ukraina Hotel, staring at the green chenille bedspread with little cotton balls on it. He couldn't stand or speak. He shut down, like a light switch.

And then, in Moscow, out of the blue, Dean asked Wiebke to marry him.

"Would you like to be my wife?" Dean said.

"I would like two days to think the situation over," she said.

He was not pleased at all by her reticence, although it was a phrase she learned from him. "I would like two days to think it over," Dean would say whenever he had a difficult political issue to deal with.

"Unless you're my wife, I can never take you places," Dean told her.

So she said OK. They got married and Dean did take her traveling. He took her to Venice. He took her to America where, like Leonard Cohen, they stayed at the Hotel Chelsea. On a plane to LA, she saw Kojak in the flesh. With Dean, Wiebke went to Colorado and Hawaii, and to New York, where she was sick as a dog in a restaurant in Greenwich Village. She told him she thought it might be fun to stay in America for a few months, maybe longer, but Dean said no.

"I cannot," he said, "I have no career here. I am a political man."

Wiebke adored Cuba, although Dean was disappointed because Fidel Castro was out of town when they got to Havana. Nonetheless, he was impressed by Cuba; it was the only country in Latin America where, as he saw it, there weren't great disparities between rich and poor. Wiebke was surprised that white people ran everything.

"The music in Cuba was wonderful," said Wiebke. "Dean made his best record with some Cubans. They have natural rhythm, you know."

Now, in the restaurant of the Stadt Hotel in East Berlin, Wiebke finished her story, staring at the remains of the kebab on her plate.

"Have some wine?" I said.

I wanted to get Wiebke to tell me what Dean was like in bed.

"No thanks," she said, "I'm driving."

We stayed on for a while, talking and drinking coffee. There were more stories, more anecdotes, more tales. Across the table I could see Leslie thinking: how in the hell are we ever going to make a film of this huge promiscuous life, about all this STUFF?

"Of course, he was a Virgo," said Wiebke thoughtfully.

I said, "I see."

"Like me," she said. "Both Virgos. Stubborn, obsessive, perfectionists. He didn't have hobbies. He didn't read much, except politics. He didn't go to the theater or the opera, or have an interest in sports. He was interested in propelling his career. He "craved attention," she added. Once we were in a boat with Victor Grossman. Dean disappeared. We got into a panic. We looked over the side of the boat, and, suddenly, he bobbed to the surface. 'Look, I've drowned,' he said and, rising from the water like Jesus Christ, he burst out laughing."

Wiebke shuddered, finished her story and signaled the waiter for a bill.

I opened my bag to get some money to pay it. Wiebke stopped me.

"Please," she said.

"It's OK," Leslie said.

"No, I will pay and, if you like, you can pay me back later," she whispered, glancing over her shoulder at the waiter. Then I understood: she wanted the dollars.

Wiebke stuck her elbows on the table and put her chin in her hands. "Sex and politics. That's all Dean was interested in. Sex and politics."

I thought of Paton Price.

Paton who had been angry with Mrs. Brown because she sent Dean to Hollywood a virgin; Paton who wrote letters to Dean in South America about the women he screwed; Paton who made him strip naked in class, and sent him to a prostitute who said Dean was a natural in bed. Dean always said: "I am no puppet." But wasn't Paton his godfather? His puppet-master? The best friend of Dean's life as he called him: Paton Price.

"Was he?" I asked.

"Sorry?"

"A natural?"

Wiebke changed the subject. The next afternoon, at her house in East Berlin, Wiebke showed us her nudie shots of Dean doing push-ups on the carpet.

Wiebke's place was in the Berlin suburbs. It was five minutes' drive from Dean's place at Schmockwitz.

We ate coq au vin in the kitchen. Over the table, a shelf held a dozen brightly colored packets of tea that were obviously precious. I asked if food was hard to come by. Only the mushrooms, she said. And oranges. You could only get oranges at Christmas.

Natasha, Wiebke's daughter by Dean, ate with us. She was twelve years old. A slight, fair, pretty girl, she had her mother's face imprinted on her like a pale photograph. She smiled shyly and hardly spoke. She refused to speak English, Wiebke said, because she was angry with Dean for leaving her. And for dying. She was mad at him for dying.

A cuckoo clock chirped from the living-room wall. Wiebke got out a box of pictures, as Mrs. Brown had done in Hawaii. There were photographs of Dean turning somersaults in the air, of Dean rolling around with the dog, of Dean doing push-ups on the rug without any pants on. There were pictures of Wiebke bare-breasted, which she showed us without any embarrassment.

Natasha crept quietly into the room and curled up in the corner of the sofa.

I tried to get another look at the picture of Dean doing push-ups bare-assed, but Wiebke had moved on and was staring at her own wedding pictures. Dean wore a cowboy shirt with an eagle on the front. Wiebke wore a muu-muu from Hawaii and platform shoes. Everyone had had such a good time that they forgot to speak English, which made Dean feel left out. He grew petulant and remote. Wiebke wondered what she was doing there.

"It was the first time since we met we didn't make love, our wedding night," Wiebke said.

After Dean and Wiebke were married, they built the house in Schmockwitz. She gave up her career. He chose women who were self-possessed and competent, but as soon as they were his, he wanted them to stay at home.

Dean could be erratic, even volatile, Wiebke said. His moods could change on a dime.

"Once he became so furious he punched the furniture with his fists. On another occasion we turned up at some cinema where tickets should have been left for him, but weren't. He could not handle it. He wanted to go home and give himself up to despair," she said. "I said, 'Dean, let's go out and have a good evening,' but he said, 'You don't know what it's like when I'm checked in this way. It makes me feel dreadful. I can't cope with it.'"

They tangled about clothes.

Wiebke said, "He wore those cowboy clothes. He had a red jacket. 'He looks just like a trained monkey,' my first husband would say."

They also fought about his music.

"Once, when Dean was practicing, I said, 'I've heard that song thirty times, I'm going into the garden.' Dean became hysterical. He said, 'Patty used to love to hear it a hundred times.' I said, 'Good for Patty. I'm not Patty,'" she said. "But I think he knew his limits," Wiebke added. "He would put on Frank Sinatra and he would say, 'I wish I could do that.'"

Wiebke looked at her box of pictures and documents and in it were bundles of letters tied together with ribbons. She took out a letter that was marked "To be opened in the event of my death."

The letter, written before a trip to the Middle East, described the necessity of his visit to the Third World. It was what a man had to do, said Dean. You could not ask others to put themselves on the line if you did not do the same thing.

"As soon as things were going bad in his personal life, he got on a plane and headed for some revolution. He would go somewhere really stupid and dangerous. He played a kind of Russian roulette," said Wiebke.

In another letter Wiebke showed us, Dean talked of the reconciliation with his father that had occurred when he went home to America in 1978. They had gone fishing together.

"I really feel I have his love and respect now, and that he now loves me more than Vern or Dale, but he never told it to me," Dean wrote.

"Getting his father's attention was the most important thing in Dean's life," Wiebke said, echoing what Dean's mother had told me. "He thought his father was very brave to commit suicide. Dean saw the movie *Whose Life Is It Anyway?* He said 'a man has a right to end his life.'" And then it ended. Dean and Wiebke split.

It was a startling change of gear. And Dean told Wiebke he was bringing a red-haired stewardess home to Schmockwitz and would Wiebke please beat it. It was 1978, and Natasha was still a baby.

"Was Renate already in the picture?" I asked.

"He knew Renate. He knew her from the time he came to East Germany," Wiebke said. "There were many women. He used to come here and say, 'Can't you teach these girlfriends of mine to cook?' He had a different girl every weekend to cook, but he liked my goulash."

Wiebke was put out that Dean didn't even bother to help her find a place to live. He had powerful friends on the Central Committee, but he did nothing. He didn't bother with Natasha. When he married Renate and adopted her son, Sasha, he bought him videos of Mickey Mouse and Donald Duck. For Natasha he bought junk.

"Couldn't he buy Natasha a Donald Duck, too?" Wiebke asked, and added, "Renate could never have a child by Dean. After we had Natasha, he had a vasectomy!"

Wiebke looked over at Natasha who was still on the sofa and had not said a word.

"Would you like to play something for us, darling?" Wiebke

asked her little girl. Natasha went to the piano and began. Then she got up abruptly and ran out of the room and Wiebke's mood changed.

"Shall I play for you the song Dean and I made together?" Wiebke asked.

They had gone to Prague together to record it. Dean recorded most of his albums in Prague. Wiebke turned on the record player. The song was called "Together," and it had a spoken interlude.

"Tell me you love me," Dean whispered.

"I love you," Wiebke said.

"Tell me you need me."

"I need you," Wiebke said.

"Tell me you respect me," Dean cooed.

"I respect you."

In spite of Wiebke's feisty style in person, the song was very sentimental, all deeply felt; she had gone all the way to Prague to whisper that she respected Dean on the mushiest of all the tracks he ever put down on wax.

"He didn't even make a special effort to get our song special plays on the radio," Wiebke said.

13

"I'm convinced it was suicide," said Victor Grossman in his flat near the Karl Marx-Allee in East Berlin. The flat was in a postwar apartment building, where, like scabs, the tiny beige tiles had peeled off the façade. Grossman's flat itself was full of books, and there was a yellow plastic shopping bag from Tower Records. Perhaps someone had brought him a present.

The suicide scenario surprised me; it had been mentioned before, but only casually. In East Berlin, Grossman had been close to Dean Reed.

We had had trouble getting to Renate, Dean Reed's widow, and Renate was the key. Leslie Woodhead and I went to see Victor Grossman, who knew her. He agreed to contact Renate. As soon as we arrived, he had called her and now we talked and waited for the telephone to ring.

Good-natured, shrewd, maybe a little vain, Victor had first met Dean at the same documentary film festival in Leipzig where Wiebke met him.

"I was called and asked to help interpret for an American rock and roll singer. It wasn't my sort of thing, but I agreed," said Victor, who was a folk music man himself.

"He was a big surprise for me," said Victor. "I really had never known a rock and roll type, a Colorado cowboy singer, to be an avid leftist. But that's what he was. And we got along very well. It was very unusual for me. And, of course, it was probably interesting for him, too, to meet an American here in East Berlin. We spoke the same language in many ways, and became good friends."

He paused, removed his glasses, and put them back on. "Dean was a star from the moment he arrived. Girls here fall for anything Western. *The Golden West*, they called it," said Victor. "One girl bragged her Italian lover gave her one hundred lire. She thought that one hundred was a lot of money."

Victor Grossman, in his sixties, wore a plaid shirt and sandals. He was enormously hospitable, but slightly fretful that day we first met. He had not yet booked his summer holiday. If you missed the final booking date, your holiday was *kaput*, even if there were still vacancies. Victor intended to visit Soviet Georgia with his wife.

In Victor's flat, which he shared with his wife—the kids were grown up with children of their own—back issues of *Mother Jones* and *Rolling Stone* were piled knee-high. Galleys of *Veil*, Bob Woodward's book about the CIA, were sprawled out on a large work table that held a computer. Dictionaries in Russian, German, and English were stacked beside it.

Victor disappeared into the tiny kitchen that was behind a curtain strung on a metal rod.

"Have some cheesecake," he said reappearing, a large metal cake tin between his hands. Shoving aside a pile of manuscripts, he put the cake tenderly on the coffee table.

"Go on, please. My wife made it," Victor said generously.

I ate a lot of cake on the Dean Reed story, especially in East

Berlin and Prague. Cake eating, as a ritual, seemed to feature as significantly in the German Democratic Republic as smoking Marlboros did in the Soviet Union, or Kents in Romania. As soon as you arrived—at Wiebke's, at Victor's—the coffeepot was filled and a cake was produced. Victor pushed a large knife into the tin and, getting some leverage on it, gently prized out huge slabs of cheesecake.

In the Seventies, when Dean was a superstar making movies in East Berlin, Victor was involved as his translator, and he could thicken up the story with anecdotal titbits: the ragged gypsy girl Dean befriended on location in Romania; his camaraderie with the stunt men (you got paid by the stunt in Eastern Europe, and Dean saw to it that everyone got an equal piece of the action); the horror of the directors when he insisted on doing his own stunts. In one case, even after he broke his wrist, Dean persisted in climbing a castle wall for a sequence in a film. He demanded that his stunts were filmed in a single shot so that it was clear that Dean himself was performing them. He often spoke of himself in the third person.

Idolized by fans, his politics acceptable to the Party, Dean became a minor but potent player in the East. He claimed to know Erich Honecker and Gustav Husak. He made speeches and was honored by the Czechs with the Julius Fucik Medallion. He played concerts in Sofia and the Bulgarians presented him with the Dimitrov Medallion. Every ghoul in Eastern Europe, I thought, the whole bunch of them had honored and celebrated Dean Reed.

We ate cake and drank coffee in Victor Grossman's flat, and Victor told the story of how Dean, on a visit to America in 1978, was arrested and sent to jail; how the East German propaganda machine clanked into action and the legend of Dean Reed grew.

In a Buffalo, Minnesota, jail, Dean began a hunger strike and he wrote a letter about his suffering to the people of East Berlin. In it, he crowed about the solidarity among the prisoners, but mentioned wistfully how he dreamed of eating goose, especially now it was almost Christmas. His letters were larded with the international socialist rhetoric he was so good at.

Obsessively, the media reported the details of Dean's detention: on November 6, *Neues Deutschland*, the official East German newspaper, gave front-page coverage to Dean's telegram of greetings to "the people of the GDR and Erich Honecker."

From his jail cell, Dean wrote to Erich Honecker. Joan Baez sent a telegram to President Jimmy Carter to protest Dean's incarceration. So did Pete Seeger and Dimitri Shostakovich.

An international incident was in the making. On November 11, 1978, the *New York Times* got into the act, reporting that a number of Soviet composers put through an appeal to President Jimmy Carter to help with the release of Dean Reed who was in jail in Buffalo, Minnesota. He was awaiting trial and had been charged with trespassing during a protest over a power-line construction site.

Trespassing? Trespassing? The infraction was so minor that even a German couldn't get exercised over it. It was more than a little embarrassing when the judge was revealed to have offered Dean his choice: a $500 fine or three days in jail. Dean made a speech and went to jail.

Every morning in jail, apparently, he rose early and, from his cell, he sang for the other prisoners.

"Oh what a beautiful morning, Oh what a beautiful day," Dean sang. It was one of his favorite songs and he often sang it when he was in jail. I could imagine him in the role of Curly; he would have been perfect in *Oklahoma*. Not everyone saw it that way.

"Give it a break, Dean," the other prisoners shouted. "Give it a break!"

Like Dean Reed, Victor Grossman was an American in Berlin. Unlike Dean, Victor was perfectly cast for his life. He did not admit to missing much by living in the People's Democratic Republic. Except maybe an avocado. And a Jewish salami. It was impossible to get a Jewish salami in East Berlin, he said.

I thought that Victor was maybe a little fed up with talking about Dean Read. Concealed behind his amiable face and the round spectacles, was a not inconsiderable guy. He, too, was an American in the East; he, too, had an amazing story to tell.

"He's an exotic here, isn't he?" asked Mike Wallace when he interviewed Grossman about Dean Reed for *60 Minutes*.

"Perhaps, a little bit. Because, of course, there are not so many of us Americans around here, you know. Basically, I'm an exotic here, too."

"That's true. That's true," said Wallace.

"I'm more exotic than he is, in that sense," said Victor Grossman.

While we waited for the telephone to ring—for Renate Reed to call Victor back—Victor pulled one leg over the other, polished his spectacles, and told his story which, like Dean's, was pretty incredible, another tale from the Cold War, another story of an American who had crossed over.

Victor, who had grown up in New York, went on to Harvard. In 1951, during the Korean War, he was drafted. The army asked if he belonged to certain left-wing organizations.

"Did you?" I asked.

"As many as I possibly could," Victor said.

"The Communist Party?"

"Yes, of course."

Refusing the draft was illegal. Being a Communist was illegal, too, if you were in the military. It was Catch-22 and Victor kept his mouth shut, joined up, went to West Germany, and served nearly his whole year without incident, although as a Jew he felt uneasy: there were still plenty of fascists around.

Then the letter came. The Judge Advocate, noting that Victor Grossman had concealed his illegal affiliations, ordered him to report to the nearest Military Court. Victor panicked.

In his head perhaps, he played out scenes of his Court Martial. Senator Joe McCarthy's voice plagued his sleepless nights: "Are you now, or have you ever been . . . ?" Maybe agents in raincoats chased him through his nightmares. Images of prison haunted him, of hardened criminals and Victor among them, a kid who grew up in New York, whose parents sold books, a commie, a pinko traitor.

Victor ran. Making his way to the Danube, the river that was still divided between East and West, he jumped in. Just stuffed his papers in his pocket and jumped, just like that, swam across, and came up on the Russian side, clutching those papers, looking to defect.

He couldn't find a Russian.

For twenty-four nightmare hours Victor wandered around the Eastern sector, holding tight to his papers, looking for a Russian. By the time he found one it was pretty hard to explain where he had been all that time.

Still, they took him in, debriefed him, and resettled him. He went to university and moved on to East Berlin, where he married Mrs. Grossman, had a couple of sons, and got down to the business of being a journalist and translator. He had an East German passport with the word "American" stamped across it.

As a Jew, he said, he found West Germany scarier than the East. In East Berlin he never made a secret of his Jewishness. He believed the German Democratic Republic made a conscious effort to reject fascist ideology. He believed the GDR made an effort to evolve a just socialist society. Victor didn't have to buy into these views, to accept the socialist package. He had grown up on it. He *believed*.

He settled down in East Berlin, where he wrote books about folk music and he took his holidays in the Soviet Union, and, after thirty years, Victor Grossman still believed. He knew that it was not paradise on earth, but his basic convictions were intact: in the East there were great gains in education and in medical care and the arts. Neo-Nazis and big business ran West Germany, Victor believed; I. G. Farben was a name that often popped out of Victor Grossman's mouth.

What about the Stasi? What about the prison camps? Perhaps, Victor said, perhaps they existed, a few of them, and they were not unlike the prison farms of Arkansas.

Leslie asked if Victor felt oppressed at all by the system, by the lack of freedom to express his opinions, for instance. Victor said that he often heard a wide range of opinion expressed in East Berlin. Maybe you didn't hear the non-leftist view in political meetings, but you heard it at the supermarket. You heard discussions of West German TV, for instance, and people watched the American soaps obsessively. There were shortages, yes, but there was music, theater, art, opera. There were world-class sports.

"I don't actually care much for sports," Victor added with a self-deprecating smile.

In some ways, I thought that Victor was a man in a time warp. In spirit he was true to his origins. You could put him in a museum with a label: Young American Communist Man, *circa* 1952. He had grown up when the Soviets were America's brave wartime allies.

His role models must have been those urban coastal Jews in America, the union organizers in San Francisco, and the New York booksellers, like his parents, the believers who hoped for a better way of life for their kids and for the dispossessed, who thought, whatever its drawbacks, and all systems had drawbacks, that the socialist ideal, realized, would feed body and soul.

"All them cornfields and ballet in the evenings," Peter Sellers had said as the union man in *I'm All Right, Jack*. That was what the American dreamers imagined when they thought of the Soviet Union and even of its satellites: All them cornfields and ballet in the evenings.

In East Berlin, Victor Grossman was one of a tiny group of Western expatriates. He did not think he would ever see America again. He still owed the US army some time, so he was afraid to go back, but, as the years went by, if Victor missed America, it became more and more remote.

"Will you ever go back, do you think?" I asked.

He said, "I think this year we shall have our holiday in Soviet Georgia," he said.

Then in Victor's apartment, the telephone rang. Speaking briefly into it, he covered the mouthpiece.

"It's Renate. She says she will see you, but not before Sunday, if that is convenient for you."

One more delay. We had a thousand questions. Victor had to get to the travel agency.

In the elevator, he was silent, concentrating on his holiday, I thought. We shook hands and agreed to meet on Sunday—he would translate for Renate. Leslie and I were going back to West Berlin for the night, and then on to Prague.

"Is there anything you'd like from West Berlin?" I asked.

Victor hesitated.

"Please let me," I said.

"Well, I would like an avocado. It is thirty years since I last saw one," he said.

The metallic sound of the goose-stepping guard at the *Memorial to the Victims of Fascism* rang out with chilling irony as Leslie Woodhead and I drove away from Victor's, looking for something to do. Leslie had hardly said anything while we were at Victor's, and I knew something was bothering him.

At the Kino, *Die Mission* was playing. I wished it were *Tootsie*, which had been a big hit in East Berlin, and I could have used a laugh. Robert De Niro speaking German did not seem an appetizing way to spend the evening. I had watched him schlep his weapons in the string shopping bag up that mountain in English already, and once was enough. As he manfully shouldered his own good-hearted message around the globe, Dean would have identified with De Niro, *Die Mission*, and the penitent's net bag.

I suggested a visit to the opera, for which East Berlin was famous. Leslie looked horrified. Opera was something fat ladies did if they couldn't get a job with a rock and roll band.

"Let's have a drink instead," he said.

A few blocks from Checkpoint Charlie was the Grand Hotel,

an island of comforting new Western decadence in the gray heart of the righteous socialist state, but a state that needed hard currency desperately in the late 1980s.

Inside the lobby, the illusion began to fall apart. It was as if hoteliers from another planet had reconstructed a hotel from a blueprint made after a single visit to Earth. The elaborately carved period furniture was imitation veneer on top of chipboard; the courteous young managers in striped pants had the beady eyes of security guards; there was a swimming pool in the hotel, but it was too small for real swimming, and the tropical solarium looked out on a sodden, chilly city.

In the café, a grave little all-girl orchestra played skillfully, but without any feeling, for the clientele were more interested in the enormous bowls of ice cream than in the pretty renditions of Brahms.

A young woman in stone-washed jeans—the uniform of the well-to-do youth of the East—sat at a table opposite her mother, who wore a hat and ate whipped cream off her spoon with her pinky raised in the air. Smiling, she nodded dreamily at her daughter, as if lost in the illusion that this was the Berlin of her gay youth and nothing at all had happened since.

When the woman in the hat got up to gaze at the cakes in a glass case, her daughter leaned over. She spoke good English.

"It is nice for her," she said to Leslie and me. "Next time, I will save enough to take her to the swimming baths, too."

I scrounged a few dollars from the bottom of my bag and gave them to the young waiter for a tip. He seemed worried. Then he smiled. He had it. "Have a nice day," he said. "Have a nice day."

The Grand Hotel accepted Diners Club, American Express, Visa, Eurocard, Eurocheques, Avis cards, Hertz cards, dollars, pounds sterling, Deutschmarks, Swiss francs, French francs, and yen.

"Money makes the world go round," went the song in *Cabaret*. Money, money, money. I could hear the jingling of coins.

Not much in the East shocked me more than the way these countries degraded their own currency. It eroded the whole structure of society; it made people willing to sell themselves for a few bucks, and I hated it. When in the fall of 1989, East Germans began jamming the trains that would take them west through Hungary, they tossed their banknotes on the station platform with contempt and spat on them.

At the Grand Hotel was an Intershop, an official hard-currency store. With their noses literally pressed against the glass, locals, out for the evening, gazed at displays of leather coats, French perfume, and Italian silks. Without hard currency, they could only look; there was nothing else they could do. Why didn't they smash the windows? Why?

What did Dean make of it, with his medals from every dictator in the East? Did he have a secret agenda? Was he working for democracy from within, the worm in the apple? Maybe he remained a tourist in Berlin and Moscow, seeing only what officials intended him to see, unaware of the corruption.

I remembered something that Dean's mother had told me in Hawaii.

"When he first arrived over there in Germany, he was like something from outer space," she said. "He never got used to Germany, though. He was always a tourist."

"How could he be?" said Leslie, who had barely said a word all day long. "How the hell could he be unaware?"

All day, Leslie drove, he took notes, he ate cake, but he kept a thin-lipped silence, which was unlike him, for he was always ready for a laugh. East Berlin got to him, and I knew he was beginning to take against Dean Reed; more than anything, he could not stand the naiveté.

"I don't get his politics, you know," Leslie said.

Dean Reed's politics were very simple: US democracy was only a choice between Pepsi and Coke; imperialism ruled the West; the East featured benign state socialism and free medical care. Dean had a rationalization for everything, even the invasion of Afghanistan by the Soviet Union; the Afghans denied women their rights he said.

He had the line down pat and was much given to shtick about the arms race and the human race. Mike Wallace of 60 *Minutes* told him he sounded like an editorial in *Pravda*.

I made a half-hearted stab at explaining to Leslie that I thought Dean was, at least, sincere. Leslie didn't care. He was also desperate to get out of East Berlin now. At the border, we discovered we still had East German money. You were forbidden to take it to the West.

The bank at Checkpoint Charlie had closed. The guard directed us to a bank back in the Alexanderplatz and we turned the car around, and started driving, peering out into the empty city, looking for the bank.

Suddenly, Leslie stepped hard on the brakes, the car stopped, he got out and I followed. He looked around the dark empty city, the rain falling in gray sheets.

"It's crap," he said. "Crap. All of it crap. The politics are crap. The money is crap. The furniture, the clothes, the schools. Crap. It's a conspiracy of mediocrity. From the Berlin Wall to Vladivostok, they've cheated everyone and everything is crap."

A man in a hat walked along the street, staring at us. The man disappeared, and all I could see was the rococo outline of the opera house against a purplish sky. In the distance, beyond the Berlin Wall, lay West Berlin, the neon dream city. It made the sky glow the way Las Vegas does when you come to it, all of a sudden, out of the desert.

Leslie started walking.

"Where are you going?" I was nervous.

Looking around once more at the empty, dark, wet Berlin street, he took all of the shitty, crumpled, greasy money out of his pockets and shoved it in a garbage can on top of all the other garbage. Then we got back in the car and fled to the West. I could hear Leslie heave a sigh of relief.

I said, "What's the matter?"

"I had a minute of panic," he said. "I thought I might be trapped on the other side of the Wall."

14

In Prague, Vaclav Nectar had been Dean Reed's best friend. He was himself an improbable rock star. A tiny, cherubic man who had trained as an opera singer, he had the direct, dimpled gaze of a five-year-old, the face of an elderly baby. *Un vieux garçon*, the French would have called him. His friends called him Vashek.

In the driveway of Vashek's little villa in the exquisitely bourgeois suburbs of Prague lay a mirrored ball from a dance hall that had closed. It seemed such a perfect metaphor for Prague: heartbreakingly lovely, sad, the gaiety and music shut down by an oppressive regime.

"I can't think of anywhere to throw it away," said Vashek.

On the other side of the drive was an ancient tree. "My wife's father planted it when she was born," he added, gazing up at the sky on a day so exquisite it seemed ironic all by itself, but almost everything was in Prague.

Inside the house Mrs. Nectar fussed with coffee cups and cakes. She had been a ballerina and she was thin and looked fragile and safety pins dangled from her apron. She also had a cold and she smiled wearily and left us in the living room with its carefully matched furniture to watch a video of Vashek's band, the Bacilli. All of the Bacilli wore masks and their biggest hit was called "The Clown."

There followed a little tour of Dean Reed memorabilia, carefully hoarded, placed in positions of honor around the house: wind-chimes from Colorado, a big tin samovar from the Soviet Union, a chromium clock from somewhere socialist, and a little brass lamp from India.

"Dean had a tremendous capacity for warming up the public," Vashek said. "He could win their trust immediately, then state his political convictions. People would take it from him. He spoke in English. He was a master at communicating. I learned from him: the public must be yours the moment you've sung your third song.

"He did the international hits. He did the Everly Brothers, 'Ode to Joy', and even 'My Yiddishe Momma', which was tremendously popular here."

In the basement of Vashek's house was a secret rock and roll museum. On a row of shelves, back issues of the *New Musical Express* were stacked tidily alongside newspaper cuttings and record albums. There was an old stereo. The walls were completely papered with posters of rock stars such as Mick Jagger, John Lennon, Elvis Presley, and Dean Reed. Cliff Richard, however, had, in a sense, made Vaclav Nectar a star.

In 1968, Vashek tuned into a radio broadcast from the Albert Hall in London and he heard Cliff Richard sing "Congratulations."

"I was much taken with it," Vashek said in his formal way. Three days later, adding his own Czech lyrics, Vashek recorded a cover version of "Congratulations." It became the anthem for the euphoric Prague Spring when the country seemed to have been liberated from its oppressive regime. In Czech its lyrics concerned spring, green trees, a girl in a nylon blouse, and young love over a

Martini Dry. Vaclav Nectar longed to meet Cliff Richard, but when he finally saw him backstage at a concert, he was too shy to say hello.

Prague was a city addicted to music: Paul Anka had played Prague once, so had Manfred Mann. So pervasive was rock and roll in the Sixties, that when the writing team of Sucy and Slitr—their hits included "Mr. Rock and Mr. Roll" and "Vain Cousin"—opened the Semafor Theater in Prague, over five years a million people came, which was equal to the entire population of the city.

In the 1960s there was a surge of Western culture; the Beatles flourished. In his book about rock and roll in the East, Timothy Ryback describes a delicious moment when, in 1965, Allen Ginsberg was made student king in Prague. Ginsberg announced that rock and roll "had shaken loose the oppressive shackles of Stalinism."

What a howl it must have been when they made Ginsberg king and carried him like a hero-god around town. He was thrown out of the country for subversion, perversion, and wearing flowers in his hair.

When the Soviet tanks rolled into Prague in 1968, everything went dead. People said it was as if you could hear the noise in the streets, the excitement, news, chatter, music, the buzz that during Alexander Dubcek's short reign had risen to a delirious hum, simply stopped. Banners and flags that crowded the city's sight lines, extolling socialism and Lenin and Brezhnev, flapped to a tuneless breeze. In Wenceslas Square, for twenty years afterwards, it was as if the soundtrack was shut off. That's what everyone noticed as the city crept back into silent submission.

The Soviet invasion destroyed the hope and the gaiety; the country was gradually strangled by dread. But it took time before all the music died. In 1969, the Beach Boys came to Prague. (In Czech, the Beach Boys were known as the Boys from the Seashore, a name in this landlocked country that seemed sweet and loony and reminded me of Shakespeare's "Seacoast of Bohemia.")

"Help me Rhonda, help help me, Rhonda . . .," the Lucerna Hall rocked all night, and Mike Love of the Boys from the Seashore said how happy he was to be in Prague. He wanted to dedicate a song to Alexander Dubcek, who was in the audience. It was called "Breaking Away."

Prague was the most beautiful city in Europe, but in those years melancholy floated like dust through the stucco-colored air and there was a slow, drifting accretion of inertia. In every window in the shabby arcades around the square, in every car, taxi, and shop, were pictures of Lenin. Slogans pasted on ravishing baroque buildings testified to the joys of socialism. Groups of children with sullen faces were herded, silently, through the Klement Gottwald Museum of Socialism.

As the hard-liners had tightened their grip after 1968 all of the rock clubs shut up and Prague's top band, the Plastic People of the Universe, went to jail. Into this lovely town stunned into weary acquiescence, Dean Reed arrived and it was like Christmas.

That day at his house, Vaclav Nectar confessed suddenly that he was not altogether sure how great Dean's singing talent was. But his fans loved him and that was his true talent, and so when you walked with Dean in Wenceslas Square, it took an hour to go half a mile.

Everything east of the Berlin Wall was relative. For many in Prague the 1970s were dead years musically, but compared to East

Berlin, for Dean it was bliss at least professionally. There was a tradition for pop and rock which barely existed in East Germany, and even when East German officialdom recognized its inevitability, it did so by establishing an organization with the chilling title *Sektion Rockmusik*. As often as not, in East Berlin, a backing band meant a hundred singing strings because, under German socialism, no musician could be unemployed.

With its recent democratic history and its bohemian passions, its love for jazz and pop and rock, Prague's musicians remembered how to do it. Dean got himself a deal with Supraphon, the state recording label, which lasted the rest of his life. In a good year, what with exports throughout the Soviet Bloc, Supraphon sold a couple of hundred thousand Dean Reed albums.

Dean's first Czech tour was a "Solidarity with Chile Tour" in 1975. Ironically, as Czechs fled to the West if they could, thousands of Chileans, in flight from the horrors of Pinochet's rule, escaped to Eastern Europe. All over Europe and particularly in Czechoslovakia, Chileans, a few of them Dean's compañeros from the old days, lived in exile.

Someone said to me, "Poor bastards, they exchanged Pinochet for Husak." It probably didn't seem that way, though, if you had just avoided having your brains bashed out or worse in a Chilean football stadium. Among this free-floating group of peripatetic exiles, émigrés, musicians, and poets, Dean was a drop-in star.

"Am I popular because I fight for peace?" Dean had asked Vaclav Nectar. Vashek did not want to hurt Dean; he would say, "Half like you for that." And Dean would say, "What about the other half?" "Because you're American."

On that tour in 1975, Dean sang "Bye-Bye Love" to rock-starved Czechs. He was sweet with the girls and brazen with the bureaucrats. He stood up for his friends. He spoke his mind. In his white turtleneck, Dean went on television and said: In life you must have love and fun. Fun! It had been a long time since anyone thought about fun, maybe not since 1968; the idea of fun itself was a revolution.

Out of the blue, when we were settled in Vashek's basement, drinking coffee, he said suddenly, "But meeting Dean didn't help me much. But I don't mind, although it aggravated my problems for the next ten years."

With the obsessive recall of the torture victim, Vashek began the long, sad, intricate tale of his relationship with a Mr. Hrabal whom he called the Master of Power. The road to Vashek's particular hell had been paved with good intentions. His life went terribly wrong, and it was full of dark corners and dead ends, like a Czech novel.

After 1968, and already a marked man, Vashek had been called by the state to testify against Marta Kubishova, the heroine of the Prague Spring, the girl who sang at the tanks in the streets and was awarded a Golden Nightingale by Mr. Dubcek. Frantishek Hrabal, as the chief of *Pragokoncert*, had complete authority over pop music. A former head of disinformation, he was a full KGB Colonel; he was the Master of Power.

"We have people to destroy you," the Master of Power screamed at Vaclav Nectar when he refused to identify Marta Kubishova as the woman in a set of pornographic pictures. Marta and Vashek had worked together in a group called the Golden Kids and they were friends.

Kubishova sued Hrabal for slander. Vashek spoke in her defense again, and his career was finished. So fragile was Vashek afterwards that, on one occasion, after he shouted at the Master of Power, his chief torturer, he committed himself voluntarily to a lunatic asylum.

"I could claim I was briefly deranged and had meant no harm," Vashek said.

There followed an incredibly complicated story about how Dean seemed both to cause trouble for Vaclav Nectar and to bail him out, but I couldn't follow the terrible events that involved *apparatchiks* and ministers and bad Communist karma. Part of it was to do with Dean's insistence on being paid for his performances in dollars, as I understood it, part to do with Nectar's rebellion against the bureaucracy.

In any case, there were periods when Dean was not allowed to perform in Prague. And it was Vashek who, because he was friends with Dean, suffered most. There were interrogations. Trips were canceled. Vashek was victimized, terrorized, worked over by the secret police. But Vashek never blamed Dean, not even because Dean's righteous outrage seemed to be only about money.

"To Vashek, my brother, friend, and comrade. I love and respect you very much. You are a very special person in my life. Until death us do part. An embrace," Dean wrote in the flyleaf of his autobiography.

Vashek showed me the book. He insisted that the last line was significant. Before he spoke, he put a record on the stereo to muffle our conversation.

He whispered, "With Dean's death my life in fear began," he said and then suddenly stopped.

In the background, the music played dully. Vashek's voice dropped as he spoke of the Czech secret police and an alliance with the East German Stasi and their desire to eliminate Dean Reed because Dean Reed was trouble.

"Dean said too much. He called the officials 'Mafia'. He had many friends among the prostitutes here. Many were informants," Vashek said. Glancing over his shoulder, he added with a meaningful stare, "One of the girls was called Ophelia," he added, and looked at me to make sure I understood he was referring to Dean's death—a murder in his view—by drowning.

Still, well before his death, Dean was finally allowed to perform in Prague again; he sang "Give Peace a Chance" and 4000 people rose to their feet.

"The popularity, doesn't it bother you?" Dean's Czech engineer had asked.

"I need it," Dean would say. "I can't live without it. It is a drug."

15

There seemed to be no way forward. The more informants I talked to, the more the mystery jammed up against itself: Wiebke described a massively moody man whose adrenalin rushes left him too drained to turn on a light switch; Victor thought Dean was a man of profound political naiveté and great glamour; and Vaclav Nectar saw him as a brilliant performer and loved him, even though he had somehow ruined Nectar's life. Dictators gave him medals; stunt men, kudos; women adored him; no one could or would really talk about his death.

I had been following his ghost for months by now. Who killed Dean Reed? Who was he? A true believer? An American rock star supplying opium for the socialist masses? Our spy, the best mole America ever had? Theirs?

The Berlin Wall was still up and even when you got to the other side, it was a police state, ruled by the Stasi, a fortress of paranoia. Information about Dean Reed was very hard to come by. I was at a dead end.

East Berlin was a city of dead ends: the Wall that kept people in; the badly drawn map on the greasy visa issued at Checkpoint Charlie, which marked forbidden territory; the midnight curfew for tourists; the worthless money which you could not export; the East Germans, noses pressed against the glass at the hard currency Intershop in the Grand Hotel, gazing at leather coats they could not buy from countries they could not visit; doormen who barred the way to hotels; the official reports of Dean's death which yielded nothing much at all except the German obsession with bureaucratic detail; the lonely house where Dean Reed had lived next to the lake where he died.

It snowed the day that we, Leslie Woodhead and I, finally went back to Schmockwitz, to the house on the wrong side of the Wall, at the end of a country road next to a frozen lake. Victor Grossman was with us; he had agreed to translate. It was March, 1988, four months since we had first come.

The wind howled around the Alexanderplatz as we drove out of Berlin towards Schmockwitz. The earflaps of his Russian hat pulled down over his ears, Victor Grossman sat in the front seat next to Leslie and recited the directions for Schmockwitz. In his lap, Victor held a bag with a couple of avocados that I had brought him. Leslie pretended not to have been down the road the previous November.

As we left the city behind, the snow fell harder. A thick mist came up and the low-lying suburban buildings turned into an endless gray blur. The dismal little East German cars slid and skidded on the highway: none had chains or snow tires. Hairdryers on wheels, Leslie called them The Trabants. I said they were like mobile sardine cans. We passed the time making up names for the Trabis, laughing nervously, not paying attention to the fact that Victor Grossman might have been offended by our jokes. This was his country, his country's cars.

The village of Schmockwitz was shut tight for winter. The pub was boarded up. At the end of the long, bleak road was the Reed house, with the carved R on a post.

We parked and, as we walked down the path to the front door, I could see the lake, gray and forbidding. Every time she looked out the window, I thought, Renate must have seen the lake where Dean died. On the doorstep were two pairs of rubber boots caked with mud. I wondered if they had been used the day Dean's body was dragged from the lake.

The house seemed silent. It had been the object of so much effort for so long that I sometimes dreamed about it. Suddenly, a light flashed on inside, the door opened, and Renate stepped out, smiled, and kissed Victor's cheek.

In black leather pants and a white silk shirt, Renate stood in the doorway and greeted us, smiling. She had an anxious, beautiful face and dark eyes. Renate gazed directly at you, kept you in her gaze, made you the center of her attention. She had that peculiar talent that people said Jackie Onassis had.

"Please," said Renate and opened the door wide and tilted her head in welcome.

"Thank you," I said, and gave her some chocolates.

"Thank you," she replied.

In the hall, Renate took my wet boots away and gave me furry slippers. A good *hausfrau*, I thought. Renate smiled; she knew what I was thinking. Still standing in the vestibule, she lit a cigarette. Her hand shook as she forced a lighter into life. But she grinned with unexpected good humor; she had a wry grasp of the situation, and I liked her instantly.

Victor, who had removed his own boots, was already in the sitting room. On a table in front of a tan corduroy sectional were blue and white cups, a coffeepot, the inevitable cake, and a plate of little chocolates.

"Décor is Biedermeier Cowboy," Renate announced winningly.

The house was full of stuff: a carved dining-room suite, a cuckoo clock, a sofa, chairs, a big fireplace with a television set, video cassettes, plants, copper jugs filled with flowers, a miniature set of fire tongs, and a shovel. Over the fireplace hung Dean's guitar, and there were horse things—bridles, bits—props from a movie. In a picture in a fancy frame on the mantel, Dean and Renate kissed for the cameras. Beside it was a brass carriage clock, with an inscription from Dean to Renate that read, "I love you more every hour."

On the floor lay a dark brown animal skin, probably a bear, I thought; it seemed to have a bear's head. I had seen a video clip of Dean near that fireplace, holding his guitar, speaking to the camera:

"This guitar, this Martin guitar, which I took with me when I left, has been in the jungles with me in Brazil and Bangladesh, and this buckle [points to his belt buckle] are the only two things that I've kept for the twenty years since I left America. They have traveled throughout the world with me day by day, they know my life."

"Please, sit down." Renate gestured towards the sofa.

I sat down and fell out of the slippers, then I ate some cake. Leslie sat near Renate and listened intently.

Renate spoke German and Victor translated, although sometimes she slipped into English. She seemed fragile and sad and vulnerable. The big dark eyes locked mine into a tremulous gaze. My God, it must have been lonely down the end of that road with only her boy, Sasha, for comfort.

Like all teenagers, Sasha, who was fifteen, seemed to be perpetually in motion. Ill at ease, but handsome and polite, he shook our hands, kissed his mother, and hurried away to meet his friends, his long, skinny legs encased in black leather pants that gave him the look of a big bird.

"He is a good man. He is my little man," said Renate. "You would like to see the house?"

It was a shrine. On a table were Dean's spurs from Chile. A saddle was tossed over the stair railing. On a wall, an American flag hung upside down; it was the flag Dean had washed in public in Santiago to protest the Vietnam War, the flag he said he had washed of the blood of the Vietnamese. It was hung upside down as an ironic comment on America.

We followed Renate up a flight of stairs, where she opened the door to Dean's study. I walked in and thought: the inner sanctum. You could almost smell him in here.

Through the window was a view of the lake and the woods beyond. On the wall were pictures and quotations from Fidel Castro and Jimmy Breslin. On the desk was his portable Olivetti typewriter and, under the glass top, snapshots. One was familiar.

"Oleg Smirnoff," I said.

"You know Oleg?" Renate smiled.

She was pleased because Oleg had been such a good translator for Dean. Dean said Oleg could do it almost better than he could. (I thought of Oleg's hatred of Germany, where, he said, the people say hello to the dogs but not to you.) Renate was happy that we knew Oleg.

Back downstairs in the living room, we exchanged pleasantries about Mrs. Brown and Phil Everly. I told her about Nikolai

Pastoukhov and his tale of Dean's first trip to Moscow, when he sang all night in the private train that belonged to Deputy Premier Tikhonov.

Lost in reverie, Renate clasped her hands and perhaps imagined her handsome husband singing in the train that sped through the Tolstoyan night as if it were a scene from a Russian novel she'd read as a schoolgirl.

"So what is it exactly that we are here to talk about?" Renate asked.

The small talk was over, the cake eaten. Renate wanted to know what we wanted. Leslie talked about the drama-documentary that he wanted to make. He said that he liked to think of Costa-Gavras's *Missing* as a model. Renate said it was among her favorite films. This was a good sign. She poured more coffee.

Leslie took charge and he was convincing.

"We want to work with you," he said. "To be absolutely candid, you are Dean's widow. You own the rights to his music. We need you."

Renate inquired politely about editorial control over the script. Could she see a script when one was ready? she asked.

"I really would like to," he said, "but I am forbidden to do so by Parliamentary law."

I had no idea if this was true, but it sounded convincing and I was impressed.

Renate nodded and she poured out white Hungarian wine into dainty Hock glasses with thin green stems.

Renate Blume was born in Dresden. She must have been a child during the firebombing that reduced the city to rubble, but she did not talk of such things. She was reserved and well bred. Her father had been an aviation engineer. Her brother was a mathematician. It had been expected of Renate that she would be a doctor. She wanted to dance, but her parents forbade it. "We are scientists in this family who do not fool around with such stuff," they said.

Still, she had her way and, having trained as a dancer, she got a place in Berlin's best acting school. Before she had even finished the course, she was cast in a film, *The Divided Heavens*.

Renate played the tragic heroines on stage in Dresden. She married a director, Frank Bayer; she worked in films and on television. For her portrayal of Jenny Marx in a Soviet series, she received a Lenin Prize.

Renate rose from the sofa now and took a mother-of-pearl box from a drawer in a table. In it was her Lenin Prize, a small, elegantly embossed medal.

"Dean also got one," she said. "He got his first, which was right, because he was the bigger star."

Shyly, she reached for the scrapbook beside her on the sofa and opened it for us. In it were fanzine snaps of Renate.

"A fan sent me this," she said self-consciously, giggling over a picture of herself in a miniskirt, her cheeks sucked in, her hair long, her lips white. "Terrible," she added. "Terrible pictures. But I have been so lucky in my work. Then I have had no luck at all when Dean died. The man I was looking for all my life and thought I would never find," she said piteously.

She first met Dean on location in a movie called *Kit und Co*, taken from a Jack London novel.

"We were lovers," she said. "But only for the film, of course." Renate was still married and Sasha was a little boy. Dean was married to Wiebke. But something stirred between them right away, perhaps friendship, Renate said. In 1975, she divorced Mr. Bayer, but she did not ever want to marry again.

"I lived without my husband and without Dean for almost seven years," she said. She did not want a star like Dean for a husband—she knew there would be problems. But it was somehow inevitable.

They were married on September 22, 1981, Dean's birthday; he wrote a song for her called "On the 22nd of September."

Now Renate pulled a large box of photographs towards her. Bending over it, the ritual began: the showing of photographs. Ruth Anna Brown had produced pictures from a trunk in Hawaii and Wiebke from her own archive and now Renate.

Leslie and I sat on the edge of his seat, looking at the box that had not been opened since Dean's death, according to Renate. She sat on the floor near the box and started pulling out pictures. Images of Dean spilled out on to the carpet as if he were a jack-in-the-box and only Renate could let him out. I sat beside her.

Pictures of Dean in performance. Pictures of Renate and Dean. Pictures of their wedding. For the wedding, Renate had worn a white dress and she carried white roses. Dean wore a suit. The wedding party was on a boat on the lake.

In the pictures, groups of people celebrated, toasting the radiant couple; he was fair and handsome, she was dark and beautiful. In one photograph, Dean wore a sailor hat cocked dashingly over one eye. He sat at the wheel of the boat. Renate gazed lovingly into his eyes, and her arms were clasped passionately around his neck. In another, Dean hugged a pig. "A wedding gift," Renate said, giggling. Then she grew serious.

"Three weeks after we were married Dean went to Beirut," Renate said now, no longer laughing. "Dean was an idealist."

Before they were married, she had accepted his need to put himself on the line for his beliefs. She understood Dean because she, too, believed. Like all educated East Germans, she spoke Russian. In working with the Soviets on *The Life of Karl Marx*, she came to understand them. With her whole heart she felt they were a friendly, peaceful race. In the Soviet Union, many people had lost their families in the War. The Soviet Union had lived through war in a way that Americans had never known upon their own soil, and the USSR would never want war again, she said.

"So many women are living alone because of wars, and have never found another husband," Renate said sadly.

Truly, Renate believed; she had also been passionate for Alexander Dubcek's Prague Spring, for socialism with a human face. So she understood his need to travel for the cause. When he went to Chile in 1983, though, she was scared and she begged him not to go. The death squads were rattling around like loose cannon and no one was safe. Renate begged Dean.

"Please, Dean. Don't go. Please!"

Before he left, he got into his car and drove all night to the Czech border to meet his friend Vaclav Nectar. There, Vashek handed him the master of a record Dean was to present to the brothers in Chile. In no-man's-land at midnight, the two rock stars embraced.

"Promise me you won't sing 'Venceremos'," Renate said when he got back from meeting Vashek and before he left for Chile.

"No, Renate, I cannot promise you. I am not going all the way to Chile to sing 'White Christmas'," Dean said.

* * *

The secret police grabbed Dean as soon as he arrived in Chile and he was informed that he could not work because he had no permit; he said he was not working for pay, only bread, so he didn't need a permit. He strode into the union hall that was filled with his comrades who had paid a loaf, if they could, to see him sing.

Fist raised, Dean jumped on to the stage and the striking workers from the copper mines began to clap for him. Their wives and their kids clapped. Striking his guitar with one hand, the other held in a clenched fist, Dean sang "Venceremos," the anthem of the revolution. No one had dared sing this patriotic song since Allende's death; everyone in the hall stood. Everyone began singing, raising their fists for Dean and for liberty. Outside the hall, the security men prowled, their weapons ready, waiting for him.

Dean spoke to the crowd in Spanish. A woman put a pendant that had belonged to her dead husband around his neck. In Santiago the next day, Dean sang "Venceremos" again, this time to a group of university students who had never heard it before, because they were too young.

Dean was arrested and deported, although there were some who said he bought his ticket out with the American Express card Paton Price had given him for emergencies. While Dean was in Chile, a filmmaker he knew recorded everything. Now, in Schmockwitz, Renate put the video on and the scene played in front of us.

Renate was scared when Dean went to Chile, of course, but by and large, they were happy. Dean made her happy. He even whistled at her when she was especially pretty; in Germany it was an insult when a man whistled at a woman, but she understood that for an American it was a compliment. They had holidays in the mountains together and she helped him prepare his television shows. She coached him in German. They went skiing. Dean adopted Sasha. He offered, but he never pushed.

"I would like Dean to be my father," said Sasha and, after a while, he took Dean's name.

Looking up at the video, Renate smiled at another image of Dean. He was on a dirt bike, which he rode standing up, playing his guitar.

"He really was crazy," she said fondly.

After they were married, Renate gave up a good deal of her own work; she had a more important role: it was her role to be there for Dean when he came back from his many trips, to entertain his friends and comrades.

Life was full: Dean performed at concerts and he made movies. His friends from America came to visit, among them Paton Price, who stayed for six months in order to act as Dean's advisor on *Sing Cowboy Sing*, a cowboy spoof.

It was shot in Romania because Romania was a terrific double for the Old West, the landscape was rugged and there were barely any television aerials in the Romanian countryside. Paton hated the food. A million East Germans saw *Sing Cowboy Sing*.

Like a fond mother hen, Renate indulged Dean when his Americans came, for she knew that he missed his own language and its jokes. When Phil Everly was at the house, they carried on like little boys, horsing around together. At a concert at Karl Marx-Stadt, Dean and Phil played "Bye-Bye Love" together, just as Phil and Don had once done.

"How did you come to play with Dean in East Berlin?" I had asked Phil Everly in the Mexican restaurant in California.

"He just got in touch and invited me," Phil said.

"What was it like with Dean in East Berlin?" I asked.

"We played some concerts. We had a lot of laughs. Dean was a real joker. He got me an interpreter, a lady who was one of only twelve Mormons in East Germany. There was nothing to buy, I mean how much caviar can a fellow eat? So I bought some diamonds, but they weren't much good. But Dean loved it."

I remembered that Phil had found East Berlin depressing.

"In fact, it had me scared when I got off the plane," Phil had said. "Of course, Dean was on the other side. Dean was so popular then, so well known that the treatment once you got in there was phenomenal. The fact that you were coming there to see them. But I was scared until I saw him. I told him that, too."

Dean took him to the Stadt Hotel, the best in town. Phil remembered, "The first room I had was so narrow, maybe as spoiled American that I am. You had to see it to believe it. And I told Dean. I said, 'I can't stay here two weeks.' Dean got me to a corner room, which was twice as big, and got me one of the two televisions in that hotel. You could see West Berlin television, so I watched *Bonanza*. In German, you know? But it was so American, I loved it. One thing is sure," Phil added. "Renate sure did love Dean. Some mornings, when he got up to go to the movie studio around six, she got up even earlier, drove her car down the road and waited, so she'd be there to wave him off to work."

By and large, life with Dean was idyllic, Renate said, conjuring up scenes of domestic bliss. They had busy lives, but, from time to time, they stole an evening together. Dean would sit near the fire and play the guitar, with Renate stretched out beside him on the bear-skin rug. They talked about *Bloody Heart* and how they would spend the summer of 1986 filming it together in Yalta, and they looked into each other's eyes.

Bloody Heart was to be *their* movie—Renate's and Dean's. Dean was to star, write, and direct the film about Wounded Knee. A German–Soviet coproduction, it was a love story, set against the Indian uprising at Wounded Knee, South Dakota, in 1973, which ended with a violent shoot-out between the Indians and the FBI. It was a perennial favorite of socialist propaganda and it had everything movie-goers in the East loved: war, horses, big set pieces. Most of all, it had Indians.

In the Soviet Union and the East, but especially the USSR, people were obsessed with American Indians. Particularly around Leningrad, kids with a taste for exotica joined Indian clubs, wore feather headdresses, practiced Indian love calls, and mourned the death of the great native culture.

Dean and Renate were to star in the film as a divorced couple, she as a reporter, he as a photographer. On assignment at Wounded Knee they are reunited, but, in the tragic finale, Renate's character is shot dead. Already in 1985 they were thinking about *Bloody Heart.*

In the fall of 1985, Dean went to America. Nothing was ever the same again, Renate said.

"Did Dean want to return to America? Would you have gone with him?"

"I would have no audience there. I would have no career, no job. I do not speak enough English, and I am not young," she said. "After his trip to Colorado he missed his homeland very much. He was very homesick. He talked of nothing else."

Dean had come back to her full of hope, wanting to live in America which, to her, was a strange land.

Renate loved Dean deeply; she loved his courage, his thinking, his personality, she said. He was the man she had been waiting for all her life and whom she thought she would never find. He was her *compañero*. Now he was dead.

"After Dean died, I put away all the boxes, all the pictures, everything. For a while, I could only look at the pictures and cry," Renate said.

She got up and wandered over to the window; it was completely dark outside. She shivered and drew the blinds against the night, then turned around and smiled.

"Are you hungry? I have some steaks I could fry," Renate said eagerly.

Looking at his watch, Victor shook his head. Perhaps he was thinking about his vacation, perhaps polite.

Renate would have liked the company, I thought. It was miserable at the end of that road, near the frozen lake in a silent house that was inhabited by ghosts. When she talked of Dean, she was perfectly loyal, but there was an undercurrent; I thought she was angry with him for leaving, and very lonesome.

We put on our coats. We left the house. Leaving Victor and Leslie near the car, Renate walked me to the little cemetery. In her red coat, she put her hand on my shoulder, as if to steady herself. A bunch of wet flowers lay on Dean's grave, where a rough stone was engraved with the words THE COUPLE REED.

Renate said softly, "When Dean was leaving for America, I was so unhappy. I thought he was never coming back. He got the stone and he showed me. He said, 'I love you and I am coming back and some day we are being buried together under that stone.'" Renate looked at me and said, "You understand? I think he believed this."

An early recording

Dean at military school

The Reed family

Dean on his way to Hollywood

Dean and friends in Hollywood

Cine-Amor

M. R.   N.º 18 — LA REVISTA CHILENA DE FOTONOVELAS   —   PRECIO: E° 0,30

DEAN REED

Chilean movie magazine

Dean and South American tribesmen

Dean being arrested in Argentina

Movie poster: Dean and Yul Brynner

Dean in an Italian film

Lobby poster for *Sing Cowboy Sing*

Dean and Vaclav in *Sing Cowboy Sing*

On set in Moscow at
Ostankino studios

Dean in Moscow

In 1973 with Tamara Terashkova, the first woman in space

Dean at World Music Festival, 1973

We Say Yes, World Music Festival

Dean on East German TV

Dean starring in *Blood Brother*

Dean and Phil Everly at Karl Marx Stadt

Dean and Yasser Arafat

Dean with the PLO

Dean with Daniel Ortega

Dean with the Allendes

Dean with Renata on their wedding day

Dean in Loveland, Colorado, with John Rosenberg

Dean and Renata on set of *Bloody Heart*

One of the last photos of Dean

Three

16

"My brother called me and said, 'Quick, turn to Channel Four, NBC News, Dean's on,'" Johnny Rosenburg reported when I visited him in Loveland, Colorado, in the winter of 1988.

It had been the summer of 1984 when Johnny took his brother's call. Now he said, "And I turned it on and, sure enough, there he was. But a big star in the Soviet Union, Eastern Europe. I couldn't believe it. I mean I can't even begin to tell you the emotions that went through me at that time."

With Dean on the TV screen, the reporter's voice was saying, "Who is this man, the one being hounded for autographs in downtown Moscow? You probably don't recognize him. Most Soviets would since he's considered to be the most popular, best known American in the Soviet Union. And most Soviets are quite startled to learn that most Americans have never heard of him." The picture cut to a Soviet woman with a few teeth missing, who said, "He is the best singer in the world."

Johnny was pretty much bug-eyed.

"My God," he thought. "It's Dean!"

Johnny's back had been giving him some pain that day, but he hardly noticed it now. He turned up the volume on the TV. Yes, by God, it was Dean. It was him. On national TV in, where? In Russia. My God. Johnny was stunned.

"Mona, Mona? Mona!" he had called to his wife. "C'mon in here."

Then Johnny got his scrapbook off a shelf and looked up that last postcard he had from Dean in 1962: Merry Christmas from South America. All those years since he and Dean had roomed together in their manager's house in Canoga Park in Los Angeles, he had had no idea if Dean was dead or alive. Since the postcard, Johnny never heard from him again. Seeing Dean turned out to be a much more fateful event for both of them than either Johnny or Dean could have imagined.

Now Johnny looked at me pleasantly. I was sitting on the two-seater couch in his living room in Loveland, near the same TV where he had seen Dean. His memories of the event and the reunion with Dean that followed were absolutely fresh.

"I sure have had a lot of company since meeting up with Deano again," Johnny said to me.

The Rosenburg living room had the couch and chair and the TV set and a coffee table. An archway led into a kitchen, where the fridge was dotted with magnets shaped like fruits. On the wall was a collection of fancy commemorative plates.

On the table next to the chair where Johnny sat was a well-worn bible, with a brass cross for a bookmark sticking out of it. From time to time as we talked, Johnny reached over and touched his bible.

In his late forties, he wore a plaid shirt and jeans and cowboy boots, and he shifted his weight in his chair like a man in constant pain. All his life he'd had the bad back. Or maybe he was just weary of the constant visitors who'd turned up at his screen door since Dean died.

Out of the window you could see the neat houses in Janice Court where the Rosenburgs lived. Beyond their yard were more houses, big green pines, and in the background the outline of the Rockies.

On the way up from Denver to Loveland, the road was dead flat and the countryside looked half-an-hour old. The snow had melted, the sun was warm and it shone on a scatter of wooden buildings set down at random on the raw yellow scrublands.

Denver wasn't a mountain town at all; it was the last stop at the edge of a huge prairie, flat as a pancake and barely domesticated. This had been the end of the world for the pioneers, the last outpost before they launched themselves with incredible will over the Rocky Mountains and on to God knew what beyond. For the early settlers, so remote was California and the coast, they might as well have been headed for the moon.

Loveland itself felt like a little covered wagon encampment made suburbia. At the edge of town were the Rockies, purple and huge and intimidating.

Johnny returned to his story. He took me back, not just to the day in 1984 when he saw Dean on TV, but to the 1950s when they first met. Memories just flooded back to him. Suddenly, it was 1959 and he was a kid with an idea, as he put it, about playing some music.

In 1959, Johnny had had his spinal operation and his folks bought him a cheap guitar to help him pass the time while he was getting better. He always had a desire to get into the music business and he discovered he could pick out a few chords and had the ability to take what was in his mind, as he said, and put it into words and music. The first two songs he wrote were "Lynda

Lea" and "Gonna Find a Girl." Eventually, "Lynda Lea" did pretty well in Japan, Johnny said.

Johnny hooked up with another kid, a guy from his home state of Nebraska named Ted Lummus. Ted was a drummer. They got to jamming together and they got a big old bulky tape recorder and went down in the washroom of Ted's parents' motel and laid two songs down on tape. You got a good echo effect down in the washroom and Ted's parents were OK about them doing it.

Around that time Johnny read in the *Recorder Herald* that there was a Capitol recording artist vacationing at Estes Park, at the Harmony Guest Ranch.

"Let's take these two songs up to him and see what he thinks," he said to Ted.

"We won't get near him."

"Well, we never will know 'less we try," Johnny said.

Johnny and Ted loaded up the old tape recorder and drove up to the Harmony Guest Ranch, where they saw Dean out by the pool with a couple of ladies. So Johnny walked right up to him and told him who he was.

"I've got a couple of songs here. Would you listen to them?" Johnny asked Dean, bold as brass.

Johnny figured at that point Dean would say get lost. But Dean just told one of the girls to go get an extension cord for the tape recorder.

After listening, Dean said, "I like those songs. I'd like to maybe record one."

Jesus, Johnny thought to himself. I don't want to be a songwriter. I want to sing my own songs. I want some of that spotlight. But what could he say?

"Well, yeah, sure," Johnny said to Dean.

On Dean's advice, Johnny and Ted cut a demo. Dean said he would take it out to his manager in Hollywood, and a few weeks later, Johnny got a call from Dean; he was back in Estes Park and he had good news. Johnny went up, Dean grabbed him by the hand and smiled.

"Johnny, I want you to know you're going to be recording for Capitol and you're going to have the same manager I've got."

Ted got dumped, but, well, that was the way these things went.

Needless to say, a young kid like Johnny from nowhere, he was out-of-his-mind excited. Soon after, Roy Eberharder, Dean's manager, flew in to meet with John and his folks and he signed John up. That was October. In November, Johnny went on out to California and signed with Capitol.

Dean was living out in Canoga Park with Roy Eberharder and Mrs. Eberharder and their son, Dale. It was one of Shirley Temple's older houses that she rented out and it was on a hillside overlooking Canoga. Johnny shared Dean's room with him.

Sometimes Johnny found himself alone in the evenings. Other times he'd be gone on the road and Dean'd be there by himself. Most of the time, though, they were both there together.

They never went around as a pair. The only time they were together was at the house, in the evenings mostly. They'd just lounge around, go out to play badminton, go down to Canoga Park, kick some dust. There wasn't much to do.

Out in California, as Johnny recalled, things were going pretty well for both of them, though they never really discussed each other's careers. One evening, Dean and Johnny were at the house. Johnny was thinking about his work, figuring he was getting on OK. He didn't think it was a bad life. Dean was crazy upset, though.

"I'm never going to get any work if I keep this guy as manager. I don't know about you, but I'm getting out on my own." he said.

Johnny told Dean he was nuts. Almost the next day, Dean disappeared. Johnny, who sometimes didn't see him for days anyway, didn't give it much thought for a while. Then he began to wonder. He went and found Roy Eberharder.

"Where's Dean?" Johnny asked.

"The SOB thinks he can do better for himself," said Roy.

Johnny let it drop. He was busy trying to keep his own head above water, trying to do his own thing.

It was the latter part of 1960 when Dean just disappeared. He wasn't a hundred percent sure of the date. Most records showed that Dean actually left around 1962.

In the house in Loveland, Johnny broke off his story. He was a self-possessed man, damaged by disappointment and lost chances, maybe, but with a humorous, long-suffering look and a great talent for storytelling. From the time I met Johnny Rosenburg and heard his stories about how he met up with Dean Reed after a quarter of a century and how Dean came home again to Colorado, I could never get the rhythms of Johnny's speech out of my head.

"This is Mona," Johnny said, as a handsome woman in jeans came through the screen door carrying a brown paper bag full of groceries.

She had a steady blue gaze and a face out of a Dorothea Lange photograph. Mona was one of twelve children. She had worked three jobs since Johnny's illness and now their eldest girl, Pamela, was in college. You knew that at the Rosenburg house Mona ran things even if she always deferred to her husband. We shook hands and Mona went to put up some coffee in what she and Johnny referred to as the 'world's loudest coffee pot'. Mona usually called him John, which was his true Christian name. When the coffee was ready, John took a cup from Mona and returned to the story of his time in Hollywood.

He crossed his foot over his leg and rested a scrapbook on it. He opened the brittle pages. There were some publicity stills of Johnny Rose, which had been his professional name. He had been as handsome as Dean in his way; Johnny had looked like a young Steve McQueen. But after Dean left Hollywood for Chile, things didn't go right for Johnny. He had just signed the seven-year contract with Capitol and was back in Loveland on a visit to his folks, when Roy Eberharder called him on the phone.

"Johnny, I got bad news for you. Capitol dropped you," Roy said.

"What?!" Johnny couldn't believe his ears.

"Well, they've got a new policy. If you don't make it big in the first record, that's it."

Johnny stopped his story to take some coffee from Mona. Then he shrugged some and said there was nothing to explain why he was dropped so suddenly from the music business in the early 1960s. He'd been doing OK; he'd won a big talent contest in New Orleans; he had even played Ocean City Park in California, where he did a show with Dirty Stevens.

"She had a big hit out at that time called 'Tan Shoes and Pink Shoelaces'. Do you remember her?" Johnny asked.

I tried very hard to remember because it seemed so important to him.

"I can't understand why things turned out for Dean and me the way they did," he said.

I asked what he thought the reason was.

"You know, it's really hard to say. I don't know. I don't understand that anymore than I understand why I was treated the way I was," Johnny said. "You know, the people that were judges on that panel for that contest, people who are supposed to be able to identify talent when they see it, they picked me and then they didn't want to work with me. There I was on Capitol along with Dean, I had songs that were doing quite well. I don't know why, all of a sudden, I was no longer around."

I said, "Maybe the business was too mean for you."

"Maybe," he said. "Maybe you had to be mean. Or very sold on yourself, because that's what Dean was. He wasn't doing that great back then. He had to pay his own way to South America, where he heard he had a hit with 'Our Summer Romance'. But nobody was sold on Dean more than Dean himself. You know that was it. I mean Dean knew some day, some way, he was going to be a hit. He knew he was going to be a hit one way or the other. I hoped I would be a hit," Johnny said, "but hope wasn't enough."

After he had seen Dean on TV in 1984, Johnny had one hell of a time running down Dean's number over there in East Berlin. He called the TV station in Denver. He called NBC in New York. London said they'd get back to him, but he couldn't wait. Up half the night in a growing frenzy, he called in succession: the State Department; the Russian Embassy, who were not very nice; and the East Germans, who were quite nice. Eventually, he got a telephone number in East Berlin. When he heard the operator's voice, he just went bananas. He taped the phone call and now Johnny put a tape into a tape recorder box that sat on the floor near him. He switched it on.

"United States calling for Mr. Dean Reed."

"Yes, this is Dean Reed."

"Dean, this is an old friend of yours back here in the United States. Does the name Johnny Rose ring a bell?"

Dean didn't remember.

Johnny reminded him they recorded on Capitol together, that his birth name had been Rosenburg, but he recorded under Johnny Rose and how they met at Estes Park, where Dean helped him.

Dean remembered. Of course, he remembered. You could almost hear Johnny let out his breath with relief that his old friend remembered him.

Johnny told Dean he had made the TV news back in Colorado. Dean asked if Johnny was still in the singing business. Johnny told him how he underwent surgery in 1981 and couldn't work. They exchanged news about their families and promised to write each other. It was almost crying time for Johnny, as he put it.

"My God, man, keep in touch, write to me," Johnny said.

That's how it got started. The renewed friendship got cranked up as they wrote each other. A while later, Dean told Johnny he was coming back to Colorado for the Denver Film Festival in the fall of 1985. Some fellow called Will Roberts had made a documentary film about Dean: *American Rebel* was its title. It was more than twenty years since Deano had been back to Colorado, but he was finally coming.

From things Dean was saying in his letters, Johnny could see he was a big star over there in the East. Big like Michael Jackson. That kind of big. Johnny realized that Dean thought a lot of people would know of him in Denver. It worried Johnny considerably.

Johnny said, "In his letters he would say, 'Well, when I get back to Denver, Johnny, maybe we can have a horse parade from the airport to the state capitol, and the governor can be there to greet me.' And I thought, Wait a minute. Nobody knows him. I thought to myself, You're a songwriter, John. You've got to do something here. You've got to tell Dean nobody knows him back in his hometown. Then I thought, Well now, wait a minute. That's a pretty good title for a song. So I sat down and I wrote this song. I called it 'Nobody Knows Me Back in My Hometown'."

"You think he'll laugh at it?" Johnny had asked Mona when he had finished the song.

Mona said, "So what? You've had people laugh at your songs before."

Johnny sent the song on over to Dean in East Berlin, and Dean flipped for it. Dean sang it at the Youth Festival in Moscow, the summer of 1985. A couple of months later, he called Johnny to say he would arrive on October 16.

Johnny played "Nobody Knows Me Back in My Hometown" for us on the tape recorder. It was really good, a classic country tune.

Johnny remembered everything about that period, and he recorded his and Dean's phone conversations and put his own thoughts down on tape. It was uncanny. It was as if Johnny knew that one day somebody would make the movie.

Johnny picked up the bible with the bronze cross from the table near his chair in his living room in Loveland. I asked him about Dean's death.

"Maybe he was the best mole this country ever came up with," said Johnny Rosenburg. "But me, maybe I'm thinking more with my heart than with my mind when I say, I think he was murdered."

17

"Welcome home, welcome home. My God, man, you kept all your hair. Look at me," Johnny said right off the bat when Dean came off the plane at Stapleton Airport that October day in 1985. He had just burst out of that plane door like the biggest star you ever saw. He looked terrific. He was forty-seven years old.

Dean was in something of a daze, Johnny could tell. There was some press at the airport but not like Johnny would have liked. Dean had written that maybe there could be a horse parade and the mayor could meet him at the capitol. He was used to that level of welcome in Eastern Europe, he said; he loved the fanfare. Johnny had called a few TV stations.

"Guess who's coming to town?" Johnny said.

"Dean WHO?" was what people had usually said back.

Johnny had the date Dean arrived engraved in his head: October 16, 1985. Mona was real excited. Their pictures had hung together on the wall at Johnny's mom's house for as long as she could remember. After staring at Dean's mug on the wall at her in-laws' house for all those years, it was thrilling for Mona to meet him for the first time.

At the airport, Mona got introduced. God, he was a handsome man! she thought when she first laid eyes on Dean.

The first thing Johnny noticed was that, to his ear, at least, Dean had developed something of a foreign accent, which the female race, including Mona, found very sexy. But in other ways he hadn't really changed all that much.

But then Dean was swept off down to Denver by the film people who were in town for the documentary film festival.

Mona and Johnny jumped in Johnny's Ford Elite and drove home to Loveland real fast to tape the news coverage. As they ran into the house, they turned the set on. They saw Dean stepping out of his limo at the Westin Hotel downtown.

The day after he arrived in Denver, Dean did a radio show with Peter Boyle. Johnny warned Dean not to go on Boyle's show. Communism was not flavor of the month exactly; no one knew much about this Gorbachev guy; Reagan was talking Evil Empire.

"Don't do it, Dean, you're being set up. Don't do it," said Johnny.

"Johnny," Dean said. "I have played my songs in thirty-two countries and I have risked my life for the things I believe. Why would I worry about one radio talk show guy?"

Dean went ahead with the interview. At their house, Johnny and Mona were listening to the radio.

"It's seven after the hour of nine o'clock on a Friday, the 17th of October, in Denver . . . you heard it through the grapevine," Boyle's voice came over the radio from the Fairmont Hotel lounge, where he was broadcasting. The music switched over from Martha and the Vandellas to Dean Reed singing, a ballad about Sacco and Vanzetti. Dean called them Nicola and Bart.

Boyle again: "It's twenty minutes after the hour of nine o'clock, 9:20. Remarkable guest in the studio, Peter Boyle on K-BIG AM and FM. That was the voice of Dean Reed. And this is going be a difficult interview. Dean Reed . . . was born right here in Colorado and now lives in East Berlin. He's back in Denver for the premiere of a documentary film about his life at the festival; he's a big star in Central America; in the Eastern Bloc . . ."

Johnny and Mona could tell from Boyle's voice that he probably didn't like Dean.

"Do you consider yourself a defector?" Boyle asked Dean on air.

"Not at all, Peter. I consider myself an American patriot," Dean said, his voice firm and cool. "I'm a good American, Peter. I can take a sword 360 degrees around my head and cut no strings. I'm a puppet of no one, Peter."

Boyle egged Dean on, asking him about Communism and if he was some kind of traitor.

Dean started getting mad.

"Peter, I resent that. Dean Reed is not what you say. Dean Reed believes in equality for all mankind. You sound like a fascist. You're talking just like the neo-Nazis that killed Alan Berg."

"Don't you ever accuse me of that," Boyle screamed.

"That's the way you're talking," Dean said.

"Get out of here! Get out of here! Take a walk . . ."

Johnny thought, Jesus, man, I told you Boyle's best friend was Alan Berg, the talk-radio guy who was murdered by the neo-Nazis. Johnny knew those old Nazi boys were going to be sitting up there in Idaho now, watching for Dean. He thought: Man, if you stick around here, you had better get yourself a bulletproof vest.

"Take a walk . . ." Boyle said.

What startled Johnny most, though, was that in the background, along with the noise of scuffling, he could just about make out Dean's voice. He was whistling.

"To me," Johnny said, "it seemed that World War Three almost erupted behind that microphone."

Eventually, I met Peter Boyle, and he said he was a little sorry he'd lost it with Dean Reed.

"I wish I had to do it again," Boyle said. "I probably would have done it differently. I don't know if I did my job correctly. It was a very raw nerve time for me. I had been, up until actually that day, I had been testifying in a murder trial of a colleague named Alan Berg, who had been murdered by neo-Nazis." Boyle was sorry he'd thrown him off the air and he recalled how intimidating Dean seemed.

"And he got up," Boyle said. "He really got up. And he was big."

Maybe it wasn't World War Three, but the story escalated around Denver, said Peter Boyle.

"Well, less than an hour later, the whole story about what had happened had changed. And it was all over the press. And Dean Reed was saying that he would be murdered in Denver that night. And if he was, it would be on my conscience. It was my fault. And I had just gone through a murder. And I thought, you know, 'My God!'"

That night, because of the Boyle affair, when *American Rebel* premiered at the documentary film festival, a squad of police cars cruised the Tivoli Center in downtown Denver.

Jesus, Johnny thought when he got there. Johnny had bought about twenty-something tickets for the show and inside the Tivoli Center's movie theater, he and Mona and their friends settled in their seats.

The lights in the theater went down, the film opened on a rain-streaked Moscow street, and then changed to Dean in Red Square mobbed by fans. The filmmaker Will Roberts' voice described how he'd been visiting Moscow when he came across the scene and asked someone what was going on.

"That's Dean Reed," the guy said.

"Who's Dean Reed?"

"Why, Dean Reed is the most famous American in the world."

In the audience, Johnny figured it was going to be OK now so he just laid back and enjoyed himself, although he wondered how Dean could expect anyone in America to reach out with open arms to him when, in one of the film's sequences, Dean was singing "Ghost Riders in the Sky" to Arafat.

"You must be kidding me," Johnny said to himself, as he was prone to do.

But considering the adverse reaction to the Boyle business in the Denver press, not to mention the Arafat thing, there wasn't much trouble that night. After the show, folks gathered to welcome Dean, and pretty soon he was absorbed into the Denver life, as if he had never been away. That was Friday night, there was another screening on Saturday, and on Monday Johnny went down to Denver to rescue his old friend and bring him up to the house in Loveland.

In downtown Denver, Dean was troubled at first because he couldn't recognize a thing. He couldn't find where he had grown up and it upset him a lot, he told Johnny.

Although he had been back to the USA a few times, he had not been home to Colorado for a real visit since his high school reunion in 1963. The only buildings Dean recognized were those he had seen on television.

Dynasty had made Denver famous. It was the perfect prime-time soap, the quintessential fairy tale for the Reagan years: rich people in big shoulder pads doing evil things to one another, while having a marvelous time spending loads of money. It was the most popular show in the world and its logo, which consisted of shots of Denver's glittering skyline, gave the city a real global presence. In Germany, *Dynasty* was called *Der Denver-Klan*. Even with the Berlin Wall still up, people in East Berlin could watch Western television because you couldn't jam TV signals.

What's more, because the West German television signals were too weak to reach beyond East Berlin, the rest of the population of East Germany made a terrible fuss. They wanted *Dynasty*, too, and in the end the East Germans were forced to run the program themselves.

On the evenings when *Dynasty* was broadcast, no one went out. In East Berlin, people pulled down the blinds, not altogether, in fact, because of politics, but because the soaps were non-*kulturny*, and Germans liked to think of themselves as cultured, if nothing else. At the house at 6A Schmockwitzer Damm, the Reeds, more than most, were glued to the television the night *Der Klan* was on. Like everyone in East Berlin, Dean watched both *Dynasty* and *Dallas* obsessively.

A friend of Dean's told me that once when he and his wife visited the Reeds in Schmockwitz they were watching *Dynasty*. "There are only two good days in East Berlin," Dean said. "The day we get meat. And the day we get *Dynasty*."

The TV shows were better propaganda for the West than any tract on democracy, better than long-range missiles; you could not buy this stuff for a billion bucks. Naturally, the citizens of the German Democratic Republic infinitely preferred low doings in

American cities to socialist documentaries about the manufacture of neon, or German variety shows featuring dancing girls in animal suits singing "Winter Wonderland." Everyone could see the good life on American TV: big cars; big blondes; fabulous homes. I always thought it was *Dynasty* that brought down the Berlin Wall.

As they drove around Denver, Dean's mood lightened. He looked at Johnny's car.

"Is that all motor?" Dean said, admiring Johnny's Ford Elite.

"It sure is," said Johnny.

"It's a typical American car, lots of power," Dean added.

"I wouldn't have a small car, they scare me to death," Johnny said.

"Renate is the same way," said Dean.

As Johnny drove through downtown Denver, Dean went on just ranting and raving about how wonderful it was.

"Well, Dean, you call yourself a country boy but you like this sort of thing. A town that has more than one stoplight is too big for me," Johnny said.

"Johnny, you just don't know how to live."

"So how come you left Hollywood?" Johnny wanted to know.

"They sold out my contract to some weird guys," Dean said.

"Are you sure about that, man?" Johnny asked, because he considered Dean's response pretty paranoid. "I don't remember it like that. I thought they were just a couple of guys from Abilene, Kansas, with a Cadillac dealership who bought you out."

Dean didn't answer. For a while, on the fifty-mile drive up to Loveland, they were silent.

When Johnny pulled into the driveway in Janice Court,

187

everyone in the neighborhood was hanging around. Johnny had explained in no uncertain terms just how big Dean was in the entertainment business but Dean just leaped out of the car and said hi and shook their hands, they nearly dropped dead of shock.

Mona came out to greet Dean. He put his belongings in the house and, grabbing his camera, climbed the ladder at the shed in the back yard and began taking pictures. The mountains were exceptionally beautiful that fall. Every time Mona Rosenburg looked out of the kitchen window, she felt glad to be alive.

She said, "You just know that when Dean looked out of our west window and saw those mountains, his heart must have had a flutter."

"During that week, we got to know each other real well," Johnny said. "That friendship that we once had was all of a sudden there again, and it grew. I would like to think that it solidified and was even more important to both of us than what it was when we were young, back in 1960.

It was sunshine and blue skies every day that week in Colorado. Mona made pecan pie. Dean and Johnny chewed the fat. It was as if Dean had come in from the cold; he had come home. During the week in Loveland, Dean rode a neighbor-boy's motorcycle, threw a football—he forgot how hard it was to throw a spiral and how much fun—ate Mona's pecan pie, gave her little love pecks on her neck, left his room a mess, and spoke German with Pamela, the Rosenburgs' daughter, who was studying the language.

Dean sang for the local kids and juggled and walked on his hands for fifteen minutes at a go. He admired the way Mona and Johnny kidded each other—they had lost a child once and joking kept them going through the hard times.

Dean and Johnny drove over to Collins to buy cowboy stuff that was on sale and Dean thought the "fifty percent off" sign was a capitalist trick. He bought a belt buckle, but he didn't have Dean Reed put on it because it was considered improper to make a big thing of personalities over there in the East. Instead he got LOVE put on it.

Dean gave interviews to the local press. He took Mona and Johnny to a party given by *Denver Magazine*, which pleased them since they didn't ordinarily brush shoulders with the type of people who went to those parties such as the DJ Gary Tessler. Mona saw how Dean held all those people spellbound with his baby blues.

At night, after supper, Johnny and Dean sat up late and talked. They talked religion and Johnny thought Dean was more an agnostic than an atheist, although he did some research and found out Marxism was a religion and Marxism was atheism. Dean told Johnny that Mikhail Gorbachev was going to make big changes; Johnny had the idea Dean had had a talk with Big Mike. Dean always called him Michael. John and Dean batted ideas around.

"Over here we have a tough freedom. A lot of people might run back to Russia," Johnny would say. "Anyhow, how come you only talk politics. You're an actor, aren't you?"

"Why can't I be both? It worked for Reagan," Dean said.

Dean laughed and so did Johnny, but Johnny had the feeling Dean meant it.

Sometimes, Dean would be laughing, kidding, and feeling he could be the first one hundred percent genuine international superstar, then his mood would drop way down. Johnny found Dean one night, reading an article that was pretty tough on him. Dean's mood turned really bad.

"It's just one article, Dean," Johnny said.

"You just don't understand, Johnny," said Dean.

But the next morning, Dean straddled his chair backwards like always and ate his Wheaties.

"Breakfast of Champions," he said and hugged Mona.

Dean was a big hugger and it made Johnny uneasy, but Mona loved it. So did Pamela and her brother, Eric, who went by the nickname of Bull.

Now Mona offered me a piece of her peach pie and we all moved into the kitchen and sat at the table. She reminisced about Dean's visit while she served up the delectable pie.

"Dean couldn't believe the way John and I dealt with each other. I'd say, 'Oh, quit' or something. And he'd say, 'You know I can't do that with Renate. I can't say, I love you, to Alexander, because there's a different set of love for the German people,'," Mona said. "I said to Dean, 'You're kidding. Well, I love you, Dean. Would that just blow Renate out of her mind?' And he says, 'Yeah, it would.'"

That same day, Johnny said to Dean, "Let's just shut down the telephone, Dean, and go up in the mountains." Most mornings that phone just rang off the hook at the Rosenburgs with people wanting to talk to Dean.

"Johnny, I'm not vacationing here. I got to lay the groundwork for when I come back," Dean said and Johnny realized coming back to America was already in Dean's mind.

When Dean took Renate's call early one morning at Johnny's house, she was scared. The Boyle radio show bust-up made the news in East Berlin and it was reported that Dean's life was threatened. Dean reassured her over the phone.

Then Dean said to Johnny, 'You know, I had a devil of a time with her. When I got ready to come over here she thought that I would never go back. What I had to do was get some friends together to bring down this great, big, huge bolder, and say to her, 'Renate, I will be back and you and I will both be buried under that bolder.' 'But Johnny, I am not going to be buried under that bolder.'"

"Well," Johnny said now, "as things worked out that's where he wound up."

That was also the night that Dean confided in Johnny he was not proud of having been married three times and that he loved Renate a whole lot. He was very firm in that, although she was awfully jealous, he said.

Renate would have been even more jealous, according to Johnny, if she had known about Dixie Schnebly, the woman who came into Dean's life in Colorado that week.

Mona put the dishes in the sink and said, thoughtfully, "Dixie knew the ropes. She was a business woman and very intelligent. She was a go-getter." Mona added, "Dixie, in my opinion, was a woman that was fascinated by Dean Reed. There wasn't anything she wouldn't do to help him, and she was maybe even in love with him. But I think her number one goal was to have him."

"Dixie Lloyd Schnebly. Yeah," Johnny said with a snort. "I don't know how many other names. She came into the picture on the Friday night at the end of the week when Dean was here."

The Rosenburgs were planning a concert in the basement of their house, and Dean asked if he could have a friend come up from Denver.

"Would you like to come up here?" he asked Dixie over the phone. "We're having a bye-bye Dean party."

* * *

For the party in Loveland, Dixie wore slacks, high-heeled boots, and a white silk blouse. She told everyone that meeting them—Johnny and Mona and their friends—made her feel so special, that she was thrilled Dean let her be one of their group.

In the Rosenburgs' yard, Dixie danced with Dean to a Phil Collins tune on a boom box. Johnny's brother shot some video. Then Dean did the Twist and everyone laughed at him because he was so old-fashioned. Dixie showed him how to dance 1985 style. "Pornographic dancing," Dean called it.

At one point Dean quit dancing, and walked on his hands for a while, then he grabbed Johnny and arm-wrestled him.

"That's the first thing I always had to do with my dad every time I came to see him. We could never really talk, so we did this stuff," Dean said to Johnny.

Afterwards, in Johnny's basement with the gold-flocked wallpaper, the oil painting on the wall, and the upright piano, Dean gave a concert. He had on his white turtleneck and a pendant around his neck, and he looked his most handsome. As it turned out, it was his only concert in America. He was wonderful. He sang practically his entire repertoire. He told jokes. He did political shtick. He kidded the little kids.

Kids, old people, toddlers, all Johnny and Mona's neighbors and friends sat on chairs or on the floor. A little apart, crouched against the wall, was Dixie Schnebly.

At the end of the concert, Dean scanned the room.

"Now I want to thank someone here. I want to say thanks to Johnny. I helped Johnny Rose back in Estes Park, then he came to Hollywood and I left."

"Couldn't stand the competition," Johnny called out from the back of the room, ducking his head with delight.

"Right. Anyway, Johnny got in touch after almost twenty-five years. He wrote this song for me," Dean said. "John, do you want to sing this with me? Come on up here."

With a diffident shrug that did not conceal the thrill he felt, Johnny ambled up to the front of the room. Together, he and Dean sang "Nobody Knows Me Back in My Hometown." Everyone clapped and cheered and Mona took snapshots of the two men together.

It was the last time that Johnny ever performed in public. After Dean died, he gave away his guitar and said it was time to grow up.

After the concert, there was ice cream and cake, and because they knew Dean was leaving the next day, people were reluctant to go. Johnny's neighbors were taken with how nice he was, and a woman called Fran who was a devout Christian, later told Johnny that Dean was the most Christ-like man she had ever encountered. As the party broke up, Dixie remained behind; she was the last to go.

All that night, Johnny was aware of Dixie, the woman Dean had met down in Denver. She was some kind of rival for Dean, although Johnny did not put it that way. She told him, "I want to let you know that I've told Dean, when he comes back, I've got a place for him to stay."

"That's real nice, Dixie. That's really nice," Johnny said, although Dean always had a place with him and Mona. Johnny would always be there for him.

After Dixie left, Dean plunked himself down on the Rosenburgs' sofa and said, "She is in love with me. There is nothing that she wouldn't do for me."

Looking at Dean, Johnny thought: If Renate was here and she looked into Dixie's eyes, and she is as jealous as you said, you'd be in a whole heap of trouble, boy.

The next morning, Dean left Colorado. Mona couldn't bring herself to go to the airport. It was a sad day for all of them. Johnny and Dean had been apart so long and no one knew when Dean would come back.

After I first met them in Loveland in 1988, Mona and Johnny sent me some tapes, tapes of Johnny's phone calls with Dean, tapes where Johnny had put down his thoughts about the reunion with Dean that October in 1985.

"Dean was a confused man," Johnny said on one of the tapes. "After he left Colorado he was even more confused. How can I convey what I felt about Dean, what my family felt? We loved him and he loved us, but we're not the only ones of this planet that he loved, I know that. If anybody ever got to know Dean, a piece of them died when he died. He did what no other American did—Dean became a superstar in a part of the world we call our enemy."

In exquisitely recollected detail, the taped accounts Johnny sent me conveyed his memories of Dean's week in Loveland. If Dean had stolen away a piece of Johnny's life when he left for South America all those years ago, he had given it back.

Letters from Johnny followed me to New York. Mona sent along a jar of her pickled beets, which I had enjoyed in Loveland.

"We're pleased to hear the tapes were acceptable. Gotta tell you it's crazy how we remember even more as the days go by," Johnny wrote.

Johnny also enclosed a note from Dean, which Mona forgot to

put in with the beets. It was from Dean to John and it was full of longing. He asked Johnny why they didn't take time for fishing, and for building a fire at night, and using the stars for the roof, while they talked about many things. You could feel how much Dean wanted to be back with his old friend. How much he wanted to go home.

18

"Hi, I'm Dixie."

Her feathery voice was tremulous, almost frightened, when I first met her in the lobby of Denver's Brown Palace Hotel. She was a good-looking woman. In her early forties, Dixie Lloyd Schnebly had on a short fur jacket and polished boots under her slacks and she looked a lot like Ann-Margret.

As Dean Reed's American manager at the time of his death, she had figured as a main character in every news report; she told reporters that he had, without doubt, been murdered. It had taken me a while to reach her; on her answering machine was an announcement that said no one was home but that there was a big dog in the house.

Now in March of 1988, around the same time I saw the Rosenburgs up in Loveland, Dixie was here, shaking the snow off her fur chubby. It was starting to snow outside; a blizzard was on the way. In the Brown Palace lobby, waiters bustled around with huge trays loaded with coffee and cake, and the bellhops rustled up large sets of leather luggage.

In the American West, I realized, everyone was big, or seemed big, and the men dressed up in Western costumes; big tall men in boots and cowboy hats, their wives in full-length minks sashaying around the lobby of the Brown Palace, greeting one another as they waited for the annual stock show to open so they could go and buy cows.

We made an odd, huddled grouping in the middle of all these big buoyant people: Dixie, her feral, rather sexy face close to Leslie Woodhead's; Dixie's friend, Greg, a burly man with an amiable manner, who was there, it seemed, as a kind of bodyguard and who also sold real estate.

Like many Western women, Dixie was self-sufficient, but she deferred to men when there were men around.

She leaned closer to Leslie.

"Gee, I'm sorry I was, like, so hard to get hold of, but you have to be careful," she said apologetically. "There are people after Deano. A lot of people are trying to get at me." Dixie often called him Deano.

I assumed she meant that people were after Dean's story, but she also had something more sinister in mind. She was very nervy. She fiddled with a pendant she wore around her neck.

"A gift from Deano," Dixie said shyly.

"It's pretty," I said.

Like a girl with her first corsage, she smiled.

"When it first came I thought it was, like, junk, you know? And then I took it into a jewelry store and they said it was worth something."

I said, "It must be amber. From Russia?"

She nodded. "I thought that was so neat."

Dixie's conversation was peppered with "neats" and "beautifuls," and she blew raspberries for emphasis. With a husky voice and a fluent way with words, she punctuated her thoughts with funny noises and she rambled, but her intuitions and insights had a loony poetic truth. Later on she did admit that she was considered something of a poet and, diffidently, showed me a few of her poems.

Dixie, or DJ as many of her friends called her, was a woman in a man's world, as she put it, and it took a lot to scare her. She grew up in Wheat Ridge, where, as a girl, she first knew Dean. She still lived in her father's house, although her father was dead and she was on her own.

After high school, she had married a Mr. Lloyd, which was how she got into the oil business in the 1970s when Denver boomed.

Things didn't work out with Mr. Lloyd. Then the oil business dried up and Dixie took up driving a long-haul rig. As often as not she was out on the road, the rig eating up hundreds of miles of Interstate, roaring across America.

At truck stops she ate with the truckers; at night, she slept tucked up in the cab of her rig. No one hassled her, because she knew her way around, she said. She said she also had her eye on the possibility of a secretarial business and she had some property up on the North Slope in Grand Junction, Colorado.

When she met up with Dean Reed in October of 1985, though, when he asked her to be his manager in the US, she set aside all her other ambitions. Dean told her that she would be his Colonel Parker.

Now Dixie rose from the sofa in the hotel lobby, then she sat down again. She seemed to be looking for someone, but she settled down and told the story of how she had met Dean Reed at the documentary film festival in Denver where *American Rebel* was shown.

* * *

The second screening of *American Rebel* was on Saturday night, the night after Johnny and Mona had been to see it. Dixie had not been able to get a ticket, but she figured, what the heck, she'd go along and if she couldn't get in, maybe she'd run into Dean anyway. She had known him when she was a young girl and he was a teenager back in Wheat Ridge.

Outside the Tivoli Center in Denver on that warm October evening, police cars cruised the area, their windows down, and their radios on. Because of Dean's bust-up with Peter Boyle on the radio and the press it got, there were plenty of cops. Dixie passed the time waiting for Dean by eavesdropping on a couple of police car radios.

Dixie could read police code. She had been to the Miami Convention in 1972 with her husband, who was some kind of player on the Nixon side and had FBI protection. For the hell of it an FBI guy taught Dixie to read the codes.

Half in the shadow, Dixie watched people going in to the show. She let her mind wander on the subject of Dean, recalling there had only been a few guys like him when she was little, real cowboy types. She remembered how Doug Dana once gave her a 1955 Wheat Ridge Annual. It had a picture of Dean in the play *Pistol Pete*, serenading the girls. The last time she had seen Dean was in 1963, when he attended a Wheat Ridge High reunion. He had been to Hollywood by then and all the kids were really excited.

In between, for more than twenty years, she had kept a scrapbook on him, waiting for him. She thought it was something anyone would do if one of their classmates got to be so famous.

And then, suddenly, right there in Denver at the Tivoli Center she saw him. Bounding out of a car, Dean strode up the steps of the Tivoli Center. Without thinking, Dixie darted out from the shadow into the light.

"Hi, I'm Dixie," she said.

Dean seemed a little nonplussed.

And then he smiled and exclaimed, "Little Dixie! Of course, I remember. *Ja*," Dean said effusively.

It was weird how he had that little German accent, Dixie thought. It was kind of nice. Dean introduced Dixie to his mother, Mrs. Brown, who had come into town for the film festival. Mrs. Brown didn't seem to remember Dixie, but Dean had had lots of friends as a kid. She greeted Dixie with a smile.

Now, in the lobby of the Brown Palace, Dixie whispered to me, "A lot of people want to harm Dean, you know. But I think I can trust you. Would you like to see where Deano grew up?."

I said yes I wanted to see where Dean had grown up. His mother, Ruth Anna Brown, had told me a lot about his childhood when I'd met her in Hawaii, and I'd seen pictures, but I had not actually seen his boyhood home.

Dixie's friend Greg peeled away to go and sell some real estate; Dixie led Leslie and me out to her pick-up truck, where she told us that she kept a gun in the glove compartment. I made Leslie sit in the middle, next to her.

Dixie drove us to Wheat Ridge, which was now pretty much a suburb of Denver; just off the exit from the freeway, a sign read: WELCOME TO WHEAT RIDGE, COLORADO, CARNATION CAPITAL OF THE WORLD. POP. 28,270.

When Dixie and Dean had been kids, Wheat Ridge, like the other small towns at the foot of the mountains, was a rural village where a lot of people still kept horses. Dean sometimes even went courting girls on horseback. Sometimes, Dean galloped over the empty fields to where Dixie waited for him behind her house. She was just a kid, still in pigtails, but she was kind of in love with Dean, the handsome older boy, and he was nice to her in a brotherly way. "Little Dixie," he called her when they rode horseback together.

"Everyone had a horse around here, even me," Dixie said. "And I was raised poor as dirt. Deano thought he was poor. But I was the poor one," she said, as if they had engaged in a "poor" competition.

The anger rose and died away in her. I tried not to look at the glove compartment where the gun was. Leslie listened to Dixie attentively.

What really rankled with Dixie was how, when Dean went to Hollywood, she could not buy his records because her mother was very strict and didn't want her to have any spending money. Her best friend, Karen, could buy Dean's records and that hurt worst of all. Dixie's mother did not approve of Dixie, never did, but her dad was always proud of her and they had had some neat times together when she was growing up. He loved goofy gifts and she always bought him a toy at Christmas, but her father was dead now and all Dixie had was the little house in Wheat Ridge.

"What about Dean's dad?"

"He was something else," she said. "He never got over Dean being a Communist. Cyril taught at the local high school and was a big womanizer. Ruth Anna Brown was one of his students. When Ruth Anna divorced Cyril, Deano was shattered. In those days, people didn't get divorced, you know?"

We drove around Wheat Ridge. Most of the shops had moved out to the big malls and it was only a shabby suburb now. Vacancy signs hung outside the Blue Swan and the Humpty Dumpty Motels. On the roof of Verne's Cocktails, a pink neon martini with an olive in it flickered, or maybe it was a Manhattan with a cherry. Across the street was a plain white church.

"I don't think there was much church-going in Wheat Ridge," Dixie said. "Dean's people were not church-goers," she added, although she herself was raised a Catholic. She took a small breath now, and slowed the truck down. She pointed at a two-story bungalow with a front porch and a tidy front yard with a low long shed behind it made of chicken-colored cinder blocks.

"That's where Dean's mom kept her chickens," Dixie said and stopped the truck.

For a while we sat in the truck outside Dean's house.

Leslie said to Dixie, "What was Dean like in high school?"

"He was very naive in some ways. He was terribly shy with girls. When he went to Hollywood, he was still a virgin. I mean, everybody did *it* back then," she said. "My homecoming queen in high school was pregnant. Everybody was pregnant."

"Was Dean very political?" Leslie asked.

"Dean was not particularly political in high school, but he was a gung-ho kid. He did track, hence the race against the mule. He was a gymnast and a swimmer. He did it like he did everything. He was a track alcoholic, a music alcoholic, whatever he did, he did with maximum commitment. When I met him later, there were two Deans, the public man and the private one, and he was definitely a political alcoholic."

Then Dixie found a pack of cigarettes in her bag and lit one and took another little breath. She told us how after the showing of *American Rebel* at the Tivoli Center the night she met him,

Dean had invited Dixie back to visit with him at the Westin Hotel. She thought it was so unique that Dean would be her friend, she said. He was the same slim cowboy she had known as a child. He spent the evening with her and sang her three songs so gently. In public he told the same three stories over and over, as if he'd memorized them, but, alone with her, he opened up. When he told her he wanted to think about coming home, he cried.

Cautiously, Leslie shifted the conversation towards Dean's death. Dixie grew wary. It was getting dark. I thought about the gun again. Leslie edged towards me and away from Dixie, pretending to reach over for a pair of gloves he had left on the dashboard. From somewhere police sirens wailed. Alongside the entrance to the freeway was a tangled mess of steel that had once been a car.

The pick-up skidded and Dixie drove badly, as if talking about Dean had drained her and she could no longer concentrate. She announced that she was taking us back to her place, and then she missed the exit that she must have taken every day. Her face glowed in the reflection from the headlights of oncoming cars. My stomach turned over.

"There are so many things I could tell you," she whispered, veering out of lane. "I know I can trust you. I think I can trust you. Can I?"

I nodded in what I hoped was a trustworthy fashion and Dixie smoked a second cigarette and told us she had given money to the Sandinistas because Dean told her it was a righteous thing to do. She let slip that she felt Fidel Castro was the devil incarnate. Her politics seemed to me a kind of American libertarianism that existed where liberalism flipped backwards to meet the right.

Colorado had its own peculiar mix of laissez-faire libertarian and far-right zealots.

This was the heartlands: there were a hundred million handguns in America and a lot of them were in Colorado and at least one was in Dixie's glove compartment. I had never seen a gun in real life.

Dixie tried to believe what Dean had believed, a sentimental socialism that was part peace and love, part free medicine. But she had been raised on the anti-Communist Catholicism of the middle 1950s in the middle of America. As a result of this stew of ideas, she was now scared of everything, including the CIA, the KGB, and CBS.

Eventually, she found the exit that she was looking for, drove off the freeway, and pulled up in front of a small gray house. She jumped out of the truck and ran towards the door. In the window sat a big sad dog with a huge pink tongue, staring out into the night.

We followed her inside and stood around in the nearly empty house.

"Say hello to Bear," Dixie said patting the dog now licking the window pane.

Leslie said hello to Bear and I realized this was the dog mentioned on her answering machine.

Dixie went into the kitchen.

"There's orange. There's cola," she called out.

"Orange, thanks," I said.

It had been Dixie's father's house. She generally rented it out, though it was currently unoccupied, and kept only a room for herself. Most of the time she lived in the mountains near Grand Junction.

On a chair was a box and Dixie picked it up and held it close to her. In it she said were Dean's letters and some tapes. It was pretty much all she had of Dean, who had told her that he loved Renate, but that he did not want to die in East Germany. It would be hard for Renate to work in America. Dixie had said she would help find Renate a job. He talked to her about his need for America, about the movie he was making, about peace and love.

From the box she took a few ballpoint pens with the legend: "Colorado is Dean Reed Country."

"Have some," she said. "I guess you could say they're a rarity now." She gave me the pens then turned to the jumble of audiotapes in the box.

Dixie had taped all of Dean's telephone calls. The answering machine was on a table and Dixie took a tape out and pressed the button. The tape began.

A phone rang. Then Dean's voice came up. They exchanged salutations between Wheat Ridge and East Berlin.

"Is that me calling you, or you calling me?" Dean's voice said. "Are you just waking up? Did you have nice dreams? Are you a member of the *Denver Klan*?" he joked. Dean seemed to be entombed inside the scratched plastic cassette case and the tapes had the creepy vitality of relics, as discomfiting as a saint's toe-bone in a glass box. Dixie suddenly stopped the tape.

I said to her, "Why did you make tapes of Dean's calls?"

"I just like hearing his voice. Not just then, but all my life."

I wanted the cardboard box. I wanted the letters and the tapes, but Dixie was reticent and said she would think about it. We agreed to meet for dinner the next night and she drove us back to the Brown Palace Hotel. It was snowing harder.

* * *

The Rattlesnake Club was inside the Tivoli Center. The restaurant where we met Dixie had fat copper brewing vats—it had once been a brewery—pushed halfway through the floors like unexploded bombs. The distressed walls looked like the consequence of a tasteful war. The waiters wore Topsiders and pink Ralph Lauren shirts, as if they were Yalies or yachtsmen. Only a few tables were occupied. Dixie, thin in her short white fur jacket, looked bewildered, as if she did not know whom to trust.

We talked about Dean and out of the blue she offered me the cardboard box with the letters and the tapes. The next day, Leslie and I went back to the little house in Wheat Ridge and took the box with a kind of obscene speed, as if she might change her mind about the treasure.

In the tapes and letters Dixie gave me, as in Johnny's tapes and letters and memories, were all the details of Dean's time in Colorado and all that came afterwards. Dean had wanted to come home to America. He wanted it so bad he could taste it, and Dixie conspired with him to make it happen. She had asked Dean if she could set up a fan club for him in America and, before he left Colorado, she was already at work for him.

19

When Dean left Colorado, he went to Los Angeles to look for a manager because, though Dixie would help, he was savvy enough to realize he needed a pro, as well. In fact, he told her, he spent most of his time talking into answering machines. Everyone Dean knew was out of town: the Everly Brothers were in Australia making a video; Jane Fonda was away. No one answered his calls and he hated the smog.

"It gets on my nerves. I've been calling people in Hollywood all day and all I get are recorded messages," Dean told Dixie over the phone.

A fellow named Levinson was interested in working for Dean, but Dean did not trust him; he felt Levinson would sit on his ass and wait for Dean to perform, then come in for his twenty percent. He told Dixie this was the America he hated, said that Hollywood was worse than the killing fields of Cambodia, because you never knew who your friends were. Dean stiffened up his morale with the political rhetoric he could wrap around him like a familiar blanket.

In Los Angeles, Dean stayed with Tillie Price, Paton's widow, who was old and unwell and sometimes referred to herself as "Silly

Tillie." He went to visit Paton's grave and missed him terribly. In the house where Paton Price once taught his students the meaning of life, Dean sat on the bed in his room, wondering if anyone would ever call him back.

A second Hollywood career now seemed a pipe-dream. Sure, he'd amassed $300,000 in a West Berlin bank from residuals on his movies, but in LA he discovered $300,000 wouldn't buy a chicken coop. Tillie gave a little party for Dean.

"Don Murray and Kent McCord came," Dean told Dixie. "I asked Kent if he could get me an agent and he said only Jack Fields, who is Ed Asner's agent, is brave enough politically. Haskell Wexler—I know him from Chile and Nicaragua—said the same thing."

Maura McGivney, an old girlfriend of Dean's who sometimes looked in on Tillie Price told me some time later, "When Dean was here, he used to leap out of bed in the morning and run out to the pool for a swim, naked, with a huge erection, singing 'Oh What a Beautiful Morning'. Tillie was embarrassed."

Ramona was the other reason Dean went to Los Angeles, he told Dixie. Ramona was his daughter by his first wife, Patty, and he wanted her to take his name. Mrs. Brown said it was true that Dean was keen on Ramona, who had visited him in East Berlin. Ramona wanted to make Dean's life story as a Hollywood movie.

I saw a snapshot once of Dean's children, Ramona, Natasha, and Sasha, and they were an oddly assorted bunch. Ramona was a healthy, pretty, self-possessed American teenager; Sasha, the only boy, wore his privilege as uneasily as he wore his skinny black leather pants; Natasha, the pale little girl he'd had by Wiebke, seemed somehow isolated.

Dean had really put his back into getting the hard currency he

needed to send some regular support money to Patty and
Ramona. According to Dixie, Ramona didn't want anything to do
with Dean around the time of the trip to Los Angeles and it nearly
broke his heart. In the spring of 1986, he sent Dixie a copy of a
letter he wrote to Ramona to commemorate her eighteenth
birthday.

He called her his "Dearest Daughter" and told her of his
sorrow that he was often not there when she needed him. He told
her life was not black and white. He passed on the many homilies
Paton Price had preached to him. The letter was full of syrupy
political sentiment. I wondered if Dean had sent Dixie a copy
because things felt more real to him if he had an audience.

"My daughter wants to become a singer," Dean told Dixie.

Dixie said she was thinking about his career in America. The
conversation had the dreamy quality of two people dawdling
down different paths, but hoping to meet up.

"Nothing much is happening," said Dean. "It's not as nice as
Colorado. The smog is terrible," he said and added that in
California he was down in the dumps.

They talked about the movie Dean was planning to make
when he went back to East Germany. *Bloody Heart* was to be the
story of the siege of Wounded Knee, the Indian rebellion that
took place in 1973 in South Dakota. Already Dixie had been on
the road looking for props that he would need and had found a
vintage Marlboro sign and some Indian artifacts.

She said, "I went to South Dakota, smart Aleck. But I didn't
know what to take. So I went to Wounded Knee and I went to Pine
Ridge and I went to Martin and talked to a kid who didn't know his
belly button from lint, and then I came home." She laughed happily
at his astonished delight over her trip across South Dakota.

"I would love to spend the night with you tonight," Dean said suddenly.

"If I thought that was true I'd trip over my own two feet," Dixie said.

"I'll be leaving on Monday to go to Minneapolis. I'm not having as good a time as I did in Colorado," he said again, flirting with Dixie, obviously wanting her to say she'd come on to meet him, without having to ask. Finally, he said, "Would you fly out and spend some time with me in Ohio?"

She said she would come to Minneapolis.

Dean went on tour across America with *American Rebel*, the documentary that had played the Denver film festival. In Minnesota, Dixie met him. It was there they agreed that she could be his only manager instead of some Hollywood guy and help pave the way for his triumphal return to America.

Dean wrote to Dixie while he was sitting at John F. Kennedy Airport waiting for his plane back to Europe. He said he wanted to write to her of his thoughts and emotions and how he felt after spending more time in his homeland than he had for a quarter of a century.

"The trip was the happiest I've ever made to America. I've seen my blue skies again and my battery was recharged." He wrote of how he had seen the mountains and the faces of so many people, and of how he had visited Denver, Los Angeles, and New York. He talked of how all people must have a peaceful future and how he would work towards making it so. He said he felt he would return to his own country and do what he had done in thirty-two other countries.

He vowed to make *Bloody Heart* an inspirational movie and said he would be back soon. He signed the letter "Dean." Dixie sent him a bumper sticker that read: YOU CAN'T HUG CHILDREN WITH NUCLEAR ARMS.

Dixie tried to call Dean at JFK the afternoon he left. She was afraid of losing track of him. She wanted to beg him to know that not all Americans were Peter Boyle. But she couldn't reach him.

After that, Dixie spent a lot of time with some friends trying to reach a righteous decision about how to help Dean. The afternoon she received his first letter, she was so relieved she cried for six hours.

"I am very happy to be part of your Colorado world and eager to make Colorado another home for you, again!" Dixie wrote to Dean, adding if she ever spoke out of turn or if she stepped on his toes, so to speak, or Renate's or Sasha's, he was to tell her plain.

By the second half of November Dean was back in Germany, and, in the weeks and months that followed, Dixie called and wrote frequently and he responded eagerly.

Often, Dixie's letters ran to six or eight pages, single-spaced. In January of 1986 Dixie wrote to Dean seventeen times. He was astonished and delighted. All the letters were about him.

Almost as soon as Dean left Colorado, Dixie went to work as his Colonel Parker, paving the way for his return. She set up a fan club and had nifty membership certificates printed; Mrs. Brown was made an honorary member and so was Renate; Dixie got bumper stickers printed that read: SO WHO'S DEAN REED?

She wrote to classmates at Wheat Ridge High; she called record companies and checked out which early songs of Dean's had been hits; she commissioned record finders to locate copies of Dean's old records, including one titled "Cannibal Twist"; she drove across the Southwest, looking for props for Dean's movie;

she had a lengthy correspondence with the South Dakota police department on the pretext that she was a schoolteacher whose class was interested in such things, and so obtained pictures of South Dakota police uniforms, badges, and cars.

Along with her letters, Dixie sent Dean packages. One contained postcards showing the Denver Mint and panoramic views of Denver. She shipped the movie props via Czechoslovakia, to the DEFA Film Studios in Potsdam. She sent him turquoise jewelry she had purchased in Santa Fe and a denim jacket from Johnny.

Dixie wrote out shipping lists very carefully; in one case at least she painstakingly translated it into German. This list included three music videotapes, one red bandanna, three copper medallions, twelve boy scout pins, one pack Skoal (chewing tobacco), one plastic ring, one 1986 calendar, one empty milk carton from the Wheat Ridge dairy (where Dixie and Dean had worked after school as kids) for a joke, one box of liquorice for Renate (just for fun). For St. Valentine's Day, she sent a cubic-zirconium heart-shaped pendant for Renate.

Dixie wrote to Dean of her progress and how she had picked up material on music videos, their production costs, and even directors in the Denver area; she boned up on music copyright laws and ordered both the Songwriters Market book and a Nashville yellow-page telephone directory.

Her letters were full of good advice and jokes; she was coy, cute, smart, flirtatious, and sassy. She chided and chastised Dean and instructed him to be good to himself. When he was feeling down, he was to look in the mirror and say "I love me." She was bossy, sweet, provocative, spirited, determined, and greedy, but only for love. The letters included sly asides and little drawings—

moon faces of herself, smiling or pensive. There was such longing in all of them, and poetry, and the sense that she was blossoming, that her world was enlarged, embellished, and lit up by Dean Reed.

Dixie wrote to Dean of her feelings for Colorado: "the inky blue darkness of the star bedecked night" and "the light blue cloudless sky of morning"; of a delicious Mexican meal she had eaten; of her snowmobile, which was a delight. She tempted him with the pleasures of an American life and wished him "beautiful blue-sky days." She said she hoped Renate would "like our weather, our little towns and big towns, our massive shopping centers filled with people who are rude, kind, happy, sad, little, big, young, and old!" In her own way, Dixie was a poet of the banal.

"In case you haven't figured it out, getting a letter from you, or a card, is better than home-made chocolate cake," she wrote to Dean. She wrote that she had even begun German classes and she signed one of her letters "Chow" because it was a word Dean often used. She asked him what it meant.

He wrote back, "It's an international word in Italian for hello and goodbye" and she wrote that that was "neat" and she was relieved to know what it meant because she couldn't find it in her German dictionary.

Dean said her letters were "jewels" and exclaimed on how many she had written. He complimented her on her humor. "I tried to translate some of your jokes for Renate, but it is difficult to translate jokes—that is my problem living in Germany . . . Humor must be in the native tongue. *Ja?*"

His letters were typed on a portable typewriter, and he noted his spelling was terrible, but blamed it on the fact that he spoke four languages. He enclosed the address of Mr. Oleg Harjardin, the President of the Soviet Peace Committee, because a friend of Dixie's had requested it.

They wrote about everything. Dean wrote about how his dog bit him, about the Sandinistas, and about his trips to Prague for recording sessions and to Moscow to negotiate money for *Bloody Heart*, his movie. He wrote Dixie when the Challenger space shuttle blew up in the winter of 1986 that he thought it was a bad omen.

Dean's letters to Dixie covered a lot of territory and revealed not only a man with an enormous appetite for work and for movement, but also a man who, in between the lines, was growing weary of it all. The letters careened between revelations of his philosophy of life, the determination to better the lot of all mankind, and the steely practicalities of the performing life: copyrights, arrangers, engineers, producers, contracts, deadlines.

As they wrote and called each other, in the letters and tapes, you could feel the intimacy build, as if they were locking into some fatal two-step to the exclusion of everyone else.

In the house by the lake in East Germany, Renate began to resent Dixie's barrage of phone calls, but she was always polite when she picked up the phone.

The calls and the letters continued on well into the winter of 1986. The manic reporting of every detail in their lives continued. Dean had begun to focus seriously on his return to America. There was also an ecstatic mention of the possibility of *60 Minutes*. The biggest show on American television was interested in Dean! In his mind, Dean fixed his return to America for October, 1987, which was only a year and a half away and *60 Minutes* would be terrific publicity.

His return, he said, would be based on the distribution of *American Rebel*, the documentary, and the release of his new LP in America, which he also intended to call *American Rebel*. In a letter to Dixie, he discoursed on the meaning of the word "rebel." Dixie looked it up in her Funk and Wagnall's Dictionary and also in her Reader's Digest *Family Word Finder*.

How to present himself to America, he wondered. There would be a personal tour; his film must be shown in the universities. He, Deano, would appear on television and radio talk shows; there would have to be an advance man to handle Deano's publicity.

He also discussed with Dixie the autobiography he intended to write; the old one was incomplete. Maybe Dixie would write it for him. Yes, why not, and perhaps they could get an advance from a publisher, although maybe that was too optimistic.

She pooh-poohed all that, and told him he should be nicer to himself. He would soon be rich, she kidded, which was just as well, because she might want a new Rolls-Royce in 1987.

He confided in Dixie his dream of founding a social democratic party in America. If there were 260,000,000 Americans and only two percent voted for him that would be considerable.

"My dedication in my life has been to use my fame and talent to fight against injustice wherever and whenever I found it," Dean wrote, then added, "I believe that there is a great commercial hole to be filled in the USA. There is a need for a new singer to fill the void which Pete Seeger used to fill."

Now Dixie had a real purpose. She called Mrs. Brown; she called Tillie Price; she talked to Phil Everly on the phone and Phil did not have the heart to tell her that she had no idea how to be a manager. As she toiled to put Dean back on the American map, she saw the pitfalls everywhere. But she had found a community.

Then relations in the community soured. There was bickering about who owned what bits of film archive in *American Rebel*. Mrs. Brown said she had given Will Roberts money to accompany Dean to Chile; Will Roberts said he had mortgaged his house to make the film. For Dean's biography, Dixie thought maybe she would write to Yasser Arafat for his thoughts on Dean because, "Wouldn't that fritz Johnny?" She was not happy working with Johnny.

To protect Dean (in case he hit it big), Johnny had had Dean sign a deal with him for residual rights. It would stop people making spin-offs, such as Dean Reed dolls, without Dean's approval. The contract ran until the end of 1988. Dixie didn't like it one bit. Dean said he made the deal because Johnny was "sick and didn't have much of a future," explaining how much it meant to John and Mona when he, Dean, came to visit and gave them his love and trust. Anyhow, Johnny had promised when the day came that Dean signed on with the William Morris Agency in Hollywood, he would tear up that contract right in front of Dean's eyes.

Dixie finally asked Dean to release her from her promise to work with Johnny. His views were on the hard right, she said.

Dean responded that "Johnny was a religious and conservative guy, who, if he did not love Dean, would never be a fan of his life." But Johnny did love Dean, Dean said, and Dean would not release Dixie from her promise. To cheer her up, he sent her Yasser Arafat's headscarf for a present.

Dean left Dixie no choice about Johnny, so she turned on Will

Roberts and told Dean that she figured Will was no friend of Dean's and that Will was reluctant to part with his material. Dean wrote to Will that Dixie was his business partner now.

There were insinuations and suspicions, and the various factions took differing views of Dean's future in the United States; no one agreed. At one point Dixie took some friends up to Loveland to check Johnny and Mona were not agents of one kind or another.

"God, Dixie, can't you see we're just poor clods?" Johnny said.

All of them dissected every letter Dean sent, as semioticians might do; they taped his telephone calls, and sent the cassettes round in carefully made packages. They copied the video cassette of Dean's farewell concert in Johnny's basement. They put his bumper stickers on their cars.

In the way that Dean's American friends operated, it was a lot like an underground network in the East. There was the hope, the desperate desire for information, the coveting of news, the fear. Cassettes of Dean's songs were copied over and over, like the *magnetizdat* which Soviet kids had once made of rock music, passing them along, their amateur quality—where you could hear the laughter in the background—making them more potent. Videos were copied, too, until they were too grainy to look at.

Letters smuggled from one partisan to another were cherished, reread and reread. There were also the aspersions cast on those who seemed to have defected. There were the relationships degraded by desire and need. At one point along the Dean Reed trail, I heard from a musician who had known Dean in Moscow that someone—perhaps it was Mrs. Brown—had heard rumors that I was working for the CIA.

In Colorado, Dean's friends were not hicks. But they had no idea what Dean's standing really was in the Soviet Union or in

East Berlin. They could understand only that their friend had become a big star. By the time Dean came home in 1985, for different reasons—Johnny's bad back, Dixie's longings—they inhabited a world that was as flat as the yellow scrublands on the way up to Loveland from Denver. Dean's presence animated it, and they could not bear to let him go.

Their delight seduced him; he was homesick; he saw an opportunity to move on one more time and he was determined to take it because it meant going home.

In trying to solve the mystery of Dean's death, I made a kind of sodden progress and there were times I had the feeling that Dean had existed only in the desires of his friends and archivists. When I heard the stories and read the letters and listened to the taped phone calls, I felt I was hearing versions of what had become a kind of folk tale, passed on from one teller to another.

Dixie saw Dean's return to America in grandiose terms. It would be the return of a great star, of a prodigal son. Dean wrote that he did not want her to be disappointed, that there were people who would be afraid of him because of his politics, and who would not answer her calls or letters.

Buried in Dean's own letters though, was a hard, cold, little core of realism, a chilling premonition that none of it was going to happen. I think that all the way along, Dean knew the truth, but he was a patsy for hope.

The next time I saw Dixie, we had brunch at the Brown Palace Hotel in Denver. She had promised me more tapes.

She had tapes of all her telephone conversations with Dean, she said, right up until his death. Interesting tapes. Important tapes. She had them at home at Wheat Ridge, she said, then changed her mind and said they were up at her other house in Grand Junction, up in the mountains. It was her safe house.

She teased with promises of information, but it was not intended as a tease and her heart wasn't in it. She seemed frayed and worn with sorrow. Her memories of Dean seemed to detonate in her endlessly like tiny land mines.

In the huge dining room, large people cruised the food, slapping mounds of scrambled eggs on their plates along with dollops of corned beef hash, stacks of pancakes, and bacon and sausage. There was butter and syrup for the pancakes and heavy cream for the coffee.

Small in her chair, Dixie ate her breakfast, absorbed in some private despair.

"Dean was going to have trouble making it back here in the music business. It was all run by Jews. Deano didn't care what a person was, of course, he didn't care if a person was pink, white, black, green, purple."

I wanted the rest of her tapes very badly. I could feel my own desperation grow. I had never wanted anything as much as I wanted those tapes, but Dixie was off on another tangent.

Dean had money in a bank in West Berlin. Emergency money, she said.

"Can you check if there have been any withdrawals since Dean's death? If there haven't, I'll give you the tapes," she asked.

"I'm not sure I understand," I said.

Dixie said softly, "I've been getting strange phone calls. I think someone is speaking Spanish. I think the calls are coming from South America." She tried to drink some coffee, but her hand shook and she put the cup down. "I want to know if there have been any withdrawals recently because if there have it might prove something."

I said, "Prove what?"

Dixie looked expectantly at the door to the restaurant and said, "It will prove that Dean is still alive."

"Dick Cheese, Mr. Cheese."

The public address system at Stapleton Airport in Denver ran through a never-ending loop of names, "Dick Cheese. Mr. Cheese. Brett Falcon. Mr. Falcon. Margaret Bird. Ms. Bird. Wayne Sick. Mr. Sick," and so on, until it looped back and began all over again with Dick Cheese.

It was snowing again in Denver the morning after I saw Dixie, and the planes were delayed. Travelers wandered around the airport looking for something to do, or to buy, or to eat. The airport was huge and so were the people and a lot of them were stuffed into down coats and vests because it was the spring ski season. On their feet they wore huge plastic ski boots in pink and baby blue and they marched around stiff-legged, unable to bend their ankles. As they bought souvenirs and ate soft ice cream, they resembled vacationing families of Yeti with pastel feet.

Among the passengers were young couples, barely out of their teens, their own babies slung casually into backpacks. Returning home, setting off on a journey, they coped with ease. Their ancestors would have come West in covered wagons. Every one at the airport was big, handsome, and healthy, and they were all traveling, because moving on was the American thing to do.

"Dick Cheese."

I was glad to get on the plane back to New York.

20

It took me a long time to get a fix on 60 *Minutes* and how their story came about and the confusion about the origin of the story made people suspicious; some even suggested that somehow it had something to do with Dean's death.

When I met Bill McClure—a producer for 60 *Minutes* based in London—in his Knightsbridge office, he told me he hadn't much liked Dean Reed. McClure had lived in Berlin and he knew Europe well.

"A very big fish in a very small pond," McClure said. "Renate was a *bona fide* star, though." McClure's neck bulged over his collar; he loosened his tie and told me that the original idea had been to do a piece for 60 *Minutes* on a number of American defectors in Europe, including Dean and Victor Grossman.

McClure thought Dean was a hustler, an opportunist without political conviction, a self-aggrandizing old crooner, with an ego the size of the Berlin Wall.

"Dean Reed was a fake," he said. "And he was approaching fifty and he was frightened." McClure's dislike emanated from every pore.

His animosity, however, I discovered, was at least partly to do with Dean's last-minute decision to defect from the show. McClure had set everything up. He flew Mike Wallace into East Berlin. Then Dean backed off. McClure sat in East Berlin with a crew and with Mike Wallace ready to go and this putz, this cowboy, this fake said he didn't want to do it. McClure's job was on the line.

"Whose version would you believe? Mike Wallace, who gets maybe a million a year, or Bill McClure, who gets maybe fifty grand?" said Erik Durschmied. "Anyway, the show was *my* idea."

I was feeling trapped again in the adhesive confusions of Dean Reed land, and this went on for months to come while I tried to follow the way the *60 Minutes* story and everything that surrounded it developed.

I met Erik Durschmied at the Intercontinental Hotel where he was staying in New York, and we went out to Murphy's Irish Pub on Second Avenue because he liked the cheeseburgers there.

Durschmied's wife, Annalise, was a long-time friend of Dean's in Europe. Durschmied was a tough little Viennese of about sixty who worked for CBS out of Paris as a cameraman. He was a legendary figure, who had made his reputation working for the BBC as a brilliant reporter-cameraman in places like Indochina. He had thinning hair and a good tweed jacket.

Erik Durschmied ordered a beer and a cheeseburger. At Murphy's, there were checkered cloths on the table and a crowd of men at the bar. Their ties at half-mast, they craned their necks to watch a football game on the TV set that was suspended over the bartender's head.

"Dean hated East Berlin." Durschmied chewed his hamburger methodically and drank some beer.

"Did you like Dean?" I asked.

"Yes, and I'm a black and cynical bastard," he said. "Dean was a feather in the wind. He was naive. But he had enormous charm. Whatever his talent as a musician, his talent for charm was never in any doubt at all."

According to Durschmied, Dean also had a sense of humor, at least about his own films.

"He knew his films were garbage," said Durschmied, "but Dean himself had no taste. He gave us some of those vulgar porcelain statues from Germany. We were touched, of course, so we kept them, but they were junk."

We talked about Dean's womanizing and he agreed that there was plenty of it, but he felt that Dean was also capable of real friendship with a woman, his own wife Annalise, for example. I had met Annalise once in Paris and it occurred to me, that, like Dixie and Wiebke, she was slender, small-boned, blonde, and sexy.

"Would you have gone to bed with Dean?" Durschmied asked suddenly.

His accent grew more Viennese with every beer and a friendly leer spread across his face. There followed an exchange about whether or not I would have slept with Dean Reed, or, indeed, with Elvis Presley. The crowd had grown noisier at the bar. I edged my chair away from Durschmied.

"Would you have gone to bed with Marilyn Monroe?" I said.

"You bet! Just think of being able to tell people." Durschmied wiped some mustard from his chin.

Leaning over the table, Durschmied whispered to me about Dean Reed, who he was, why he had died.

"Remember, it was the American Embassy that got Dean free in Chile when he was arrested there in 1983," Durschmied said.

"Why would the embassy bother with some commie type who'd gone over to the other side? Ask yourself why."

"Why?" I said.

Durschmied was silent for a moment and I asked myself what he meant. Was Dean a spy for us? Was that what Durschmied was saying? Was he CIA, the ultimate mole?

It was a tantalizing idea, the corn-fed blue-eyed boy with his crew-cut and Chevrolet Impala, his mule races and silly songs. Did Paton Price run him? Was the sudden move to Latin America exquisitely planned? Was the socialist rhetoric a perfect cover for an agent? In his tight pants, with the guitar slung over his shoulder, with his merry antics and goodwill, he had certainly converted plenty of Russians to America.

Was Dean Reed, then, the Tab Hunter of the secret world? Was he, as Johnny Rosenburg had once suggested, the best mole our country ever had? But even Johnny didn't believe that and neither did I.

For the hell of it, Durschmied also tried out the notion that Dean Reed was still alive and living in the Soviet Union. I said it seemed unlikely that a six-foot American rock star had gone to ground so easily in Gorbachev's Soviet Union, where Western news crews were now to be seen everywhere. Durschmied giggled. It was provocative stuff, but it was small talk.

"The whole thing is a jigsaw puzzle, and you're looking for a bit of sky when the sailboat is right in front of you," Durschmied added mysteriously.

He clamped his mouth around some French fries and wouldn't say anything about the sailboat, what it was, or where it was. It was clear he didn't know much, but his urgent whispers had a kind of adhesive quality and the spy stories were tempting.

Then he said something really interesting.

"Dean Reed was a man without a language. Without a language. *Ja.* Like me," Durschmied said.

In the tapes I had with Dean Reed's voice on them, his English was stilted, as if something essential was sometimes missing, and people in Colorado had talked of how he had a little accent when he came to visit.

Durschmied went on. "Look, I was only fifteen or so when I left Austria. All my vocabulary for subjects before fifteen is German. Everything else, which means my entire professional life, my political life, is in English. The same with Dean. His American vocabulary was pre-1961. Everything else was in a foreign language. Spanish. German. His musical life, his political life, his married life, his whole adult construct was foreign."

It was true. Dean spoke English, German, Spanish, and a little Russian. The gaps in his languages matched the gaps in his experience. The old-fashioned slightly stiff English went with the smiling countenance and the belief in peace and freedom. It was always 1962 in Dean's world. The clock in his head had stopped when he left America.

In a letter to Wiebke, Dean had once written that being in America had made him happy because he could speak his own language. This was so astute it turned my head. Dean was not a subtle man, but he had poignantly diagnosed what ailed him: he was a man without a language.

Durschmied got up now and so did I, and we headed out of Murphy's.

"Of course, you know Dean and Renate were planning to go to live in Rome," said Durschmied.

Rome? Rome! No, I didn't know about Rome; there had been

no mention at all of Rome. Another alley to follow looking for Dean Reed. Another dead end, I thought.

"Rome?" I said, but Eric Durschmied was half a block ahead of me, singing a Tom Lehrer song in counterpoint to the noises of the New York night.

"They're rioting in Africa, they're starving in Spain," he sang and disappeared around the corner. He never said another word about how the 60 Minutes piece on Dean Reed came about.

In the corridor at the 60 Minutes offices at CBS News on West 57th Street in New York, before I saw Mike Wallace, I heard his voice. It was the same voice that came out of my TV every Sunday night, the voice that had introduced me to Dean Reed in April of 1986.

When I got to his office, Wallace was talking on the phone and he looked up and smiled and raised a hand in greeting. He looked exactly like Mike Wallace and I was pretty awestruck and more than a little nervous. I was here to interview the most famous and toughest reporter in the country.

He hung up the phone and shook my hand. He said that when they had first met, he thought Dean was a bit of a fraud, but after a while felt that was probably an unjust assessment and that Dean probably did believe the things he talked about. He was naive maybe, but he had conviction and he was charming.

"Was Dean intelligent?" I asked.

"Intelligent enough. He was certainly no dummy, though he had a learned rhetoric and could do the Communist number; but he adjusted his view as we went along. It wasn't merely a kind of parrot repetition; there was some real involvement. Of course, he had done this interview plenty of times and he knew the words and knew how to express himself in those terms," Wallace said.

"Did you like him?"

"Yes, I did. He was politically naive, but he was honest," Wallace said.

On February 9, 1986, Mike Wallace flew into East Berlin. Bill McClure was already there, wringing his hands, wondering if Dean Reed intended to do the interview.

Dean had tentatively agreed to the interview, but he did not like Bill McClure much, so he changed his mind. Dean felt that *60 Minutes*, along with his movie *Bloody Heart*, was his ticket back to America. He had spent some time on a recent trip to Moscow with Oleg Smirnoff rehearsing for the interview, with Oleg playing Mike Wallace.

"Why are you a Communist, Mr. Reed? Why do you believe in the Berlin Wall? Call yourself an American? What about Afghanistan?"

Oleg and Dean trudged around Red Square.

"Hit me harder. Ask me another question." Dean said, "Pretend you're Mike Wallace."

Oleg had no idea what he was doing.

"Hit me again," said Dean, obsessed with *60 Minutes*.

Dean called Dixie: "In four days in Moscow I spoke only English," he said. "I was getting ready for Mike Wallace. Johnny has begged me not to do the *60 Minutes* interview. Johnny says *60 Minutes* goes deep into the past."

Johnny was more worried about *60 Minutes* than Dixie. He knew that Dean just did not understand the type of people at *60 Minutes*. He did not get that America had no love for communistic people like himself and that the interview would not do him any good.

"These people dig deep into your background," Johnny said on a tape he sent to Dean in East Berlin. "Stay away from 60 *Minutes*. They're gonna cut you to pieces."

Renate was outraged. "What kind of a friend is this that comes down on you so hard and tells you not to get this publicity?" she said.

Dean and Renate arrived at the Palast Hotel, where VIPs stayed in East Berlin, to meet Mike Wallace, Bill McClure, and Anne de Boismilion, the associate producer who worked for CBS in Paris. A woman from East German television was with them. Dean was fretful but Mike Wallace did not object to Dean's playing hard to get. Unlike Bill McClure, he found it neither objectionable nor manipulative.

"The guy was scared. Many people on the verge of an interview try to back out and then come back again. I harbored no hard feelings about that," Mike Wallace said to me.

Dean said to Renate, "Please help me to say no," and then the three women went to the restaurant. Half an hour later, Dean came back in, grinning sheepishly. "I've agreed to do the interview," he said.

In the end, Renate was impressed with the undertaking and Wallace was deeply impressed by Renate. He felt in her a profound solidity. She was a considerable woman.

The 60 *Minutes* crew shot a huge amount of footage over three days. They shot around the Alexanderplatz, near the Berlin Wall, in Schmockwitz. They shot film of Renate, Dean, and Sasha. Wallace generously let me look at the out-takes. It was compelling stuff.

Towards the end of the three days, the Reeds and the *60 Minutes* people were shooting in the Reed house in Schmockwitz. Renate spoke with great passion to Wallace about Dean and his causes.

"You are just as eloquent and just as much an idealist as your husband," said Wallace.

Then Dean talked about Germany. Dean insisted that travel was not a priority for most people. Wallace asked why he thought so many East Germans wanted to go to the West and Dean was silent. Wallace told him that ten to fifteen thousand East Germans emigrated every year and that a million more wanted exit visas and that the East Germans traded political prisoners with the West for hard currency every year, like cattle, at between $15,000 and $40,000 a head. Dean said he was unaware of such exchanges.

Dean asserted that there was freedom to worship under Communism and he and Wallace talked about his career. Dean grew a little testy.

"I don't like being called the Johnny Cash of Communism," he said. "I'm Dean Reed."

"But you know what it means."

"I know that it means they're trying to say that Dean is as famous there as Johnny Cash is here . . . They call me the Red Sinatra as well. It bothers me because I'm not the Red Sinatra . . . I'm Dean Reed and I'm a very very popular man."

Dean told Wallace how much he missed America. He said he stayed in East Germany because he loved Renate.

Wallace asked, "Why do you become the captive of the women with whom you have spent your time?"

"Aren't we all captives of our women, Mike?"

"The main motivation of your life is what?" Wallace asked.

"Love," answered Dean.

"We've heard your cowboy songs. We've heard various songs. Would you sing 'My Yiddishe Momma'?"

"That is one of my favorite songs, Mike. I've sung it, for my mother, in every country of the world. My mother is not Jewish, but I think this song is one of the most beautiful songs of all time for a mother," said Dean.

"I understand you had some difficulties with that song in the Soviet Union."

Dean nodded. On Dean's second tour in the Soviet Union, a little man who said he was from the Ministry of Culture told Dean it was forbidden to sing "Yiddishe Momma." Dean told him that Lenin would roll over in his grave if he had heard him say that because no Marxist could be anti-Semitic and, though he, Dean, did not agree with Zionism, he loved the Jewish people. He had even said this to Yasser Arafat.

He told him, "Yasser, I always include 'Yiddishe Momma'."

"That's OK, Dean," Arafat said. "I have nothing against the Jewish people."

So Dean told the little man from the Ministry of Culture that if he was forbidden to sing "Yiddishe Momma" he would leave the Soviet Union and never return. Mme. Furtseva, the Minister of Culture, who had once tried and almost succeeded in getting the Beatles a Soviet date, came to see him a few days later.

"Dean, it was all a terrible mistake," she said. "Of course, you can sing anything you want to in our country." She added, "If anybody ever tells you to change something that you say or do, you come to me and I'll hit them over the head."

"You sang it?" Mike Wallace said to Dean.

"I sang it. And I continue singing it," Dean said, "I do it a cappella."

"Oh, perfect. Do it a cappella," said Wallace.

"Can I sing it 'Yiddishe Poppa' and sing it to you?"

"You can," Wallace said.

That night, when they talked, Dean told Dixie that he had sung for Mike Wallace and that Wallace had cried. "We did three days' shooting," Dean said. "Then he came into the house and we shot for four hours. "You know, Mr. Reed, I wasn't expecting a man as intelligent as you," Mike had said. "We're going to do the portrait of you now, twenty minutes from Dean."

Dixie thought it was neat.

In his office at CBS, Mike Wallace scanned a letter from Dean.

"He concludes by saying, 'And maybe we can also solve the problem of the "Yiddishe Poppa,"'" Wallace said.

"What does that mean?" I said. I wanted to hear Wallace's version.

"I'm a non-practicing, non-religious Jew. A bad Jew." Wallace smiled. "I was incredibly moved and I nearly burst into tears. After that, frankly, the piece was really a valentine to Dean. Sitting there in East Berlin with this cowboy from Colorado . . . there was this terrific yearning in him to come home."

The 60 *Minutes* piece was scheduled to go out the following fall, so Dean put it at the back of his mind after Mike Wallace left Berlin. In the six weeks that followed Wallace's visit, Dean was increasingly busy, preparing his movie, recording music, on the road playing concert dates.

There were more calls and letters between Schmockwitz and Colorado. In March, Dean wrote to Johnny, "Sorry if I don't write. There are TV shows and films. I'm damn tired and I feel old at times . . . Fifty will be coming along . . . Keep your fingers crossed for Mike [Wallace], ex-Mack the Knife." To Dixie, he wrote, "*60 Minutes* is not finished yet. Did I tell you? I spoke to Mike Wallace. They're gonna hold it until the fall, when they will have the biggest public," said Dean. It was early April.

"Beautiful," said Dixie.

As usual, Dixie and Dean bantered and giggled down the phone.

"You have a beautiful day," Dixie would say.

"Have a nice week," said Dean.

"Say, I love me," Dixie said, signing off.

On April 20, 1986, *60 Minutes* went on the air with the piece about Dean Reed. For one reason or another, maybe scheduling, it was not held over until the autumn but went out in April. That night, Dean was fast asleep in Moscow and had no idea that the piece was on the air.

I was at home in New York, watching *60 Minutes* that night. Johnny and Mona Rosenburg sat in their living room in Loveland, glued to the TV. The title of the piece on Dean came up. It was called "The Defector." Sweet Jesus, thought Johnny. Dear God.

The resonant voice of Mike Wallace began the piece: "When we think about Americans who defect to the other side of the Iron Curtain, we usually think about traitors or spies. Dean Reed is neither. Colorado born, American bred, he now lives in East Berlin, just because he likes it better over there. An entertainer who's become the Soviet version of a superstar. He sings. He acts.

232

And he speaks with what seems to be genuine conviction to the Soviet line. The Kremlin has even rewarded him with their Konsomol Lenin Prize. There is just one thing missing for him. He yearns to duplicate his success behind the Iron Curtain with a similar success back home."

There were shots of Dean's concerts. There were lovely shots of Dean and Renate in matching sheepskin jackets, walking hand in hand in the woods near their house and talking with Mike Wallace. When Dean sat down with Mike Wallace to talk, Wallace asked, "You equate Ronald Reagan with Joseph Stalin?"

"I equate the possibilities of Ronald Reagan with Stalin. I say he has the possibilities to do the same injustices and much more by incinerating this planet through an atomic war."

Wallace asked, "Do you think Mr. Gorbachev is a more moral man, a more peace-loving man than Ronald Reagan?"

Dean nodded.

"Why was the Wall put up in the first place?" asked Mike Wallace.

"The Wall—the Berlin Wall—was put up to defend the population in the first place," said Dean.

Johnny just sat there and listened to Dean defend that Wall and it burned his butt so bad! He could feel himself wanting to be sick. Johnny was in a rage; he felt his knuckles go white as Dean denied that East Germany was a colony of the Soviet Union. Dean talked about maybe being a senator from Colorado . . . if Gary Hart was going on to the Presidency, why not?

Johnny was horrified. "I think it was the next day I called him to tell him it had been shown over here, and I said to him, 'It has done nothing for you here, Dean. The one thing you can't do is defend that Wall in this country.' And he sort of laughed and said, 'Well, I guess I'm going to have to come back and explain things.' And I fired back at him, 'Well, if you do that, you better wear a bullet-proof vest.'"

Four

21

In November of 1988, I went to Leningrad to see Boris Grebenshikov play a rock concert. Grebenshikov was the first authentic homegrown Russian rock star, and his band was playing in the USSR in public with Western musicians. AQUARIUM AND FRIENDS '88, the show was called. Fifty rubles a ticket on the black market.

Jo Durden-Smith, who had been with Leslie Woodhead and me on our first trip to Moscow, was making a documentary about Grebenshikov. Leslie was hoping to film some of the concert himself to use as background for the Dean Reed drama-documentary. I was interested in the music because in some ways the increasing popularity of Russian rock written and performed by young Russians had eventually made Dean Reed irrelevant.

In that April of 1986 after *60 Minutes* was broadcast, when Johnny sat in his shed in Loveland chewing his liver and trying to convey to Dean how angry he was, what was mostly worrying Dean was that he was feeling old.

He worried about his voice failing; he worried he was too old to be a pop star; he realized that the Soviets and even some of the Eastern European countries had their own fresh music, their own young stars, local kids. Even Dean's own stepson, Sasha, didn't like his music. He wrote to Dixie, "Sasha calls me 'old man'." He sent her a picture of himself and wrote a note saying hopefully that he thought he looked rather young. "Oh, it is nice to have a baby face," Dean wrote. He was forty-seven.

"Guess what?" Leslie said as our Aeroflot plane lurched through a winter storm.

"What?"

He looked around the interior of the plane, and at the window and smiled knowingly.

"Guess," he said again.

But I closed my eyes, then opened them, terrified as the plane fell through some hideous air pocket. Outside the window it was black.

Leslie smiled at the stewardess, who did not smile back, but delivered a tray with a cup containing what tasted like swimming-pool water and a single toffee in greasy waxed paper that passed for lunch. Several drunks, cans of beer in hand, roamed the aisle.

How dull travel in the Soviet Union would be one day without the terrors of Aeroflot and without the drunks, the horrible hotels, and the listening devices. Small talk would dwindle badly; dinner parties would grind to a halt.

The plane shuddered. I closed my eyes and thought of photographs of Dean Reed's early trips to Russia. He was always moving, in a plane with fur-hatted commissars, jumping out of a plane door after it landed, standing on top of a big Russian express train, riding backwards, and strumming his guitar and singing Woody Guthrie songs. "This train," Dean sang astride the moving cars.

Now, the Aeroflot plane bumped to a halt on the runway and

we got out and trudged into the terminal, which resembled something from the 1950s. It was three in the morning. Jo Durden-Smith was waiting to meet us because he had arrived earlier, and in a blinding snowstorm we somehow got to the Pribaltiskaya, a modern hotel on the outskirts of town. It was very depressing, Soviet Modern, probably *circa* 1980. It had endless corridors with ugly patterned carpet. Every time you turned a corner, you tripped over a drunken Finn.

Helsinki's drinking laws had become so draconian—the politicians were trying to get the people to dry out a little—that on weekends a lot of men flew into Leningrad, hired some girls, got laid, got drunk, vomited, and passed out where they were, sometimes in the hotel corridors. They lay there until they sobered up enough to get up and go home. That night I didn't care. I wanted a bed. In my room, I fell asleep with half my clothes still on.

The next morning, I went looking for Art Troitsky, who had come from Moscow to Leningrad to meet us. I gave him a bottle of Advocaat liqueur I'd bought in the duty-free shop on the way out. We had coffee in the dining room, and Art said he had just been to London, Paris, New York, Los Angeles, and Graceland, and that he had enjoyed the West. Still, he said, he wished he had escaped the USSR illicitly in the bad old days, wished he had done it in a balloon. Traveling business class on a 747 seemed pretty tame to Art and even though this was one of his conceits, the rock life was becoming a little dull for him.

Once rock and roll had been a dangerous game; Art's writings were banned; people were condemned for listening to what was called "Musical Aids." Now in 1988, even the *apparatchiks* were listening to the *metallisti*.

"Hmm, Metal," they would say, stroking their chins. "Very interesting."

"My Father is a Fascist" was currently the biggest hit in Leningrad.

After breakfast, we went over to the sports stadium where the concert would take place. Around the makeshift stage were half a dozen British musicians in leather pants, shades, and ear studs; they lolled among the lights, amplifiers, guitars, trunks, suitcases, backpacks, drums, and cases of Perrier that had been trucked in overland from Helsinki. Dozens of film people lurked, waiting for orders from Michael Apted, the director of the documentary. Apted wandered around, the local rock promoter in his wake. The rock guy introduced himself to everyone as Fat Lev. "All you need is Lev, eh?" he said to everyone he met.

Even Fat Lev couldn't supply black paint, though. There were tons of equipment, but no black paint for the stage, not a single can in Leningrad, an industrial city of four million people.

Leslie Woodhead had imported yet another crew to shoot the footage he wanted for the Dean Reed drama-documentary, and his production manager, Craig McNeill, wandered around the sports stadium, with a pair of cowboy boots under his arm, looking for a Dean Reed stand-in. Everyone was drinking coffee and complaining about the hotels and the black paint and the weather, and wondering if the Russian musicians would ever show up.

The Russians were late, except for the cellist, who sat on the stage, sawing at his instrument like a dentist trying to get at a difficult tooth.

Keeping order, more or less, was Dave Stewart of the Eurythmics. A small hirsute man, Dave had produced Boris Grebenshikov's first Western album.

The percussionist was Ray Cooper. A big man in a fine suit with a shaved head, Ray kept his drumsticks in a silver champagne cooler. It was Ray's second trip to the USSR: he had been on tour with Elton John in 1979, the first Soviet tour by a Western rock superstar. From time to time, Ray went to the Kirov Ballet with his roadie.

Cooper started testing his cymbals. He made me think of the man in the title sequence of J. Arthur Rank movies. As if in response, Boris Grebenshikov appeared. He was four hours late.

Slim, pale, with big Slavic lips and long blond hair, Boris was thirty-five and he could look incredibly plain, or light himself up and be unspeakably handsome. While Dean was promiscuous with his smile, Boris saved his up, waited, watched, held back, letting it come very slowly. I introduced myself; we had almost met in New York. For a second more, he calculated the smile, then he gave it all away. He had really nice manners.

"Yes, I know your name quite well," he said politely when we were introduced, though I was pretty sure he didn't know who the hell I was at all.

Meeting Boris made me really understand how out of date Dean Reed must have seemed, how much his star had faded. Dean became an official superstar in the Soviet Union because he was American and because of his looks, because he seemed forbidden. He was, in fact, official. He not only spouted the Party line, he was also a believer. But towards the end of his life his music seemed dated; he was yesterday's man. I saw a clip from a TV program Dean made in Moscow not long before his death. He wore a kind of silky waistcoat and a shirt with puffy sleeves, an outfit a disco guy of the 1970s might have worn. Oleg Smirnoff did the translating.

"We are not too old," Dean said to the audience. "I know how old you are and I think we should be symbols to the young people." He smiled. Then he did a little dance routine to the tune from *Ghostbusters* and the audience, in a desultory way, joined in. It was one of the saddest things I ever saw.

Boris Gribenshikov, the mathematics student who became the first authentic Russian rocker, was young and he was good. His earliest memories were of the distant sound of the Beatles, the illicit seductive crackle of great Western music broadcast by the Voice of America. Boris was a rebel because nothing else gave him peace. If Dean had become a star by joining the mainstream, Boris became a star by inhabiting the underground, the unofficial world. In the years when Dean was on officially approved tours across the USSR, Boris, like a character out of a Dostoevsky novel, wandered the Leningrad streets after dark, looking for trouble and finding it.

In 1980, at a concert in Tblisi, he had famously lain down on the stage embracing his Fender Stratocaster. He got up a legend.

"When Boris lay down on the stage holding his guitar on his stomach, the entire judging committee stood up and left the hall," Art Troitsky said. "The officials said, why did you bring those faggots here?"

People who said they believed in the spiritual wrote to Boris to ask about his karma. Kids regularly crossed the Soviet Union, two, three, eight time zones, to see Boris. They climbed the stairs to his sixth-floor squat on Sofia Pereovskaya Street in Leningrad, where they wrote poetry on the walls and where Boris kept a picture of the Beatles in his place as a kind of shrine. He believed in the spiritual. He believed in the Beatles.

Boris and his band, Aquarium, made great music, they could play any style. It was Boris's lyrics—religious, sentimental, satirical, and utterly Russian—that made him a hero; next to a good meolody, which is why Russians fell so obsessively in love with the Beatles, they were crazy about good lyrics. It was a long way from Dean Reed's stuff, the early pap like "Twirly Twirly" and the platitudes of his political numbers.

Boris Grebenshikov was the perfect hero for his generation, for whom the significance of rock and roll was intense, emotional, political in the widest sense, and practically religious. Break the rules, the rock mantra went. Keep the faith. As Art Troitsky put it, it gave a generation its identity.

"It meant fight your parents," Art said. "It meant: you are free to do what you want, no matter what the seniors say. It was a form of fighting back, a reaction to oppression, a catalyst for change. It taught people how to be themselves and how to oppose the rules."

Everywhere in the USSR, kids copied Boris' underground album on to cassettes. A million of them. Ten million. Boris' music was unofficial and hard to get hold of and, therefore, in Soviet eyes, more valuable. Maybe Dean's popularity declined because he had become too easy.

"After *Glasnost*, from 1985 or 1986, local rock and roll heroes became available to the public," Art said, "and American rock and roll, even if it was Prince and not Dean Reed, became less popular."

"Only in a very provincial and very isolated country, could a figure like Dean Reed become a big star," Art added thoughtfully. "Gradually, Russia, the Soviet Union, and Eastern Europe, got closer to the world community culturally and in a very humanitarian way. In the light of new information, Dean Reed's figure was getting darker and darker."

243

In 1987, Boris went legit. Melodiya issued an album by Aquarium made from underground tapes and it sold 200,000 copies in a couple of hours. Although no Soviet had ever personally signed a contract for himself and all contractual issues, especially with foreigners, were handled by the state agencies, Boris signed his own contract with CBS Records.

Boris went to America, where he was enthralled and confused; he sat in a closet in an apartment in New York's East Village, listening to music. He sat by a pool in Hollywood and felt disoriented. At home, his fans wondered if Boris had sold out and despaired.

Art had been friends with Boris for a long time, but even Art was a little cynical. He said that within a decade you would hear Boris's music in the elevator of the Moscow Hilton. Even Art's mother liked Boris.

Art Troitksy was unhappy in Leningrad. Like many Muscovites, he despised it and called it the "City of Bad Memories." I didn't like it either and I didn't quite understand why at first, maybe the fact that insistently beautiful cities make me uneasy. I felt that in spite of its beauty, or because of it, I was imprisoned in a mad imperial theme park.

A port city blasted from a swamp by slave labor in the eighteenth century—Peter the Great was obsessed with making a European city—it was gorgeous but crumbling and somehow sinister, like Miss Haversham's wedding cake. Its *fartovshiki*, the two-bit criminals, hustled you relentlessly.

Still, it was a Georgian wet dream of a city, with its matched sets of pastel buildings and the gilded griffons on the bridges and the pale green Winter Palace iced with snow. In November, when it got dark early and the snow was dirty, it was a melancholy place.

What I remembered best about Leningrad was the freaky wax statue of Peter the Great with his own hair in a glass case at the Hermitage and the waiter at the Metropole Restaurant with jars of black-market caviar shoved in the pockets of his pants under his worn tailcoat. At five bucks a pop, it was cheaper than Moscow. I remembered the fact that, under siege by the Nazis during World War Two, Leningrad's people ate wallpaper paste.

On our one afternoon away from the sports stadium, we went to the Hermitage and when we got back to the hotel and disembarked from the bus, our guide shifted his feet unhappily and refused our gift of Marlboros. It was a kind of protest. All afternoon he had listened to us casually abuse his country, commenting on the bureaucracy and the crappy food and lousy toilets.

Finally, he said, "Are you with the rock concert?"

"Yes," I replied.

He said, "I met Boris once about eight years ago, but he's very famous now. He wouldn't remember me."

That evening, before the concert began, a group of little girl gymnasts appeared at the back of the sports stadium presumably for a practice session. Twirling, spinning, and tossing Indian clubs, they launched their perfect childish bodies into outer space like tiny sputniks. The band was tuning up. The little gymnasts seemed oblivious to the music and I wondered if rock and roll was already unremarkable to these little kids of seven and eight.

I wandered into a dressing room where tinted photographs of the heroes of Soviet sport—ice skaters in spangles, footballers in jerseys stiff with sweat—were on the walls. A member of the Russian band was there.

His hair draped over his ears, he stared into the mirror, reciting his mantra. The room was choking sweet with pot. It smelled like 1968, I thought, and then I left and went backstage, where I had a good view of the band and the audience. The hall was packed.

"Sing it in Russian!" the crowd yelled, and Boris Grebenshikov, dressed entirely in black and in command of the stage with his band around him, sang in Russian.

Twelve thousand people clapped and wept, and some of them pushed up almost to the edge of the stage and linked arms and lit candles. A pale young girl, turning her face up to him, held up a picture of Boris, an icon in a plastic sleeve.

"Sing it in Russian!"

Boris finished the number. He introduced Dave Stewart and Ray Cooper. These were his friends from the West, he said, and they were going to sing some songs in English.

"Sing it in Russian!"

Film crews in sneakers raced silently around the stage and recorded everything. News crews were there, too. Foreigners loved rock and roll in Russia. It was the sexiest image of the decade. The revolution had come and it sounded good. It sounded great. It was noisy. It was vivid. It looked like us, and you didn't go to war with your own, so we felt safe for the first time in our lives. We Cold War babies knew for sure now that they weren't going to nuke us. The music seemed to literally tear up the terrors of seventy years and toss them over its shoulder with wonderful abandon.

Boys punched the air. Tall girls with fabulous cheekbones and pale big lips, the Slav beauties who had suddenly appeared everywhere in the USSR, waved and sang along. In the best seats, officials clapped politely and tried not to wish they were listening to Tchaikovsky. People threw flowers. People unfurled Soviet flags and the hammer and sickle waved to the sound of Ray Cooper's chimes. A boy in a yellow satin jacket turned his back so everyone could see the slogan on it. It read: GLASNOST '88, as if *Glasnost* were this year's Woodstock.

In the middle of the swaying sea of bodies, a young Russian soldier in uniform got on to his girlfriend's shoulders and loosened his tie. He made a V-sign. Seeing us standing at the side of the stage, he gestured wildly. He wanted Leslie to take his picture. Then the boy whispered to his friend, who got on *his* girl's shoulders and the two of them made V-signs and laughed like crazy and yelled and yelled, probably calling out, "Take our picture."

Boris sang his anthem: "Rock and roll is dead, but I'm not yet."

Dave Stewart called out, "I'm from Sunderland, Boris is from Leningrad. We meet. It's just a tiny thing. But it's better than killing each other."

"All you need is love!"

We all sang along and believed for a while that it was really true. All you need is love. How Dean would have adored it all.

Or would he? Would he have been thrilled by the noise and good will? Was it what he had wanted? Or would he have felt old, a has-been, a man from a different time, a guy out of step with these tall girls in miniskirts and boys in ponytails? I wasn't sure he would have understood their rock and roll that was such a Russian mix of sex and poetry and religion. Maybe GLASNOST '88 would have left Dean on the sidelines, an old man. But, of course, by November, 1988, Dean had already been dead for almost two and a half years.

"Sing it in Russian!"

22

In the spring of 1986, Dean was working like crazy on *Bloody Heart*. June 24, the start date for the movie he'd been working on for five years, was coming at him like a train down a track. As he said, there was no stopping it, no changing the date, and if the deals weren't done and the production not ready, it would be over for him.

From Leningrad I went on to Moscow to try to find out what had happened to the movie, because the deal had been negotiated in Moscow, and I knew that something had gone horribly wrong, something I was now convinced led to his death in the lake near his house in East Germany.

Bloody Heart was going to change Dean's life. It was the crossover picture that would make him a real contender as a director in the East. Having been to America, he was obsessed with making a real movie with good production values instead of what he called "a piece of garbage where you could punch your fists through the sets." *Sing Cowboy Sing* had been an enormous hit, but Dean was fed up with playing an idiotic cowpoke, as he put it. A new career as a director would also release him from life as a fading pop star.

On May 30, l986, Artemy Troitsky organized a concert in Moscow to benefit the victims of Chernobyl—the nuclear power plant had blown up on April 25–26—and it was the first event of its kind. Everyone signed on, all the biggest bands and singers. There was a rumor that Dean Reed showed up and stood backstage at the concert and nobody asked him to play. Nobody cared.

For the whole of the spring, Dean led an increasingly frenzied life—the film, concerts, albums, television shows. He was always on the road—Potsdam, Prague, Moscow, Berlin. He sat up late in Schmockwitz, reworking the script for *Bloody Heart*. It was never out of his mind.

Renate would star with him in *Bloody Heart*. They would be together all summer long. They would have a chance to patch things up and get past the quarrels they'd been having which were nagging at Dean like his ulcer.

He was also desperately involved in the complications of pre-production; making a realistic movie about America in East Germany and the USSR meant he had to attend to a million details and he did it obsessively. Dean cast his "Indians" in Alma Alta in Uzbekistan, and from a collective farm that was populated entirely by North Koreans. American police cars and jeeps, as well as period sedans, were hired from vintage car clubs that flourished in the Baltic cities of Riga and Tallinn. Already that spring, a credible version of an American church was under construction in Yalta in the Crimea, which was to be the principal location for *Bloody Heart*, but the wood had to be shipped in from Riga because wood was scarce in the Crimea.

He was determined. When *Bloody Heart* was finished, Dean would show his movie in America and he was convinced that it would be his ticket home.

"It was really a dream world in some ways," Victor Grossman said. "But Dean had high hopes and met someone in America who was willing to manage him, a woman who talked about fan clubs and making pencils and all kinds of things with 'Dean Reed' on it." He meant Dixie, of course.

In Potsdam, Dean struggled with the changes at the DEFA Film Studios, which was his professional base. The great Berlin movie studios, where films like the *Blue Angel* had been made before World War Two, had been taken over by the Communists in the 1950s as part of the socialist network of movie facilities.

By the 1980s the studios were a mess. On DEFA's vast back lot, broken Roman columns lay on the ground. Inside the studio, the sound stages were shabby and so were the sets, except for one improbably imperial bedroom and bathroom constructed of fake marble.

DEFA was in trouble. Erich Honecker still ruled East Germany, but hard currency was increasingly what mattered, and the producers at DEFA dreamed of deals with the West. Maybe Dean thought that *Bloody Heart* was the perfect vehicle for his return to America, but the smart money at DEFA knew the West wasn't interested in a movie where the FBI were the bad guys.

Bloody Heart was cut back. In the Soviet system, everything on a movie was painstakingly planned because everything was so expensive, even the lousy film stock. You had to calculate the number of shots—there were two and a half meters of film per shot—and submit your plan. At almost seven hundred shots, *Bloody Heart* was two hundred more than the norm. Dean was planning a movie that would run over two hours.

"I must show the American life with all the details. There must be lots of short scenes," said Dean who, like all movie directors, dreamed of movies with thousands of extras. He was forced to scale back from a cast of six hundred to a cast of sixty.

Dean needed Soviet coproduction money to make his film. In fact, half of the money was to be Soviet, but, even more than in Germany, in the Soviet Union money for old-style socialist movies was drying up. In spite of his impossible schedule in the winter and spring of 1986, until the week before he died in June, Dean shuttled to and from the USSR as if his life depended on it. He was worried, frantic, his face lined, Lilia Liepine told me when I met her in Moscow. She had been Dean's production manager on *Bloody Heart*.

In her pink angora sweater, Lilia looked like Mrs. Brown and she said she had mourned for Dean like a mother. She was from Riga. In the Soviet Union, the production of every movie was assigned by Moscow to a regional studio. *Bloody Heart*, a German coproduction, was given to the Riga studio, in part, at least, because in the Latvian capital most people spoke German.

"Dean felt we were like Germans, that we were too polite, too reserved for his taste," said the good-natured Lilia.

She told me sadly that, in the Riga studio, the boxes of props for *Bloody Heart* were still stored, including a cracked Coca Cola sign and the footage, which Dean had shot on Denver's skid row when he was in Colorado.

He had been convinced that it would give the movie a real feel of America, and the tale of the filming was already added to what he called "The Annals of Deano." He loved telling how he found himself in the middle of a burglary that day on Larimer Street where the bums lived, how a real American cop stopped him with a big riot gun, how he, Dean, bravely kept the cameras turning and got the real goods, how frightening America sometimes was, with its hundred million handguns. Dean was frightened by the guns, but exhilarated at the same time.

Possessed by the vision of the professional American film, but doomed to make it in two countries where every piece of equipment was forty years out of date, Dean himself oversaw the casting and the sets and even the make-up tests and the animals.

He chose a horse for himself at a collective farm in the USSR where wild horses were broken. Month after month, he traveled the whole of the Soviet Union with Lilia Liepine, restless, anxious. In Yalta, mobbed by fans, Dean gave an impromptu concert at the end of a long hard day and Lilia said to him, "How can you stand it?"

"I like it," he said. "I need it."

Then the tank was late arriving from North Vietnam.

Hanoi was the only place you could put your hands on an American tank. People filming in the Soviet Union who needed a US tank had to buy one from Hanoi. I remembered that I had seen a photograph of Dean with some North Vietnamese generals. He appeared to be joking around with them and maybe it was how he had finagled his tank. I asked Lilia Liepine if people would be frightened by the sight of an American tank being driven down a road in the Crimea.

"USA, USSR, there isn't a lot of difference between tanks," she said.

"Of course, in the end, the Soviets canceled the money for *Bloody Heart*," said an American diplomat who had known Dean and was retired and bored and happy to talk. "The Soviets killed the movie," he said with absolute certainty. "Everyone knew," he said, "the movie was *kaput*."

Kaput. Finished. If it were true, the emotional fallout for Dean would have been like Chernobyl.

In Moscow at the end of 1988, I discovered just how much the new freedoms in the USSR were changing things. *Perestroika*—the restructuring of the economic and political institutions—meant that, where movies had once been completely subsidized by the state, every studio now had to turn a profit.

Movies had always been big in the Soviet Union. The Soviets went to the pictures all the time—as much as nineteen times a year, some people said—largely because there wasn't much else to do. Their flats were crowded and the restaurants were disgusting; at least the movie theaters were warm and you could make out in the back rows.

Even before Gorbachev took office in 1985, people were fed up with the crap that came out of the Soviet studios. State censorship, the yes-men of the Brezhnev era, and the decades of stagnation meant that movies ran largely to provincial romance and costume drama. The Russians were crazy for costume drama and heroic space pictures, including *Cosmonaut #2 in the USA.* The Russian version of *Mary Poppins* had been the biggest cinematic event since *Battleship Potemkin*; the Sherlock Holmes movies, too, were very popular.

A sign of change, and there were people in Moscow who read these signs meticulously, obsessively, was the election of Elem Klimov as head of the cinematographers' union. It took place a few months after Gorbachev came to power. Klimov's films had been banned for years; then, suddenly, he was official.

Censorship crumbled. Movies once considered irreverent were screened. Sexy movies. Political movies. Soviet film stars began appearing in *Playboy*. In 1987, Juris Podnieks made *Is It Easy to Be Young?* and it was another watershed because in his dark, tough picture, he portrayed hostile punk kids and their passionate desire above all else for money and good times.

One night I met a writer at *Dom Kino*. Moscow's film house was jammed and the stylish crowd of movie people drank and kissed the air a lot and Nikita Khrushchev's grandson, a balding, plump young man in jeans, ate ice cream. Over vodka, the writer looked at the crowd and said, "Just remember, these people who now dance to the Gorby Gavotte, used to do it to the Brezhnev Boogie and before that, in some cases, to the Khrushchev Carioca."

Mosfilm, the city's main studio, was in the Lenin Hills on the outskirts of Moscow. Leslie and I went with our guide, Vera Reich. As we drove up to the studio gates, Vera said that she worked mostly for film people and that her last client had been the director Roland Joffe. Leslie Woodhead said we knew Roland and we'd seen him recently in Beverly Hills. At this Vera's face lit up: this connection with Roland somehow made us all friends.

Even in her tiny high-heeled leather boots, Vera Reich was very short. She was curious about everything. She had a genuine smile and she was completely incorruptible.

"Film is our most important art," Lenin said, and it was inscribed over the front door of the studio. The studio was vast; it had offices, sound stages, prop shops, costume stores and a huge back lot where vintage trams lay rusting in the dirty snow.

The lobby at Mosfilm had the silvery, stylized feel of an RKO set with *Art Moderne* corridors, the kind where Fred Astaire and Ginger Rogers might have danced; black-and-white photographs of great Russian movie stars lined the walls. I couldn't find Dean anywhere on the wall of stars.

The man in charge of foreign coproduction wore a very good suit and had an office as big as a conference room with a map of the world on the wall. He looked like a producer. He did not introduce himself or respond to a request for his name, or maybe he didn't understand. Anyway, I never knew his name and I thought of him as Mr. Big. He addressed himself entirely to Leslie Woodhead because Leslie was also a producer in a good suit and a Western coproduction of any kind was a juicy prospect.

Mr. Big wanted to talk deals. He wanted to talk to Leslie about the prospect of his shooting Dean's life story at Mosfilm and how much stuff—lights, sets, costumes, crew—he could sell. Production at Mosfilm was way down. Times were tough.

Mr. Big ordered his secretary to bring coffee. I wanted to talk about Dean Reed, but he yawned, interested only in the deal, and so I drank my coffee to cover my boredom.

"You'll want to see a script, of course," Leslie said.

No, Mr. Big said and offered him a Havana cigar.

Nothing was more astonishing than that no one in Moscow asked to see a script anymore; they asked how much money you had to spend. Leslie had been sneaking around Eastern Europe for years in order to make his ground-breaking drama-documentaries and he had met secretly with Soviet dissident generals in back alleys and taken illegal photographs of the Communist Party headquarters in Prague and the shipyards in Gdansk. Suddenly, in the heart of Moscow, all anyone talked to him about were below-the-line costs and exchange rates.

Hopeful, Mr. Big pushed his box of Havanas at Leslie.

"Cigar?" he said in English.

"Can we film in Red Square?" Leslie said for the second time.

Sure, you could film in Red Square, although the Kremlin is heavily booked years in advance.

"What did you think of Dean Reed?" I finally said.

Mr. Big shrugged his beefy shoulders. It had been Dean's ambition to play John Reed, the American who took part in the 1917 Russian Revolution. Around 1980, the director, Sergei Bondachuk, had planned to make a Russian version of John Reed's life and Dean promoted himself for the part. Bondachuk went to California and, language notwithstanding, offered the part to Warren Beatty. Beatty subsequently made his own version instead and called it *Reds*.

According to Mr. Big, directors were interested in Dean as an actor, but only up to a point. Dean would only work for hard currency. "We'd love to use you," directors would say, "but currency is what we lack."

As I pushed the conversation in the direction of *Bloody Heart* and as Mr. Big watched Leslie, trying to decipher his intentions, the door opened and a man, maybe sixty-five, ambled in. He wore a shiny blue suit, a greasy yellow shirt and a tie that might have come from a Soviet production of *Guys and Dolls*. He looked like Harry the Horse. Like Mr. Big he didn't offer his name.

Harry slumped into a chair. His back permanently curved, as if he'd spent too much time shooting craps, he held his cigarette between this thumb and his forefinger. In preparing *Bloody Heart*, Dean had come to Mosfilm to look for costumes and Harry the Horse was his minder.

Harry accepted a Marlboro from me.

Mr Big said, "Dean wasn't such a big star, but the young girls were crazy about his looks. He became in the end a little bit

256

yesterday's man. Many actors are gifted, but stupid. Dean saw what was going on. Dean was not stupid."

Realizing that no money would change hands that day, Mr. Big lost interest in us and looked at his watch. Harry the Horse took charge.

"You would like to see studio?"

It smelled of make-up and cigarette smoke. We traipsed across a sound stage at Mosfilm with a set for a fairy tale that was in production. Mismatched green plastic leaves dangled from Styrofoam trees and a few actresses in pink tulle smoked cigarettes. The cameras were as big as dinosaurs, the lights as big as tanks.

In the make-up department, a group of women in cotton smocks and hairnets worked silently with pots of paint and powder. Like everywhere else in the country, there were shortages in the movie business. Good blood, stage blood, was hard to come by. The youngest girl in the room had a Walkman on and she jiggled to the music while she worked. Across the room in a glass case were a pair of false limbs, the exquisite work of the prosthetics team; in another case was Rasputin's wig.

The costumes were stored in a separate warehouse. In one section alone there were hundreds of military uniforms and, at the end of every rack, a detailed diagram of the uniforms it held, including the period, the size, and the rank and order of the soldier or officer in question. The Nazi uniforms were crowded together. They looked old and smelled stale, and for a minute I had the feeling they weren't costumes but captured uniforms. German caps were piled on a shelf; black and brown leather gloves lay in tidy pairs in a carton on the floor; in another, larger box, jackboots, tied together by their laces, were neatly stacked.

I had to get some air. We went out into the snow where, clutching his pack of Marlboros, Harry the Horse escorted us to the back lot and left us there underneath a gallows with a rope dangling from a post. Next door was the London Street with quaint shop fronts and nineteenth-century signs; it was falling down; Baker Street had begun to rot.

Out in front of the studio, our car and driver were waiting at the front gate. The driver looked like Karl Malden. Every day, he expected and we gave him Marlboros. Cigarettes, especially Marlboros, were like currency in Moscow. You could even hail a passing car—a regular car, not a taxi—by holding out a pack of cigarettes and the driver would stop and, after negotiating the number of packs, give you a lift. There was always a lot of debate about how many packs you had to hand over.

I said to our driver, "You know what? You look just like a famous American actor."

"So what are you giving me tomorrow?" the driver asked.

I talked to more nameless film people in Moscow and a few were convinced that the final contracts on *Bloody Heart* had never been signed. There was apparently only one person who could really help, a lawyer who was unavailable until the end of the week. We passed the time hanging out with Art and Svetlana, and then the lawyer called and invited us to meet him at Sovinfilm, the state production bureau. The lawyer's name was Boris—he didn't mention a last name, just said to call him Boris—and we sat in the same conference room where Boris and Dean had negotiated the deal on *Bloody Heart*. Lilia Liepine was with us.

Boris was the legal advisor to Sovinflim, he wrote the contracts and witnessed them. A nice man with a good smile, he had a head like a skull. He had been fond of Dean, he said. He had been really emotional after he died because he liked him.

"Was the contract for *Bloody Heart* canceled?" Leslie asked. "Was *Bloody Heart* shelved?"

Boris wanted to reminisce.

"I have a friend who is very similar in appearance to Dean Reed—my friend and I were buddies in the army—so I felt friendly towards Dean," he said. "Dean was always enthusiastically welcomed, a permanent friend of the Soviet Union. Yes, he always had nice photos of himself in a bag, ready to deliver when anyone asked. He behaved himself. He was a good guy."

"Completely?"

Boris was a lawyer and he shifted into a moderate gear.

"Dean was temperamental—he scolded, he shouted—but he was a good guy all the same," he said again.

Boris reiterated what we already knew: how important *Bloody Heart* was to Dean; how he was obliged to take a codirector; how the codirector got cancer a few months before filming began, leaving everyone in the lurch and the film companies in East Berlin and Moscow nervous.

But what about the contracts?

The first *Bloody Heart* script had been approved as far back as November, 15, 1984. Boris dove into a large leather bag, looking for the contracts. Leslie and I waited, not looking at each other. If the contracts had not been signed, if *Bloody Heart* had been shelved, it would have been the end of the road. It would make you believe Dean's death might have been suicide.

We had been on the road for a year, looking for answers. I was impatient. I sat on my hands while Boris put aside his bag and knelt down to open the bottom drawer of his desk.

"I've found it!"

Triumphant, Boris emerged with a sheaf of papers. On June 10, 1986, the final contract for the Soviet–German coproduction of *Bloody Heart* had been signed by a Mr. Gerrit List, a representative of the German film studios at Potsdam. Boris passed the contract down the table to us.

I stared at the bits of paper written in languages I did not understand, signed a few days before Dean died. Suicide seemed much less likely now. He had been working for years towards the movie and it had been given the go-ahead. Green-lighted. It was OK.

Had Dean been murdered then? And why? It didn't make sense. None of it made any sense. Maybe it had been an accident after all.

Boris shuffled more paper. Shooting was definitely to have begun on June 24 in East Germany and on August 11 in the Soviet Union.

"Everything was set," he said. "Even the music director, who was from Prague. He was called *Svoboda*. Everybody in Prague is called *Svoboda*. Unless they are called prisoner," he added with a straight face.

I didn't get it.

"*Svoboda* means freedom," Leslie whispered.

"When Dean died, everything was canceled," Boris said. "Without Dean there was no movie. He was the movie."

Boris produced another piece of paper. It was a termination contract for *Bloody Heart*. It was dated July 15, 1986. The contract for the picture was declared null and void. Dean's body was discovered on June 17, so they hadn't wasted much time.

The room was quiet. Lilia Liepine wiped her eyes. Vera stopped translating. Boris looked sad and for a minute he sat perfectly still, lost in some impenetrable Russian reverie. Then he smiled cheerily and packed up his lawyer's briefcase.

"Things change," he said.

23

By 1988 there was a cooperative toilet with real toilet paper and piped-in muzak in downtown Moscow and for fifty kopeks you could sit peacefully for as long as you liked. People said this was *perestroika* at work, a sign of financial restructuring, the coming of a brand new form of private enterprise. You couldn't see it in Moscow's hotels, though. I knew someone who was thinking of making a documentary about them and calling it *Hotel Fawlty*.

We were in the Hotel Budapest. My room had a drain in the middle of the floor and indolent cockroaches lazed in a puddle in the bathroom. Something unspeakable discolored the sheets and the only amenity was a green plastic radio beside the bed, which bore the mysterious sticker: "Inspected by Mildred."

Leslie Woodhead's room wasn't much better. It had a large refrigerator that did not work. The orange paper curtains on the window didn't meet and, when he opened the window, they fell on his head. Vera Reich, the translator who had become a friend was determined to do better for us, so now we stood in the lobby of the Rossiya Hotel. It had 3000 rooms and a concert hall.

When John Denver came to Moscow in 1985, he had played

the Rossiya. People in the Soviet Union liked Denver for his music and his politics, though some of them made fun of his pimples. When he heard Denver was scheduled to play the Rossiya, Dean flew in from East Berlin on an impulse. He didn't have a visa, but he was Dean Reed after all and he felt he was a kind of soul mate of John Denver's. The officials at Sheremetyevo Airport kept him waiting and, by the time he got to the Rossiya, he had missed the show.

"Why can't I be John Denver? I'm from Denver, too," he often said.

In the cavernous lobby of the Rossiya I fantasized that Dean was alive and would come striding in. Laughing, he would make the crowds at the check-in desk laugh. But Dean was dead, and it was all just idle speculation to help kill the time, and all there was in the lobby of the Rossiya was a sign for Diners Club that read: RUNNING OUT OF RUBLES?

As she negotiated with the reservations clerk at the Rossiya, outrage crossed Vera Reich's face. Then she turned to us.

"Everything is fixed, you have rooms here," Vera said, wiping away her make-believe tears.

"How do you do it?" I said.

"I just keep talking until they can't stand me anymore, and I cry," she said, and then we all went upstairs.

The Rossiya was so big that you literally needed a map to get around, but having navigated the corridors, we found my room and sat down there and drank a lot of Scotch out of the one glass from the bathroom. Vera talked about her memories of Dean Reed.

At Vera's language school in the early 1970s, rumors began to go around that Dean Reed was coming. All through the school you could hear the whispers. Along the corridors, before class began, in the recess, at lunch, they whispered it: Dean Reed. Dean Reed.

"Dean Reed is coming."

"Like the Pied Piper," said Vera.

"Was he good? Was he a good singer?"

Vera grinned. Who could tell? Who cared! He was so handsome and he was wearing very tight pants. He sang rock and roll. He brought us this gift. He was American.

"I guess Dean was also popular because he espoused socialist values," Leslie Woodhead said.

Vera chortled politely.

"What you must understand is that we believed the exact opposite of the propaganda," she said. "If the television said, America is slums, poverty, crime, we believed the opposite." It was what Vladimir Pozner had said. "May I ask you something?' Vera inquired delicately.

"Sure."

"How it is that some people in United States have joined the Communist Party?"

I told her that everything was not quite perfect in America. I said that there were many people who were illiterate, hungry, and homeless.

"But, surely, they are just bums," said Vera.

For the time being, I left Vera to her dreams about the streets that were paved with gold.

"I guess Dean's problem going home to America was that people in America weren't too keen on socialism," Leslie said.

Vera said, "They're not too keen on it in the Soviet Union either."

She pulled on her knitted hat. Vera was going home to some remote corner of Moscow and would pick us up the next morning. I thanked her for fixing the rooms and tried to give her a box of fancy soap, but she shook her head and refused.

"This is my job," she said politely.

Vera visited the West for the first time that year and she wrote to me to say she didn't care for the supermarkets in England because the variety of goods made her hyperventilate. What she loved most about the West was that relationships were not degraded by need. Vera loved the West for its friendliness. Eventually, she went to live in Arizona.

The next day I met Xenia Golubovitch, a sixteen-year-old Moscow student who had met Dean Reed first when she was a little girl. Xenia, dark and intense, showed me the poster of Dean on the wall of her bedroom.

She said in perfect English, "He was the embodiment of the whole country's dream about America. In their secret hearts, people have the American dream. The point was that they were trying to project the way they wanted America on to Dean." She pointed at the poster and read out the hand-written dedication on it: " 'To Xenia, I thank you for your love and friendship and for your tears. Be brave, plus happy, plus truthful, love Dean Reed.' That's what he wrote to me when I was five."

The poster had been on her wall all of Xenia's life. As a five year old, Xenia had seen *El Cantor* on television. (It was the story of the Chilean folksinger Victor Jara who had been a friend of Dean's and was murdered in the soccer stadium in Santiago by Pinochet's goons.)

Xenia said, "I saw Dean Reed in a film about Victor Jara on

Soviet TV and they killed Jara and I cried. They were such humble people and I have such an image of them and their ponchos."

Her mother asked Xenia what she wanted for her birthday that year and she said, "I want to meet Dean Reed."

Now she added, "My mom dressed me up like a little doll and took me with her to the Rossiya Hotel where Dean was performing."

"Do you want me to dance with you?" Dean had said to Xenia when they met. "What do you think of me?"

"In my kindergarten, some people think of tables, some of chairs. I think of you," Xenia told Dean.

Showing off, she had begun counting in English for Dean and he laughed and she nearly died of embarrassment.

Xenia's mother Yelena Zagrevskaya was Jo Durden-Smith's girlfriend. After I had seen Xenia's Dean Reed poster we all sat down in the kitchen of the apartment and Yelena's mother made us lunch.

Yelena was a brilliant translator and interpreter. Since our first trip in February of 1988, Jo had been back to Moscow a lot and he had fallen in love with it and with Yelena. In his cowboy boots, his big leather bag flapping on his shoulder, and a cigarette in his hand, Jo had become a familiar figure around Moscow.

Jo was a writer, witty, charming, talented, and skeptical, though when he had left London for America in the 1960s he told a friend, "I have to commit myself to the Revolution." (He subsequently wrote a wonderful book called *Who Killed George Jackson?* It was about the reality and, most importantly, the illusions of the 1960s in America.)

"The Sixties are alive and well and living in Moscow," Jo often said.

Russia was his new love, his new discovery, the place where the culture was up for grabs and rock and roll was playing in every bar. It wasn't just that Jo liked to be where the action was—which he did—there was something about the Russians that touched him in the way that America had once done. It was nothing at all like the cozy, comfortable, middle-class England that Jo came from and that he loathed.

In Russia Jo could lose himself. He loved it and he loved the people. He loved sitting around all night drinking and smoking and talking philosophy with poets. Most of all he loved the fact that he could claim the place as his own at exactly the moment when you could actually feel history happening. Here it was all over again, the 1960s: the politics; the rock and roll; the shifting values; the wild nights; the fabulous characters; the conflict between old and young; and the booze and parties.

Jo shuttled in and out of Russia. It became more and more exhilarating. Westerners flooded in: movie producers did deals; Western comics did stand-ups in Red Square; businessmen grabbed what they could—I met at least one business guy who felt salvation for the Soviet Union lay in potato chip factories. In Moscow, at least, *Glasnost* had also begun to liberate the Russians, not just from fear, but from nothingness, from the dead stagnant years.

The drama was all there, and the melodrama and the excitement and the theater, and people bellowed with rage and sometimes with laughter. Even the women who guarded the floor at the Rossiya Hotel were moved by it all and they smiled shyly and hoped you would offer them a lipstick or some pantyhose.

Jo was crazy about it. He was endlessly tolerant of the poets and musicians—I called them the Wispies for their chin beards—who could talk you to death, and for the hoods who could get you diamond earrings cheap, and the famous pianist with a marvelous dacha outside Moscow, who was a connoisseur of seven-star brandies. There was never enough talk, never enough late nights.

With Yelena to translate, Jo now knew his way around Moscow: he could get you into the Bolshoi Ballet through the back door, where a man waited to ply you with cakes and sweet champagne; he knew where to buy a good steak; he knew everyone in Moscow and everyone knew Jo.

Like any number of Westerners before him, George Bernard Shaw and Paul Robeson and folk singers and hippies and artists and spies, Jo was seduced by Russia.

"The Sixties are alive and well and living in Moscow," Jo said and I repeated it portentously to anyone who would listen.

I gave Yelena's mother a box of scented soap and she went into the other room with it and through a half-open door I saw her perusing the label carefully, decoding the legend of this box from New York City.

Like everyone, the family hoarded stuff, and the kitchen where we ate lunch was strewn in profligate disarray with shortbread, Scotch, and Chanel nail polish.

We ate lunch. We ate stroganoff, kasha, pickles, eggplant, cabbage, cookies, chocolate cake, and bread and butter, and drank beer, wine, and whisky and soda.

Xenia ate and then she talked about the last time she had seen Dean Reed. It was in 1986 at the Olympic Velodrome at Krylatoskoye, which was Stas Namin's old discotheque. Suddenly, Stas himself had appeared. He clapped for attention.

"We have a friend here. We have the famous Dean Reed," Stas said.

Xenia went on. "There was an uncomfortable silence and, half a beat too late, the crowd obediently rushed towards Dean, who strode into the spotlight. From his pocket, Dean took pictures of himself and began signing them, handing them out to the dancers in the club, who took them politely."

Sitting on a box that held the equipment that made smoke for the disco, Xenia had watched, a little aloof.

Now she said, "Once he was handsome, and he was trying to keep his romantic American image," she said. "But he realized the game was over. It reminded me of an F. Scott Fitzgerald story, *The Last Beauty of the Self*."

An intense feeling of sadness had come over Xenia. That night in the discotheque Dean reminded her of her grandfather who could not face the truth.

"Grandpa grew up under Stalin. Grandpa was a spy during the War. When he worked for the KGB, he felt it was real and virtuous. If you take their work away, men like this have nothing. In the end, he had nothing to live for. He was just like Dean Reed. Grandpa was a true believer."

That same night in the discotheque Dean asked Xenia, "What do young people really feel?"

"My attitudes had changed, of course," Xenia said. "We are the small brothers and sisters of Boris Grebenshikov. We had all our principles changed. We have none left."

"Why did you keep Dean's poster on your bedroom wall?"

"He was a hero created by publicity and I understood all the power in this country is shit, but I believed that he believed. When I heard he had died, I was not surprised. I thought:

everyone has to pay. But the poster was a bright impression of my childhood. Dean was our first American."

Xenia remembered thinking as she looked at Dean that night in the disco that time had passed quickly and he had not noticed and now it was too late.

"I thought he was the saddest man I ever saw," she said. "I saw how all these fake rock and roll teenagers started smiling, as if to say: We don't have anything in common with this silly, pro-Soviet bullshit. But then it betrayed the slavery of the whole thing. They, they started massing around him. They rushed to him, not because they were sympathetic, but because there was this impact. What impressed me was he had this great big pack of photos of himself that he was distributing. And these photos that he was carrying told me a lot about him because it was the Dean Reed who is of no use to anybody. He is just lost."

"Dean bloody Reed," Art Troitsky said that night at the Blue Bird café in Moscow.

At the Blue Bird café, the musicians, in their wide-boy pinstripes, like visitors from the past, produced the poignant ripple of "Autumn in New York." It had been a famous rock venue and was now a jazz club and the smoke was thick. Crowded around the little tables in the cellar, the jazz fans, like jazz fans everywhere, bobbled their heads knowingly over their black turtleneck sweaters.

The introductions were in English. "English is the language of jazz," said the manager.

"Jazz is the language of democracy," said the tenor sax player who called himself Alexander Mouscou and whose hero was Charlie Parker. Mournfully, he returned to the stage, where he played "Moonlight in Vermont" for us.

From the next table, a man with a hard face hailed us and said that he had been to jail once for listening to *Willis Connover's Jazz Hour* on the Voice of America; not for the first time, I thought ruefully about my own naive leftie adolescent contempt for the Voice of America. The arm of imperialist 'Amerika', we called it. In Moscow, I discovered that jazz and rock and roll on the Voice of America had been so important, people felt it was the only thing that had made them feel alive. Like Dean Reed, I had been a sucker for an ideology.

"Dean bloody Reed." Art was mumbling into his glass of Advocaat.

From the moment Art Troitsky had said, "Come to Moscow, I will introduce you to those who knew Dean Reed," he was the perfect guide. He stage-managed everything, producing girl-friends, rock stars, and information. He translated brilliantly. He was intelligent, cynical, and smart, and he was always surprising, his views complex and unexpected. He was tough, cosmopolitan, and urbane. He hated nationalism. Art didn't need some crummy clod of earth to claim as a home and he rarely went on about his Russian roots: his home was wherever his friends were. I had recognized all this in him almost from the beginning, because he seemed to me a kind of metaphorical New Yorker, though maybe that was just fantasy on my part. Art had also been an impeccable reporter: objective, candid, and precise. Now in the Blue Bird he raised his glass, drank it dry, and a stream of venom poured out of him.

"Dean Reed was a bastard," Art said quietly. "At first everyone welcomed him. He looked like an American and he sang like one. In the early Seventies drastic changes happened. The generation of young Soviets split into the Stupids or Rednecks and the

271

Non-Stupids or Underground. For another decade Dean was cheered by the Rednecks for whom he remained the only real star."

"Rednecks?"

"The working class and peasant young people who took what culture they were given by the state. Dean Reed was like a token American on Soviet TV. Dean Reed was all there was.

"The Rednecks believed what they were told by the Soviet media—that Dean Reed was very big in America but that he sacrificed his popularity in the US after discovering Communist ideals. We understood he was nothing in America . . . I personally realized that quite well. I read books, I followed the music charts. A fucking American Soviet traitor." Art said and sat up very straight and spoke softly, but he was furious.

"I shared the one hundred percent ironic and despising view of him which existed in the Soviet underground. He was a traitor to our rock and roll idea because we simply could not understand how a person who represented Western culture, which for us meant freedom, how a person who came from that culture, could be such a bastard."

Suddenly, I remembered a story about Dean traveling across the Soviet Union to give his moral support to Brezhnev's campaign to open new regions for development. Dean was an enthusiastic propagandist for the enterprise, but it was always a sham, a façade, a hollow endeavor, a Potemkin railway. A decade after the new railway lines were begun, nothing had changed; workers along the railway lines still lived in shacks with open sewers beside them.

Art said, "I think that after a while some people began to consider Dean a traitor, a traitor of the rock and roll idea, because, for us, a person who would kiss, really kiss, Brezhnev, you know, on the mouth like this, smack, really passionately, would never be a person who had anything to do with rock and roll. Brezhnev was anti-rock and roll. And so was Dean Reed. Any guy who put our rock and roll ideas into the big shit called Communism. A totally stupid person who couldn't understand good from bad, black from white, Brezhnev from Mick Jagger, and so on.

"He shakes hands with Soviet officials, appears in concerts with the most hideous Soviet pop stars, singing patriotic songs, awful patriotic Young Communist singers . . . For some, he was young, he played the guitar, he occasionally did something like "Blue Suede Shoes." For us, it is a betrayal. How can he be on the same base with all these small Communist Soviet bastards? He was on the one hand for rock and roll, and on the other for everything that we were opposing."

Art looked at me, ordered another drink, and said, "We couldn't understand because he was a person who digs rock and roll, wears cowboy boots, who was born in the USA, the land of the free, the home of the brave and Chuck Berry. He was perceived as the ultimate bastard. It was weird. It was just weird."

24

Towards the end Dean told Dixie that *Bloody Heart* was coming unglued. The money for the movie was late coming from Moscow. He said someone was following him. He said that he had plans to "flee to the West." Once a week he crossed through Checkpoint Charlie to call Dixie from a telephone in West Berlin.

"I don't know my status anymore," he said. "I'm frightened," he told Dixie from a public telephone in West Berlin. "I am frightened."

He called Dixie every Tuesday from Schmockwitz and every Friday from the West. He was scared to death.

On one occasion at least, according to Dixie, Dean went into West Berlin wearing a false wig and moustache. He also used a phony name. But why? Why would Dean use a disguise? Why did he really cross the Wall to call Dixie from a public phone that stank of urine? It was the stuff of melodrama and Dean loved a good piece of theater, but this time he was driven by real panic.

Maybe he crossed to get to the Berliner Bank, a branch within spitting distance of the Wall, where he kept his hard currency account. A few weeks before shooting began on *Bloody Heart*, Moscow had still not committed the money. Johnny was angry. Renate was more and more anxious, worried, frayed.

Did Dean's love affair with America make him careless? Did he provoke the Stasi? Was somebody listening in on his phone at home? After a bitter fight with Renate, Dean slashed his arm. He told her, that unlike his father who killed himself, he didn't have the guts.

I found the phone booth where Dean had called Dixie and from it you could see the barbed wire and the Berlin Wall.

Leslie Woodhead had gone to make a film with some Pacific Islanders and I had been side-tracked from Dean Reed for a while by other work. I had come back to the story now, still desperate to know how he died.

The phone in the phone booth was broken. It was a hundred yards from the Berlin Wall. At Checkpoint Charlie the sour, pale guards were in shirt-sleeves, but nothing else had changed. Nothing would ever change here, I thought, not in my lifetime. It was the summer of 1989.

Even on a beautiful warm afternoon, the crumbling stretch of West Berlin had a doomed, uninhabited appearance. I had come back here because I knew that whatever killed Dean Reed lay across the Wall and through East Berlin and down at the end of the road in Schmockwitz.

In the weeks before he died, things got worse and worse for Dean. Anxious and exhausted over the contracts for *Bloody Heart*, he and Renate fought more and more often and his letters to America were punctuated with expressions of fatigue. He felt old. Incessantly, he looked for gray hairs in the mirror. All through the winter and spring, Renate had been unhappy about the calls and letters from Dixie.

"She's so insecure," Dean said to Dixie.

"She's a little girl, Dean. Don't blow it."

"How's your love life?" Dean asked.

"I don't have one. I haven't been looking."

"Paton Price used to tell us you can't look for that."

Over time the tension grew. When Dixie called, it was often Renate who picked up the telephone. She was always polite.

"He is home, but wait a moment, please," said Renate and went to get Dean.

"I had some problems with Renate today," Dean said to Dixie.

Sensing his bleak mood, Dixie said, "Pick yourself up."

"It's a little bit more difficult. It was your telephone call. She said we talked for one and a half hours. I said it couldn't be. She's jealous sometimes. She's crying now."

"I want to be her friend," said Dixie.

"I know she's scared," said Dean. "She's not accustomed to someone sending so many letters back and forth. I tell her very often, but it doesn't help."

"You go on down and put your arm around her, go tell her that we want her," said Dixie but she stayed on the phone.

Dean had asked Dixie to write to Renate and months earlier she had written a letter. She wrote about American customs and how everyone would hug Renate; how Renate would like the climate; how she must not cut her hair because American men liked women with long hair; how she must not be sad.

In March, Renate replied.

She explained how certain conflicts between herself and Dean had come about. She talked, as she often did in those days, about how Dean had gone to America and fallen in love with his homeland, and how much she had missed him, but that she had had no picture of what he was experiencing. She said he had come back to her wanting them to live in America. It felt foreign to Renate. He said he had met a woman—Dixie—who would help him make a career in America.

She spoke frankly to Dixie about how much Dean talked of the United States, and how he spoke to her, Renate, unfairly about East Germany, her homeland.

Renate understood how he longed for his native country. But conflicts arose, and nerves were frayed. Even on a rare evening when Renate and Dean could be alone, he might be thinking of America. She added that she had known Dean since 1973 and that she loved him most deeply.

It was a desperately affecting communication and I felt for Renate who seemed stranded now. But she asked Dixie for a photograph of herself and said she wished for her friendship.

A week later Renate wrote again, a cheery note, thanking Dixie for her friendship and noting that she had a cold and could not kiss Dean.

Dean did talk to Renate about America a lot, about the special smell of Colorado, its blue skies and smiling people, and his longing seemed insatiable.

He seemed like a man sorting through his life, clearing things up, cleaning out the past. He visited Wiebke at her house, where on a hot day in spring she sat in her bikini in the garden, typing translations. Smiling, Dean pushed open the gate.

"I've been thinking things over and I want to leave a present for Natasha," Dean said.

He gave Wiebke 3000 Czech crowns.

"That's very generous, Dean," Wiebke said.

He said he wanted to see Natasha more often now because he

was going to the United States in the not-too-distant future.

Dean said, "I want to come back and talk. Maybe I shall come back soon," he said.

"He never came back," said Wiebke. "I wish I had just wrapped away my typewriter and said, 'This is a good time, why don't we talk now?' But the moment passed and we didn't. That's the last time I ever saw him."

Doggedly, Dean continued his work on *Bloody Heart*, but he also wrote to his high school classmates, who were gathering for a reunion. He told them he missed them and felt it was not fair that he could not be with them at the high school Ole Gym, where they could play basketball. He missed the picnic. He loved hamburgers and potato chips. You could feel how homesick he was. I felt it more than I had ever felt his passion for politics. There was something terribly naked about this peppy communication with his high school classmates.

He wrote of his destiny and how it had taken him to thirty-two countries, that he spoke four languages (English the worst!), sat in prison, fought injustice, made his mistakes, and favored the human race over the arms race. He wished his friends much peace, love, courage, and happiness, and signed it, with an embrace, "Dean 'Slim' Reed."

Bloody Heart was scheduled to begin on Tuesday, June 24— Tuesday because, as Gerrit List told me, it was bad luck to start a picture on a Monday.

In East Berlin I met Gerrit List, who was a producer and production manager at DEFA and had worked with Dean in East Berlin almost from the time he arrived. I got the impression that he had considerable power inside the film business.

I met him in the lobby of the Grand Hotel, which had become my refuge in East Berlin. List was a middle-aged man in an anorak and the gray leather shoes East German men seemed to wear a lot. He smoked Camels. With Dean, he had made *El Cantor* in Bulgaria and *Sing Cowboy Sing* in Romania. List could effectively manage the complicated life of a location; he could work in Soviet Karelia in winter and in Cuba in the tropical summer heat.

Once he had waited patiently in a Cuban port for a ship that was three weeks late because he did not have the hard currency to expedite the baggage by air—that was sometimes the price of working in movies. He had a nice time in that sunny Cuban port, though; "The Bay of Pork," he called it.

It was a Saturday morning when we met, and although he refused even a coffee—I think he wanted to get on with his shopping—he talked freely about *Bloody Heart*. By June of 1986, there were already ninety people at work on pre-production in Yalta and List was looking forward to the three-month shoot.

"The Crimea looked a hundred percent like South Dakota!" he said with the tidy pride of a good production manager who has accomplished the impossible and reinvented the world: Bulgaria for Chile, the Crimea for South Dakota. "Riga was a very fine studio and I have developed very hearty friendships in the Soviet Union," he added.

It was true. Everyone in Russia liked Gerrit List.

Crossing his plump legs, he exhaled some smoke and I asked him if the trip to America had changed Dean. He nodded.

"He was filled with impressions. 'My country is so great. People are so good. Politics are so bad.' He tells me Dixie will organize a concert tour. He says he wants to do it."

Dean wasn't much of a singer, Gerrit List said and confided that he himself was a Dixieland fan.

"Dean just played himself," he said. "In the beginning, some people asked, 'Why does he stay here in the GDR?' I think, and this is only my opinion"—Gerrit List put his hand lightly on his breast—"he stayed for love. For Renate." He added, "In the Soviet Union Dean was like God. Here it was no longer so. A lot of people felt he wasn't so big."

I told Gerrit—he asked me to call him by his first name—that even in the Soviet Union his status had changed, that in the big record store on Kalinin Prospekt in Moscow by 1986 you couldn't find a single Dean Reed album. I mentioned that, at Supraphon in Prague, production of Dean's albums had dwindled almost to nothing. In 1979, 1980, and 1981, ninety thousand copies of his records were issued. With *Country Songs*, the 1986 album Dean had set so much store by, only a couple of thousand were sold and, after that, nothing. Gerrit List looked sad at all this.

I remembered that Dean had told Mike Wallace that he had espoused the socialist way because it offered, above all, security. Not even the security of socialism could protect him from the defection of his fans or from his own middle age. More than anyone else, Renate knew it.

25

Renate was waiting at the front door of her house, smiling. On the lovely summer's day when I crossed into East Berlin and then driven out to Schmockwitz, the house and the woods looked as they must have looked around the time Dean died.

The sky was blue. Boats bobbed on the lake. There was the sound of lawn mowers and the smell of new cut grass. A large man in short shorts and Dr. Scholl clogs appeared. His name was Hans and he had produced and directed Dean's television shows. He lived just across the lake.

Just then a boat sputtered up to the dock behind the house and Sasha and his friends tumbled out and clattered up the walk into the house. Renate smiled and went to get them a meal. In summer, crowded with children and the windows open, the house felt much less lonely, though it had been summer when Dean died.

Renate cooked for the pack of Sasha's friends and they gorged themselves while I talked to Hans.

Yes, he said, Dean's popularity as a singer was going and he was sad about it. He knew that tastes were changing.

But the kids skidded out to their boat, and Hans went away

with a basket of strawberries that Renate had given him to his red Peugeot that matched the fruit, his Dr. Scholl clogs going 'clock, clock, clock' down the garden path. Suddenly it was just the two of us.

Renate told me little things at first. She spoke in English that day and she told me how, when Dean's codirector on *Bloody Heart* got cancer, the blow was enormous. She showed me Dean's own copy of *Bloody Heart*; the script was painstakingly annotated in English in his schoolboy handwriting. There were notes about casting, but also notes about the best place to buy plastic cups in West Berlin, and you could feel Dean's immense weariness. He was the star, the director, the writer of *Bloody Heart*, and, still, he had to get the plastic cups. Real directors didn't buy their own plastic cups.

On the floor several boxes lay half open and Renate sifted through them as she talked. After Dean died, she had received a telephone bill for 2800 marks or fifteen hundred dollars. She said that most of the calls had been to Johnny in Loveland, but I thought they were to Dixie too, and that Renate knew it because her voice was so bitter.

Renate was a realist about what Dean's chances in America might have been. She knew that on the university circuit, with a few songs and the story of his extraordinary life, Dean might have made a small go of it. Dixie and Johnny wanted to turn him into a commercial pop star and take the politics out.

"He was not good in that way," said Renate simply, lighting a cigarette and tossing back her luxuriant black hair, she said suddenly, "It was *60 Minutes*. The letters." She foraged in one of the boxes.

The night it was shown, Dean had been in Moscow and Renate

couldn't get through to him on the phone and she was frantic. America had just bombed Libya. There was a lot of anti-Arab feeling in America and Dean dancing around with Yasser Arafat would not go down well. She knew what was in the program, even . though it was broadcast only in America. My God, she thought.

Dean came home the next day and, when Renate told him that *60 Minutes* had been transmitted and what she was feeling, he went crazy. His mood went black. Everything was over, she said. "*Kaput*," she said now. Renate used the word *kaput* and put her head in her hands.

Miraculously, it turned out for the best or so it seemed. In May, *60 Minutes* sent a videotape of the show to Schmockwitz and Dean watched it and was happy. It was fair-minded, he thought. Dean was quite chipper. Mike Wallace forwarded a few nice letters that viewers had written. Dean wrote to Wallace to thank him and suggest that they work together for world peace.

Dean didn't hear much from Dixie or Johnny for a while and it worried him a little, so he wrote to say he hoped the show had not changed their relationship.

Did he suspect that Dixie was losing heart and Johnny was sitting at home, his butt burned over what he saw as Dean's betrayal? Dean whistled a lot and made plans, Renate said.

It must have been in the week or two before Dean's death that the rest of the mail to *60 Minutes* was forwarded to Schmockwitz by the CBS bureau in London.

Renate shuddered, as if death had come into the room, and she wrapped herself with her arms. The letters! Oh God, Renate remembered, the letters.

Every night, glasses slipping down his nose, Dean sat up in bed, reading the letters over and over and over. He read them out loud. He couldn't stop reading the letters that called him a traitor, a terrorist, and a fraud, letters that said keep away from America, no one wants you here, go home to Russia.

Worse still was that not all the letters were inarticulate or written by crackpots or right-wingers. The cruelest letters criticized Dean, not for his politics, but for his hypocrisy, his ego; they called him an opportunistic man of little talent who could only make it east of the Berlin Wall.

Dean wouldn't let go of the letters and Renate literally snatched them from him and tore some of them into little pieces.

Even Victor Grossman knew.

"Did Dean plan to defect?" I asked him the day after I saw Renate.

"He didn't have to defect. He had an American passport," Victor said. "He wanted to go home. 60 *Minutes* was going to change his life, but it all went horribly wrong."

"What went wrong?"

"Dean thought he had done so well on 60 *Minutes*. Then Dixie—you've met Dixie?"

I said I knew Dixie.

"Dixie wrote to him to say, It's over. You can't come home again. You did so badly on 60 *Minutes*, you blew your chances. Dean lay on his bed in a darkened room unable to function," Victor said. "His movies were less popular. This is a country of twelve million people and a lot of them began to dislike Dean. How long, in a small country, how long can you go around performing concerts? Once, twice, but the third time? Also people who were becoming more and more disillusioned with or opposed to the system here naturally didn't like somebody who supported it," Victor went on. "What happened was that fewer and fewer people went to his concerts, and this troubled him greatly, I'm sure. He liked to be the star, and, you know, it's not so nice being a star playing in an empty theater." Victor paused. "By the mid-1980s, Dean heard the doors shutting one at a time," Victor said.

Like Dixie, Johnny phoned Dean regularly to tell him how bad it was for him in America after the 60 *Minutes* program, after he went on the show and defended the Berlin Wall.

Dean wrote: "Dear Johnny, I realize the problems that are now going through your mind, Johnny. You are in a pickle, as the cowboys would say. You and your friends and family met a guy named Dean Reed after twenty-five years of absence. You and your friends liked what you saw and heard. But then this guy named Deano goes and declares himself a Marxist or Socialist. By his enemies he is called a commie!"

According to his own way of thinking, Johnny felt he was Deano's close good friend, and he worried more and more for him. He was convinced if Dean came back to America after the 60 *Minutes* broadcast, he would get his head blown off. Johnny spent a whole lot of time in his shed out back of his house in Loveland trying to figure a way to tell Dean what was what.

Mona Rosenburg told me that, just before his disappearance, Dean phoned the house in Loveland very early one morning. She took the call. Dean asked if everything was all right because he hadn't heard a word, he said. Mona said they had all had the flu bad.

Dean said if they were in any kind of trouble, he would come back there and fix it. During the whole conversation Dean acted as though someone was listening in, looking over his shoulder. Something was wrong, Mona felt, but she didn't know what it was.

What did the call mean? Mona didn't know. Maybe Dean was looking for a reason to come back. But it was early in the morning and she was feeling lousy and the line was bad.

Johnny finally knew what to do, though, and he went out to his shed and after a while came back to the house with a new song on a cassette.

"I wrote a song for Dean and here's a kind of mystery," Johnny told me. "I've been accused of foreseeing Dean's death by writing this song. But after the *60 Minutes* episode, after how shook up he was and how shook up I was, I sat down and wrote a song called 'Yankee Man'. It's about Dean. I sent it about two days before he died, and of course he never got to hear it. I've often wondered who over there got to hear it? Did Renate hear it? Did the authorities hear it?"

Johnny sent me a copy of "Yankee Man." The song was addressed to Dean—to Yankee Man—and it said that even if he said he was proud to be an American, he couldn't tear his country down. That if he couldn't find "nothin' good to say about the USA," he should stay where "You are in the land of the Big Red Star."

The song was Johnny's way of telling Dean that he would always be his friend, but that he was scared for him, that he wished "you'd turn yourself around." If he didn't, and he came home, someone might "place you six feet under ground."

It concluded with the poignant line: "Yankee Man, you've walked upon the wrong side of the world for just too long."

The package with the cassette was postmarked June 11, 1986, the day before Dean disappeared. It arrived in Schmockwitz after he was dead and only Renate heard the terrible song.

26

"Shall we eat?"

Renate and I had driven from her house to a little camping site a few miles away, down a bumpy lane near the lake. It was dinner time and kids in shorts ran and played among the chalets and tents. Their parents sat outside and smoked and called them in to bed.

It was a fine summer evening, humid, soft—the way it must have been the night Dean died. Renate apologized for the restaurant, but I liked it. It had piney walls and checkered tablecloths. The waitress smiled. I had a beer and Renate had champagne. We both ate dainty little steaks with mushrooms and Renate was still looking for a particular word in English.

"I am missing this word," she said, grimacing, balling up her fists, opening a package of cigarettes, and then crumpling the cellophane.

"Damn. A word. What is the word I am thinking of?"

I asked her if she felt she could talk about Dean's death at all and it was as if something in her snapped like a rubber band that had been holding her together and then she couldn't stop talking. She hinted again that she didn't believe Dean's death was an accident, but she had to believe it because otherwise she couldn't bear the pain, otherwise it would have been . . . what was the word she wanted?

There was no acting, it wasn't a performance, only a woman talking about loss in a flat matter-of-fact way. I felt like an intruder, a voyeur, desperate for her to go on and feeling ashamed of it. Renate's hands were steady when she lit her cigarette.

In the last week of Dean's life, he had had what she called a heart attack. I couldn't know how serious it was because we didn't have an interpreter and the technical terms were hard to translate.

Renate and Dean were at home in Schmockwitz. Dean was reading his script and making notes when he suddenly clutched his chest and sat back hard. He told her not to call the doctor; he was a week away from the biggest film of his life and it would have been stopped if a doctor got involved. They argued. Finally, he slept. The next morning, Dean wouldn't talk about it and it was that week the tension got worse and things escalated and they had the murderous fight about the lawn.

It was how such things happened, Renate said and asked if I understood; I said I did. It had been a very hot day. The lake was filled with boats. The sound of the lawn mowers all across Schmockwitz gave off an insistent buzz. Renate asked Dean to cut the lawn and he refused.

You know how these things are, Renate said again. Again I said that I knew.

Dean had a bad temper and he was enraged. Renate said she, too, had a temperamental side, though usually she could balance things. On the day she asked him to cut the grass she couldn't— how shall I translate, she asked—stand it, hack it, bear it, how did you say? So there was the terrible fight about the grass cutting.

Dean stormed upstairs to his study. A few minutes later, she followed and to her horror his door was locked. Dean never locked the door. Never! Renate knocked.

"Please Dean, please let's talk," she said. "Talk to me!"

There was no answer.

"Please!"

As if in slow motion, he opened the door and she saw him reach for the machete—a prop from one of his films, but a real machete—from the wall where it hung and then he held it and began to slice at his arm. He cut himself over and over.

"My father was brave enough to kill himself, but I can do nothing," he said to Renate.

Dean stood in his study and then slowly sank to the bed. Sasha ran up the stairs to see what was wrong, but Renate barred the door.

"Go back downstairs," she told Sasha. "Go downstairs! Go!"

Now at the little restaurant, Renate smoked and told me that Dean had only nicked himself. He made a lot of cuts on his arm, as many as fifty perhaps, but they were no more than scratches and there was no real blood. I wondered if these were the "Canuto's trial cuts" referred to in the autopsy report that Dean's mother had given me in Hawaii.

Renate sipped her champagne and offered me a cigarette.

What should she have done, she asked? Should she have called for medical attention when Dean wounded himself? Should she have halted work on *Bloody Heart*? But Dean . . . he, what was the word she was looking for?

* * *

On Thursday, June 12, 1986, Dean and Renate had dinner. Dean took a sleeping pill, as he had done every night of his life since he was twenty. They argued again, bitterly this time but not as violently as on the day when Dean had slashed himself.

At about ten in the evening Dean called Gerrit List, who had just returned from Moscow. Gerrit said he had news about the contracts for *Bloody Heart*. It was the news Dean had been waiting for and he couldn't wait until the next morning when he would meet Gerrit at the studio. He said he would come over to his place right away. He was excited. He told Renate he would spend the night at Gerrit List's house and then in the morning the two of them would go right to the studio. List's house was only a few minutes from the studio and the Reeds were forty minutes away. Dean would meet Renate at the studio, he told her. He had to talk to Gerrit. He couldn't sit still.

At about half past ten or just after—Renate couldn't remember exactly—Dean left the house in Schmockwitz. He got in his car and drove away.

On Tuesday, June 10, 1986, Gerrit List had signed the contracts for *Bloody Heart* in Moscow and then he flew back to East Berlin. He went to the studio from the airport; there was a lot to do on the movie. Special effects were in the works. Among the first sequences filmed would be a night scene shot during the day. The "American Night," Gerrit List called it.

According to Gerrit, he definitely called Dean at home in Schmockwitz on Thursday, June 12, although the police reports recorded that Dean had called Gerrit. It didn't matter. They talked. They exchanged greetings and Dean said he was coming to spend the night with Gerrit.

"We can speak and I can sleep, and tomorrow I am already at work," said Dean.

"My wife was away, so I made up the bed in the sitting room," Gerrit List said. "It was not good manners of Dean to ask to stay over. He didn't ever sleep at my home before. It was not usual. But my family was on holiday and he wanted to hear the news." Then Gerrit added, "But Dean never arrived."

When Dean didn't show up after Gerrit had gone to the trouble to make up the bed in the sitting room, he was mad. But he just figured that Dean had changed his mind again and went to bed. Or maybe he didn't want to phone the Reed house in case Dean had gone somewhere else. He was always going off on escapades. Gerrit wasn't worried. He went to bed. The next morning, Renate drove herself to the studio and Gerrit was waiting for her.

"Where is Dean?" she said.

Gerrit told her that Dean had not come to his house the night before and she got very nervous. He was angry at first; Gerrit was sure it was one of Dean's stunts. Dean was always doing stupid things on impulse, Gerrit List thought. On another film, Dean had disappeared for a while because he felt like a break or because he wanted to be in the mountains or for the hell of it.

"This is not good to suddenly make a holiday when everybody at the studio is waiting to work," List said angrily. He was quiet, but he was angry.

Renate did some make-up tests for *Bloody Heart* and then Gerrit sent her home to Schmockwitz to rest up and wait for Dean. In these things, as he put it, he was Renate's producer, too; it was his job to look after her.

Gerrit List was a mild-tempered man, but he was furious as he phoned around looking for Dean. He was also worried. Dean had called him the night before, and now it was Friday and he didn't know where Dean, his director and star, was.

Renate called Gerrit; he could hear in her voice she was upset. She said, maybe there had been an accident. Gerrit List drove to Schmockwitz.

Dean always drives so fast, Renate said to Gerrit. Maybe an accident. Gerrit picked up the phone.

He called Prague, where he talked to Vaclav Nectar. He made calls around Berlin, to Potsdam, and to a Baltic island hideaway where Dean sometimes escaped. No one knew anything. Gerrit's heart sank. He began to think it was an accident. He thought about a car crash. That evening Renate was so fearful that Gerrit felt he couldn't leave her. He drove home, got some clothes from his house, and then went back to stay with her.

It appeared that the police were not called initially because there was no reason to suspect anything other than an accident or that Dean had maybe taken off on one of his jaunts.

I put together what happened in the next forty-eight hours leading up to Dean's death from what Renate Reed, Gerrit List, and others told me. What happened was that for two days Renate and Gerrit sat in her house by the lake and called all over Eastern Europe, desperate, hunting for Dean. She was terrified as she surveyed the clutter of Dean's life in his study. She was sure he was dead, then uncertain, and then worried he was with another woman. Then she thought, "Please let him be with another woman, but not dead."

The next day Gerrit called a girlfriend of Renate's and asked her to come over because Renate needed help. Then the English journalist telephoned. My God! An English journalist!

"Did the guy from the *Sunday Times* reach you?" Dixie had written Dean.

The guy was Russell Miller. On his way through Denver earlier that year on a book promotion tour, the *Sunday Times* journalist appeared on a radio show. He was looking for good ideas for his next book, he said casually. Dixie said it was she who had phoned in to the radio station to tell Miller about Dean Reed, although Johnny said he had called the station first.

Eventually, Russell Miller arranged to interview Dean for the *Sunday Times*. The interview was scheduled for Saturday, June 14, 1986.

Miller arrived in West Berlin on Friday afternoon, June 13. He called the Reed house, and Renate said that Dean had been taken to hospital that morning. In the evening they spoke again and she said the doctors thought Dean had an infection and he was not at all well.

Renate was presumably in a state of confusion and fear when she talked to Miller. The last thing she needed was a foreign journalist intruding on a personal crisis, so she tried to fob him off with an explanation about Dean being ill. At the other end, Miller suddenly found himself talking to a man who had apparently taken the phone from Renate. He told Miller he was Mr. Wieczaukowski, the codirector of the movie Dean was due to start in a few days. He confirmed Dean was in the hospital and might have to stay for several days.

It was Gerrit List who had taken the telephone from Renate.

"I was for these things Renate's producer, too," he said again.

The last thing he needed was an English journalist. My God! Dean is not at home, he said. He is lying ill in the hospital. Either in that conversation or a subsequent one later that day or the next, he told Mr. Miller the interview would be rescheduled. His only thoughts were to help Renate and Dean. In his heart there were forebodings and he had to get rid of Mr. Miller. He gave Miller a phony name and telephone number.

"I said the first thing that came into my head. I was Mr. Wieczaukowski," said Gerrit List, who didn't want Renate to have to deal with a journalist.

"My wife and I, we left Berlin," Russell Miller said. "And that was that, we left without thinking anything was wrong. It was only actually here in England on the Tuesday morning that I picked up the *Guardian*, I think it was, and there in the obituary column was Dean Reed, just a little paragraph, and I said, 'This is unbelievable.'"

Miller called the number Mr. Wieczaukowski had given him in Potsdam. A woman answered and said it was a private number and no one called Wieczaukowski lived there.

On Saturday Renate and Gerrit continued to look for Dean, still hopeful. Sunday was much worse, Gerrit said. On Sunday, June 15, the employees of the lifeguard station for the Zeuthener See and Schmockwitzer Damm informed the German People's police that an automobile had been standing about twenty meters behind the lifeguard station since at least Friday morning. The license plate number was ILT 8-05. It might have been there earlier, but they would not have seen it until the morning of the 13th when they came on duty. It was Dean's car.

After the car was found, Renate's mood changed constantly. Dean was alive, she thought; he was dead. She knew he was dead. She said it over and over: he's dead, he's alive. Gerrit List didn't know how to help her.

Increasingly distraught, Renate trembled a lot, smoked cigarettes, and was white as death, Gerrit said. On Monday a neighbor phoned. She had seen a lot of police cars near the lake. She had seen the Red Cross. Maybe Dean had drowned, she said. No, no, said Renate, Dean was a good swimmer. It was a shallow lake. It was high summer. He was a good swimmer. Please let him come back. Please. Oh God!

"I am missing this word," Renate now said again to me as we sat in the restaurant near her house in East Berlin in the summer of 1989. We sat late into the evening but it was still light out. "What is this word?"

We left the restaurant and walked for a while and you could smell the pine from the woods. Renate lit a cigarette and told me a story she said she had not told before.

Some years earlier, Renate and Dean had taken Sasha on a skiing holiday. It was a lovely holiday, Renate said. One afternoon she and Sasha were fooling around in the snow, playing and laughing with Dean.

He went inside the chalet to take a telephone call. It was the news of Paton Price's death, but Renate didn't know and she and Sasha kept playing and throwing snowballs and giggling together. After an hour she wondered what was going on and said they ought to go back to the chalet.

When they got inside, she found Dean fast asleep. An open bottle of sleeping pills was beside the bed; it was empty.

Renate ran to another chalet where she knew there was a doctor. He came back with her and looked at Dean and at the pills. He said Dean hadn't taken enough to kill himself. Just let him sleep it off, the doctor said.

Be watchful, the doctor added. Dean may wake in the night, he said. Dean did wake up. Naked, he stumbled toward the door; it was twenty degrees below zero. He was full of sleeping pills and he would have frozen to death if he had gone outside, said Renate.

"If you go out there, you will not only kill yourself, you'll kill Sasha and me," Renate shouted, pulling him back into the chalet with all her force.

It would have been a betrayal.

That was the word she had been looking for all day. Betray. Yes. Betray. That was it.

I waited. Clearly, Renate had never had anything to do with Dean's death, nothing at all. She had felt he was her partner, her lover, her man, as she had once said on a videotape. She had loved him; she still did. She had to believe his death was an accident, not a suicide. If it was a suicide, he had betrayed her love.

Just before he died, in spite of all their fights, silly fights about mowing the lawn, he told her how much he loved her. If he then went and killed himself, it was betraying her trust. She was very fierce about it. It was something that had been preying on her mind for a long time.

We walked together for a few yards, along the rural lane near the lake. It was two years since Dean had died on a summer night like this. I looked at the lake. I said I hoped that Renate would meet someone else nice some day.

"No," she said. "I hate men."

It would have been a betrayal.

On the morning of June 17, 1986, Renate's neighbor came across the lawn to Renate's house. Renate could see her from the kitchen window and went outside to meet her. The neighbor smoothed her apron awkwardly.

"I think they've found Dean," she said.

Earlier, at 8:20 a.m., his body had been discovered in the Zeuthener See. "It was approximately 300 feet from the lakeside," noted the police report. Accidental death by drowning was the official verdict. No one believed it.

27

In Wheat Ridge, Colorado, the telephone rang in an empty house. A machine with Dixie's voice on it answered.

"Dixie, this is Ruth Anna Brown, Dean's mother. Damn this machine! You never call me back, but I guess you've heard the terrible news about Dean? Call me this time, Dixie," she said.

"Hi, Dixie. This is Johnny. Call me! For God's sake, Dixie, call me!"

A reporter in Leipzig telephoned Vaclav Nectar in Prague. His life in fear, as he put it, began with that call; the news made him crazy; he felt Dean's death was a terrible omen for him.

Oleg Smirnoff heard the news in Moscow on TV.

"Dean first, me next," Oleg thought.

In Paris, Erik and Annalise Durschmied were in the Metro and he was reading the *Herald Tribune* when he turned so white he looked like a man in the middle of a heart attack. When the train stopped, he pulled Annalise onto the platform.

"What is it?" she asked urgently.

"Dean is dead," he said.

In the little house where they lived, Wiebke told Natasha as best she could that her father was dead. Natasha had seen

Bobby die on *Dallas* and she knew that Bobby wasn't really dead.

She said to Wiebke, "Maybe Daddy is not really dead at all. Like Bobby on *Dallas*."

Gerrit List was put in charge of the funeral. Renate was drugged like a stone. He sent her to a sanitorium, where she slept and slept. He organized everything. He notified the relatives. He received Mrs. Brown when she arrived. He collected Ramona and Patty from West Berlin. At Checkpoint Charlie, the daughter from Dean, as Gerrit called her, was weeping.

"My father is dead," she kept saying.

Patty told a Denver journalist that the authorities in East Berlin refused to let her or anyone else view Dean's body. It had been in the water for four days and had been partly devoured by fish. It was shocking and was not fit to be seen, the officials said. They were perfectly proper, but not forthcoming, and Mrs. Brown couldn't get much out of them. She said that the policeman she met with was mightily pompous.

"In the GDR we do not have crime," he said.

Eventually, the officials relented and days and days after Dean died—no one was sure exactly how many days—Patty went to the morgue. Renate couldn't bear to go.

In the morgue, in order to get a good look at Dean's body, Patty knelt down beside it as if she were praying. It was Dean's body, she said. She was sure. She told the *Denver Post*, "They were Dean's toes. My daughter has his toes."

Then the body was cremated.

Mrs. Brown had a lot of questions: If Dean meant to defect why did he take his important papers with him on the night he disappeared, but not his passport? Why was he wearing two coats on a warm June night? Why was he cremated so quickly? But it had been Gerrit List who gave the order for the cremation because it was the proper thing to do once the autopsy report was complete. Will Roberts, who had made *American Rebel*, the documentary about Dean, arrived in town and went a little nuts from grief. He said that Dean was murdered.

The night before the memorial service, there was some wrangling over the disposal of the remains: Will Roberts wanted to have parts of Dean sent to places he loved like Chile and Nicaragua. The women were horrified. Things were so tense in the house in Schmockwitz that Mrs. Brown couldn't stand it and went to stay in a hotel.

The memorial service was finally held on Tuesday, June 24, in East Berlin, the day that had been scheduled for the start of *Bloody Heart*.

All of the Reed women were there: Ruth Anna Brown, Patty, Wiebke, and Renate. They declared themselves sisters. They were all Reed women, they said, and held hands.

All of the children came, too: Ramona, Natasha, and Alexander, whom everyone called Sasha. Friends came from abroad, including Vaclav Nectar.

It was like a big Hollywood funeral with the bereft beautiful women, and famous faces, and powerful dignitaries who packed the hall and included the Deputy Minister of Culture, the Director-General of the DEFA Film Studios, a member of the East German Communist Party Central Committee, the First Deputy Chairman and General Secretary of the German Democratic Peace Council, and the President of the Committee for Entertainment.

The service was organized by Gerrit List and his colleagues at

DEFA and everything was correct, Gerrit said. It was a hero's send-off; Dean had been a hero in the DDR, honored, officially approved, supported, and loved.

Pink carnations decorated the hall and the overwhelming smell of the flowers made Wiebke feel sick; she had never been so queasy in her life and she thought she might faint. Renate was drugged like a stone. She used the expression over and over. She was up to six Valium a day.

Suddenly, Will Roberts got up, faced the crowd, and delivered a funeral oration. He said that Dean's ashes ought to be tossed across the oceans of the countries he loved. He said everyone should stand up and give a big hand for Dean and started clapping, but no one joined in. Gerrit List was mortified. It was not the way things were done in Germany. It ought to have been a somber occasion. There was a form to these things. But he rose, too, and began clapping and everyone else clapped now. It was surreal and a little macabre, the sober Germans in their dark suits, the Party officials, the Americans, all of them clapping for a dead man at his funeral.

As the service ended, Dean's peppy singing voice came over the loudspeaker. He was singing "Gimme me a guitar . . .' Many of the family stood and applauded. Mrs. Brown rose and said that Dean must be buried in East Berlin; here were his friends, she said.

To himself, Gerrit said, Please God, no more applause.

A hundred people went to the Reed house in Schmockwitz for coffee and cake. Patty was nice to Renate. Renate felt Patty had really helped her understand Dean's moodiness and was truly a sister. All the wives embraced.

"We are all Reed women," they said again to one another.

Mrs. Brown wondered why there was no candlelight parade through the streets of East Berlin for Dean. She couldn't understand why no one held a big parade or a vigil for Dean.

"Like they did in New York for John Lennon," she said.

When there were just a few people left in the Reed house, Gerrit finally went home and got into his own bed.

"It is all over," he said to himself and slept.

28

It wasn't over.

There were a dozen theories that grew into a hundred conspiracies. On June 18, 1986, an Associated Press item appeared on the obituary page of the *New York Times*. I read it at home in New York; it caught my eye because I'd seen the *60 Minutes* piece on April 20. I couldn't believe it. That's the guy from *60 Minutes*, I said to myself, the man who brought rock and roll to the Soviet Union.

The obit was short and uninformative, noting only that the East German press agency had reported that Mr. Dean Reed died from a "tragic accident." Then someone sent me a piece from the London *Sunday Times* by Russell Miller, dated June 22, five days after Dean's body was pulled from the lake. Miller described his efforts to interview Dean and his mysterious conversations with a Mr. Wieczaukowski.

So little news came out of East Germany that the mystery Miller reported became the basis for other articles, the centerpiece really of a web of theories. Mike Wallace had a stab at a follow-up piece but he abandoned it after a couple of phone calls. For *60 Minutes* it was only another story.

Until I met Gerrit List in Berlin two years after Dean died, no one identified him as the disappearing Mr. Wieczaukowski.

"Accidental death by drowning," the official report read. No one accepted it, because it was intolerable: it meant Dean's death had no meaning. Only Gerrit List clung to it. He insisted that Dean had gone out on the pier on the lake because from the end of it you could see a bungalow on the other shore that looked American. Dean thought it might work as a set for *Bloody Heart*. You couldn't get to the end of the pier, though, without going through a corrugated metal gate, but the gate was locked. According to Gerrit List, Dean had tried to climb it, flipped over, fell into the water, and drowned. No, said Renate firmly. That gate was always open.

Questions were raised about the autopsy. There was a Valium-like substance in Dean's blood. Enough to kill him? It depended. His liver was as enlarged as an alcoholic's, said the report, but Dean never drank.

Then I met Clive who was a British stringer for *Time* in West Berlin and he said, "You knew about the reports?"

"What reports?"

"They were pretty convincing, the reports I read about Dean having treatment for cancer in the last months of his life," said Clive.

There was nothing about cancer in the autopsy report, and the rumors spread and the mystery grew and any firm ground turned into a swamp. All dead ends, I thought. I couldn't get any real fix on Dean's death. And, why was Dean wearing two coats on a warm June night, if he was? When his body was found, Dean was wearing a jeans jacket Johnny Rosenburg had given him, as well as an overcoat. Or maybe just the coat. It wasn't clear.

Was it because he planned to flee? What about his passport? Had it been stolen? Wiebke said it had been stolen, but how did she know? Or did Dean leave home, discover he had forgotten it or lost it, and then fly into a rage and slam his car down towards the lake?

Another theory about the extra clothing ran like this. Obsessed with authentic detail on *Bloody Heart*, Dean wanted to break in his costume. There was a kind of precedent for this because in Loveland Johnny had once found Dean banging up a brand new camera bag in the backyard.

"What in the name of heaven?" said Johnny. Dean said he was breaking it in. You could not have brand new gear in a movie. It looked phony.

In Dean's car were copies of *Mother Jones* which Ruth Anna Brown had sent him. Dean also had his dad's last letter there.

How could it be have been an accident? How could he have drowned? Dean was a great swimmer. Everyone said so. As a kid he had been a lifeguard at the pool at Estes Park in Colorado. At forty-seven he was in top shape and could walk on his hands, Phil Everly said.

Mrs. Brown had 2006 scenarios, she told the *Denver Post*.

Everybody had a scenario. There were those who believed that the East German Stasi or the KGB killed Dean because he wanted to go home to America. Because he lost faith in the system. But why had he lost it now, in 1986, when *Glasnost* was delivering hope for change and Gorbachev, in whom Dean passionately believed, was in power? And why would anyone bother? He wasn't important enough to kill, said Vladimir Pozner. Pozner was talking about the Soviet Union, though; in East Germany even as late as 1986, the Stasi controlled a lot of people, a lot of territory; it had enormous power. If Dean got out of line, wasn't it possible that someone in the Stasi pushed him into the lake?

Leslie Woodhead could just imagine a scenario in which a police official made his displeasure with Dean unofficially known to an ambitious—or drunken—underling, who then took it on himself to get rid of Dean.

"What I mean is that perhaps it was made known but never overtly. The turbulent priest scenario," Leslie said. "As in who will rid me of this turbulent priest? Maybe it was like that. Maybe someone did it to please a superior without actually being asked."

"Unlikely," said Georgy Arbatov in Moscow. "It would be too big a risk for any policeman without explicit orders from his superior."

Did Dean know some awful secrets about Erich Honecker's lavish lifestyle that weren't revealed until the end of 1989? Was he going to tell? Or was Dean part of it? The Countess had said that Dean did errands for the bigwigs in the GDR, that he took money to Swiss banks for them. She said he drove a Porsche, but no one else ever mentioned it.

Others said it was just a screw-up, a blurry East German version of a Mafia hit. Dean knew important men. Once you were in, you couldn't get out, people hinted, and everyone cut his theories to suit his politics. I remembered Mrs. Brown had whispered to me that the CIA was on notice to do a "wet job" on Dean if he got out of line. Wet job? Did she mean assassination? Did she mean killing by drowning?

Vaclav Nectar believed it was the Czech secret police and the Stasi together who killed Dean. He said Dean had come to fear for his life in the East and that once, on his way to Prague, a wheel mysteriously came off his car when he knew it had just been screwed on tight.

After Dean's funeral, Nectar went to see Gerrit List in East Berlin and they sat together on a bench in a park, talking. Although in public Gerrit insisted it was an accident, he told Nectar that he believed "someone helped Dean die."

I even heard a theory that the KGB and the CIA got together, decided Dean was a nuisance, and acted together to get rid of him.

"Hogwash," said a retired diplomat who had known Dean in Berlin. "The KGB and CIA conspiracy theories were hogwash. Dean's death was accepted as an accident until those people from Colorado got involved."

Then there were the really wild theories: homosexual triangles; jealous women; jealous husbands; and skinheads, the louts who hated foreigners and roamed the fringes of East Berlin society. Most exotic and certainly the most absurd was a rumor that Renate fingered Dean to the Party because he wanted to go home to America. It wasn't true, of course, but there was no end to it.

In the US, Dean's friends and relatives were beside themselves. Dixie Schnebly said she spent $37,000 to send two private detectives to East Germany and wanted to go to a hypnotist herself to see if she could recall anything significant from her subconscious.

Johnny Rosenburg was convinced that American neo-Nazis killed Dean as they had killed the DJ Alan Berg. But how did they get to East Berlin?

Dixie didn't entirely disagree with Johnny's theory because back when she was still trying to help set up Dean's return to America, a bunch of kids came after her at her country property up near Grand Junction, Colorado. Dixie said they were from the Aryan Nation and they were after her because of Dean. But a Boulder journalist named Jennifer Dunbar, who had met Dean at the Denver Film Festival and was now writing about him, said they were just rich punks.

On the other hand, Dunbar said—and I knew yet another wiggy scenario was in the works—how come when Dixie called the police, twenty-eight FBI agents turned up?

So many people were suspect; so many were part of a perceived conspiracy that every scrap seemed to become evidence. Even the truth about the origins of the 60 *Minutes* piece appeared confusing. The truth about 60 *Minutes*, of course, was simply that it had been, as often happened with stories, suggested separately by Erik Durschmied and Anne de Boismilion, the staff producer working out of Paris.

The mystery about Dean's death came mostly out of a kind of desperation to make it important. Like Moscow's intellectuals who towards the end of 1989 sat around the cafés promising themselves civil war and chaos, the more terrible the scenario, the more seductive. Who wanted to settle for the ordinary when you could have a revolution? Or for a messy accident when you could have a political murder?

"He would never get old. He said he would take a gun and go to some revolution," a friend of Dean's said. "He would have loved a famous death."

* * *

The paranoia became rampant. A West German reporter said she saw Dean alive the day after he died. Someone else saw him buying pencils in Schmockwitz the next week.

There was plenty of evidence that Dean was alive, if you looked for it, except that none of it had any real substance. There were some who pointed to the fact that the man described in the autopsy report was taller than Dean. But there had always been a discrepancy about his height right back to his 1970 passport application, where he put his height at six feet four, when his 1961 application had it as six feet one. I was pretty sure the precise Germans had taken their data from the later document.

"The whole of Berlin was talking about the mock suicide," said Vaclav Nectar, who believed, among other things, that the arm slashing had been partly a publicity stunt on Dean's part as well as a tactic to psych up Renate for her performance in *Bloody Heart*.

Others said Dean wanted to flee, but to spare Renate he faked his death and that the body in the lake belonged to a certain singer who looked a lot like Dean. I loved the idea, it made a great story, but I wondered how Dean could have got hold of a spare body.

I remembered that Dixie had once asked me to check Dean's account at the Berliner Bank to see if money had been withdrawn since his death, because if it had it would prove that he was alive. After his death, she started hearing voices over the phone, mysterious voices. The bank account was checked: nothing had been withdrawn.

Still, it spooked me for a while. It got so I almost expected to pick up the phone and hear Dean Reed's voice.

For a long time Dixie Schnebly was in regular contact. She

helped me out with information, sent letters and tapes, and was generally cheerful. When she disappeared, I figured she was driving a rig on one of her long-haul routes across country.

Some time in 1989, my phone rang early in the morning.

"Hi," said a familiar voice muted by pain.

Dixie.

"I just wanted to stay in touch, be friends. If Dean's alive, which I still believe, he won't be able to get in touch with me unless he gets in touch through friends in Minnesota." We wished each other well and I hung up. I never heard from her again.

"Towards the end Dean could hear the doors shutting, one at a time," said Victor Grossman. "I believe it was suicide."

Johnny could not accept it.

"I think the chance of his committing suicide is about as good as my putting on my shoes and walking to the moon," he said. "I just do not believe Dean did not want to push his shoeshine one more time across this earth," he added.

I felt it was what Renate believed in her heart, though.

Drowning was a common enough form of suicide, the forensic pathologist at Manchester University said. It was common and quite easy; you sucked in a little water and gave yourself up to it.

The cuts on Dean's arm revealed a classic suicide attempt said the pathologist. Fifty cuts was a classic number, he said. He said there was nothing fishy in the autopsy report. The report might have come out of the GDR, he said, but it "was German, nonetheless" and, insofar as death was concerned, the Germans were meticulous.

Finally, I came to feel that Dean's death was a kind of un-intentional suicide, a bumbled, messy panic attack that led to the lake behind the house in Schmockwitz. He was a man running out of time, his career drying up, his voice fading, his marriage coming to pieces. Dean missed America, but there was nothing in America for a forty-seven-year-old cowboy rocker. America didn't want some commie cowboy who went on *60 Minutes* to defend the Berlin Wall.

Dean looked to the East and saw a dead end there, too. The Russians were listening to their own music and his record sales were down. As passionate as he was for *Glasnost*, it gobbled up the ground from under him and left him with nowhere to stand. But, as a scenario, suicide was unacceptable to Dean's family because it was a betrayal.

It was hard to untangle Dean Reed, the man, from this mess. Leslie thought him the dupe of two cultures, too easily taken in by both myths, a rebel only by stance. Leslie couldn't really forgive Dean for his willful disregard of political reality.

Like a flame, Dean sucked you in, but delivered no heat. There was a malign magic to it all, Leslie thought; it infected everyone who came near the story. Everyone was enlarged, changed, disarrayed by contact with Dean Reed. For them he was a star.

By then I cared much more about what Dean Reed had done than about how he died. If it was suicide, you could feel for him, for his anguish, for the messy life. I liked him not because he was a martyr to his cause, but because, while almost everyone he grew up with stayed home and watched TV, he did something. But there was no way I could tell his mother that.

"I believe it was probably a suicide to end it that way," said Victor Grossman, "and, although he was a good friend and a really nice fellow, I think, perhaps, by departing this world, he saved himself an awful lot of heartbreak in the years that followed."

Gerrit List put it even better. "It was, perhaps, the times that killed him," Gerrit said. "His star was going down. Maybe it was the right moment, but who is to say so? Maybe it is better to say, that's show business."

29

Clink, clink, clink.

Between the summer night in 1989, when I said goodbye to Renate at the lake, and the beginning of 1990, everything changed. Mikhail Gorbachev had been in office since 1985 and he was doing things "His Way," as his spokesman said and called it the *Sinatra Doctrine*. Gorbachev met Ronald Reagan. Reagan went to the Soviet Union; Gorby came to America. He walked through the crowds and charmed us in a way almost no foreign leader ever had.

The whole planet shifted on its political axis. Hungary declared itself a republic. In Poland, Solidarity became a government. In Prague, where Vaclav Havel, dissident playwright, was made president, Alexander Dubcek, the now elderly leader of the Prague Spring and an epic figure, returned from exile in the countryside and appeared on a balcony in Wenceslas Square at Christmas. With the Velvet Revolution, the soundtrack went on again in Prague and the streets were vibrant with music and talk, discussion and politics.

And in Romania, where Dean shot some of his movies because the countryside looked a lot like the Old West and had hardly any television aerials, the television station became the headquarters for a revolution. After Ceauşescu was executed, Romanians went into his office and rolled ecstatically around on the priceless Persian carpets, grinning, their Kalashnikovs beside them.

November 9, 1989. The Berlin Wall fell.

It was breached by a bunch of kids with some hammers, and then they partied on top of it, dancing all night long.

Clink, clink, clink: you could hear the sound blocks away from Checkpoint Charlie.

"The sound of freedom," I said.

"The sound of money," said Leslie Woodhead and then took it back. "I don't want to be cynical," he added. "Not yet."

I went to Berlin in the middle of November. I got to Checkpoint Charlie and stood and gaped. What a prophet I had been. Even the summer before when I'd visited Renate, I was convinced nothing here would ever change, and now, just before Christmas, Bloomingdales was selling chunks of the Berlin Wall at twelve and a half bucks a pop in New York.

Clink, clink, clink. It reminded me of something but I was so dumbstruck by the thing itself, I couldn't come up with it at first.

Then, I remembered. The sound of the Wall coming down reminded me of a noise I had heard in Moscow when I passed a dog decked out with war medals like a little general. The medals went clink clink clink.

For a while after the Berlin Wall was torn down, a handful of idealistic East Germans imagined that there was a *Third Way*—a kind of fantasy combination of socialism and capitalism. It lasted

inside. Victor ordered a pair of steaks with brandied peaches on them like two big yellow breasts; Renate and I ordered steak, too, but she hardly touched hers.

Victor still believed in socialism and he was worried that the big West German companies would wipe out the gains made by East Germany. He was right. The West Germans moved in fast and took over pretty much everything, and they left a lot of East Germans feeling crushed, defeated, and lost.

What gains? I wanted to say. What bloody gains? News of the corruption inside the GDR was coming out every day. There were stories about the gold hoarded by government officials in Swiss banks and the grandeur of their country estates, the rigged football games, and the sale of arms to South Africa and human beings to the West for hard currency. Honecker had spent four hundred thousand dollars of state money for a watch that had belonged to Lenin.

Dean Reed had always criticized Imelda Marcos and Ronald Reagan. He talked about the horrors of capitalism, about its corruptions, but what about Honecker? He shook hands with Honecker, he took his lousy medals, he celebrated the triumphs of socialism in the GDR. Dean believed!

Gains? All I could see was the misery.

In those weeks after the Wall came down, a fog seemed to slide away from over East Germany, revealing a nightmare landscape: women forced to handle chemical wastes without gloves; a countryside poisoned by sulphur dioxide; secret police who destroyed thousands of people.

There were also frightening outbreaks of feverish violence on all sides: a mob in Leipzig, screaming "Communist swine," threatened to lynch the Stasi; delirious with freedom, a pack of hoodlums accosted a Jewish girl and cut the Star of David into her flesh with a knife.

What gains? And how many other Victors were there, how many true believers left behind in the East, stranded by their politics. What gains, I wanted to shout over lunch, but I knew there was no point. With the whole rotten enterprise revealed as a sham, Victor and others like him, having made a lifetime enterprise of their beliefs, were impaled on the necessity of believing. We ate and Renate listened quietly.

After lunch that day at the Moscow Restaurant, Renate dropped Victor off at his building. She took me back to Checkpoint Charlie but she seemed reluctant to let me go. I was sorry to leave her.

I asked her how Dean would have felt about the Wall coming down.

She was correct, cheerful, and loyal to her dead husband.

"He would have been happy for a multi-party system, but worried about many problems, for he understood the need for the Wall. People in the East are very, very frightened. Everything is coming apart."

"And you?"

"Hitler, Stalin, Honecker, we believed them all. Now we believe in nothing. We know everything is bad. That we are bad people. We don't know what to believe."

A middle-aged couple nearby were kissing as if no one else existed. They kissed for a long time until, with a doleful gesture, the woman turned back towards the East and the man went through to West Berlin, and I remembered that Renate's first role was in a film called *Divided Heavens*. In it, a couple were separated by the Berlin Wall and because of the Wall, love died.

I started towards Checkpoint Charlie on foot and then turned back. Renate was standing near her red car, watching. She waved. I waved back. Then she got in her car and drove away. I crossed back to the West, where I looked at the phone booth where Dean had made his last, desperate calls to Dixie. The sheer sweep of his life got to me. I was glad I was alone.

It had never been his politics that hooked me. It was the scale of Dean's life and his determination to make something of himself, to be loved, to be a star. He had the aspirant energy of America in its prime. I wished he were alive.

For a while I walked along the Berlin Wall and watched people hammering out little pieces and listened to the clink, clink, clink. Something irrevocable was going on. It would change everything. The seeming certainties of the Cold War were over.

Then I put my hand through the Wall. I had no idea why I did it. I just went up to the concrete monolith and stood next to a teenager from New York City who was working away with a little hammer and chisel. He said hi, and I said hi back, and then I stuck my hand through it. It wasn't as thick as I had imagined. It felt like a prop wall. The remnants of another world.

It was getting dark. The November evening was setting in over Berlin. I poked my arm through the Berlin Wall one last time, put a few pieces of it in my pocket, and then I went home.

30

All through 1990, as the nightmare world of the Stasi was exposed, a billion pages of files on every aspect of life in the GDR, uncovered, it became clear that so many citizens had been involved one way or another, the files would have to be carefully archived, permanently sealed, burned. Some people thought it was simply wisest to burn the past.

Some files had already been shredded by the Stasi as the Berlin Wall was coming down, and people would spend years trying to paste the bits together again. If you wanted someone's records, you had to be family, you had to apply. There were too many possibilities for revenge. There was no way I could get access to Dean Reed's files.

But some time late that year, a letter surfaced. I heard about it long before I got it. I talked to Anne de Boismilion at CBS in Paris, who said that she, or maybe it was her researcher, had had a phone call from Will Roberts to say that someone, perhaps Renate, had seen Dean's Stasi file in Berlin.

As always, news of Dean came in a phone call carrying a rumor of a possible sighting by someone I could not reach because it would be the middle of the night in Berlin and anyhow the lines were always busy. It was all speculation, it was all hearsay, it was all a whispering gallery, but now there was talk of a suicide letter in Dean's files.

Under the US Freedom of Information Act, I finally got hold of Dean's FBI files—it had taken two years—but as always with these files the interesting stuff was blacked out. The rest I knew by heart.

One of the weird things was that nobody had ever bothered me, no one had ever asked any questions, and it made me wonder if any government agency could have been involved. No Stasi? KGB? FBI? Not even in East Berlin had I ever been approached. Maybe I had read too many spy novels; maybe Dean Reed no longer mattered. Then suddenly, out of the blue it came back to me how one afternoon, probably in 1988, when we were driving out of an underground parking lot near the Grand Hotel in East Berlin, a man on the sidewalk had taken a picture of us. I called Leslie.

"Just a tourist," he said.

"Taking a picture of you and me in a Hertz rental car?"

Still, it seemed to have happened in the past in another age. Everything had changed. The drama-doc script we'd been working on was out of date, and instead Leslie Woodhead and I were making a documentary about Dean Reed for the BBC because at least with a documentary you could try to keep up with the changes.

In an astonishing poll, sixty-two percent of Americans said that, with Gorbachev in power, they trusted the Soviet Union. It was as if Darth Vadar had not only pulled up his vizor, he'd taken off the whole damn costume. Journalists who had covered the Soviet Union and Eastern Europe yearned for the old days, when they could take a night off for poker instead of working a twenty-hour shift because now everyone in the country had a story to tell.

When I got back to Moscow, this time with a documentary film crew, it was early 1990. Sheremetyevo Airport was awash in electronic junk as the new-style Soviet traveler returned from New York, humping his toys—computers, videos, television sets—fresh from Uncle Steve's warehouse on Canal Street. Uncle Steve's stocked answering machines geared specially to Soviet-style telephones.

Moscow itself was throbbing with *Glasnost* and *Perestroika*, free speech, anti-Semitism, hamburgers, hookers, private enterprise, and long lines that led to food stores which were completely empty—as if the city were trapped in some frenzied halfway house: it couldn't go backward; it couldn't go ahead. At the Sovincenter, half the lights were out.

The Sovincenter was Moscow's first mall. The huge complex on the banks of the Moskva River included a conference center, a hotel with see-through elevator pods that slid up and down its walls, an atrium with plastic trees, and a clock in the shape of a cockerel that crowed at regular hours. It had a credible imitation of an English pub with plaid carpets that purveyed stale beer and soggy fish and chips. Those who had the hard currency hurried in and out of the shops, buying fresh fruit, Tampax, and air tickets.

What had originally been a glistening testimony to the glories of free enterprise, the Sovincenter was in disrepair: the lights were out; hoods loitered in the lobby; hookers called rooms at random in the middle of the night and occasionally I got a call from Lovely Natasha. A BBC journalist I ran into told me about the night he opened his eyes to find a Lovely Natasha and several of her friends actually in his room, staring down at him from the foot of his bed.

The Sovincenter was the ugly face of *Perestroika*, this crappy steel and glass building, which seemed a miserable imitation of the West.

Outside, the chauffeurs smoked Marlboros and leaned against the Chaikas and Mercs, waiting for their clients. Ordinary Russians, who could not enter because they didn't have the hard currency, pressed their faces against the glass doors.

"At least when Stalin was in power, there was a real man and we had food on the table," said Vera Reich.

I met up with Vera and she told me that was what she heard in the line for meat. She heard it two or three times a week: "If only we still had Stalin."

"I am the Jesus of Cool," Art Troitsky said one night as we took the subway to Moscow University for a rock concert. When we got there, the auditorium was half empty. "People are scared to go out at night because of crime. Rock is dead in Russia, anyhow," he said, no longer laughing.

It was hyperbole; people still listened to rock. But as a political act, as the music that let you declare your otherness, when the state withdrew its opposition, rock and roll lost its heart. Fed up, even Boris Grebenshikov left Leningrad and went to London, where he wore baggy brown corduroys and spent most of his time painting pictures and drinking malt whisky.

"I'm tired of being the ambassador of rock in a country that's got no rhythm," he said.

All the myths were banging around in some crazy, unpredictable fashion and Art was gloomy. He could hear the sound of breaking *Glasnost*, he said over and over. "Breaking *Glasnost*."

Good line, I said, and he nodded agreement, and we said it one more time in unison: BREAKING *GLASNOST*.

Art felt that civil war was coming to the Soviet Union—Lithuania, Azerbaijan, and Ukraine, all ready to rebel. Art could not quite explain how it was coming, but it was inevitable.

"Why don't you leave?" I asked. "If what's coming is what you say and you stay, it's a prescription for your own death."

He said, "But if I'm wrong, I want to be part of it. Wouldn't you?"

So we toasted *Glasnost* and Gorbachev.

So much stuff was going on in Moscow that it was hard to get Dean Reed into focus again. Intellectuals found him loathsome or ridiculous, if they remembered him at all; the "peasant young people," as Art had called them, had other things on their minds like finding jobs and food.

They were cynical about everything, these Soviet kids. Someone took a poll of young Soviets; in the eyes of the young, the most desirable job was that of "racketeer." This was followed by hard-currency hooker and croupier at a gambling club.

When the Australian Embassy offered to process emigration forms, half a million Muscovites came to the gates. They had been promised better times for seventy years and better times had never come and they were fed up to the teeth. They wanted to have some fun before they died.

"The best thing for this country is to sell it off a piece at a time to the highest bidders," Art said as we strolled into Pushkin Square.

Oh, McDonald's!

It shimmered there, all the neon, the yellow and red arches, the backlit signs, the shiny floors and surfaces, the stainless steel palm trees, and the pop music playing. It was the biggest McDonald's I had ever seen. I didn't know whether to laugh or cry. There was a line outside every day. People waited three or four hours because they knew when you got inside, unlike a lot of places in Moscow, you actually got something to eat.

Beeg Mek. Yum. I ate my first Big Mac in Moscow. I went very early one morning to avoid the lines. Tolya Schevshenko, the rock fan who had once bought a Chubby Checker record inscribed on an X-ray plate, came with me. We ate cheeseburgers and fries, the hot apple pie, and vanilla ice cream. Tolya asked why I had never eaten this food before and I tried to explain that, in a place like New York, fast food was mostly for kids and poor people. Tolya was not convinced. I ordered more fries.

McDonald's was the new People's Palace. My own skepticism about my country disappeared for a while. In Moscow, all things American were, more than ever, hugely desirable.

The more often I went to Moscow (I went again and again through the early 1990s), the more often I met Americans who, like me, could not get enough.

A lot of us were the grandchildren of Russian immigrants, the children of the old American Left. We were urban coastal Jews who had grown up during the 1960s. We had been cynical about mainstream America most of our lives. Now we had seen the other, we had seen the Soviet Union, and we were cynical about it, too, but also seduced by it. We were ineluctably drawn towards this mess of a country.

I talked about it with Joe Klein, the journalist, over a lunch at Doc's in New York. Like me, Joe was busy calculating how soon he could get back to the Soviet Union. Like me, he had his own friends, his Svetlana and Art, his Tolya. He had his favorite stories, his favorite restaurants, his own account of the first time he had seen Red Square. Joe made me see why it was so irresistible; for one thing, they wanted us. They loved us, and in a way always had, for our jeans, our dollars, our hamburgers and music, our movies and literature, our Coca Cola and our Constitution, and our friendliness. I remembered that Vera Reich had loved the West above all for its friendliness.

They loved us, as Americans, and we loved them back for it. It was also a kind of relief, at least for someone like me who had put in time in the 1960s and 1970s obsessed with the evils of America. We were off the hook. Going to the Soviet Union gave us back America. In Moscow I took a picture of McDonald's.

"Not allowed!" shouted a uniformed boy.

Pictures were not permitted except by special arrangement, he said, casting a sharp eye on the squads of young Soviets scrubbing the floors religiously.

These were the rules and in this, I thought, McDonald's, the result of perfect regimentation, was ideally suited to the Soviet Union. This was the company built on the inviolable principles of the University of Hamburgerology. Outside Moscow, in specially equipped factories, any bun that did not meet its standards was killed.

On the way out I looked at the long line. McDonald's now fulfilled the longing for America. It was my conceit that in some ways McDonald's had replaced Dean Reed as the American icon.

The next day I saw Oleg Smirnoff, who now represented Pizza Hut, which was coming to Moscow.

No longer did Oleg have a row of ballpoint pens in his shirt pocket; no longer did he speak the Party line. He wore a navy blue blazer from Next. He talked about "Communist assholes" and about his advertising agency. For the Moscow opening of Pizza Hut, his biggest client, he planned to commission a song about pizza. I suggested "That's Amore."

"When the moon hits your eye like a big pizza pie, that's amore!" I sang. Oleg seemed nonplussed.

We moved on to Dean's death. Oleg was no longer reluctant to talk to me.

"His death was played down and made little of in the USSR, which made everyone suspicious," he said. "Dean talked about America a lot. Maybe somebody in East Berlin got pissed off."

In the spring of 1986 Dean told Oleg, "I can go home again, Oleg. I met people in Colorado who told me they remembered me. I can have a career there. I can go home." It was the last time the two met.

"Dean, at the end, was a man who could not acknowledge that he had wasted his life. It was too late for him," Oleg said. "He was an idealist."

Oleg and I drank coffee in the Savoy, Moscow's newest hotel, where the chairs were covered in turquoise nylon brocade; the dissident poet Andrei Voznesensky ate steak in the restaurant there, I heard. All around us, men sat on the little chairs and signed deals that would never come to much. Upstairs in a casino, pimply boys, in tuxedos, worked as croupiers.

At long last, more than two years since I'd first met him in the club in Gorky Park, Oleg offered me his videotape. When I looked at it, it was mostly a memorial concert in honor of Dean Reed.

I wandered around Moscow by myself a lot. Svetlana was away in London. Art was considering his career. Tolya dreamed of

Malibu. I thought of the eight hundred thousand children dying from leukemia from the spill at Chernobyl and of the mutant babies with six toes who were born there and the trees that grew upside down. And I thought of Vera, who was leaving for America because her husband was afraid of the anti-Semitism. It was one of the ironies of *Glasnost* and of the break-up of the whole Soviet Empire: with freedom of expression, people felt free to hate each other.

I asked Vera to show me her passport. In plain Russian it was marked: Jew. On days when the *Pamyat* scheduled pogroms—it was physically shocking to write the word pogrom in 1990— Yelena Zagrevskaya's mother put a scarf over her head and stayed indoors. I read that, in the main square in Vilnius, a sign had appeared: *Lithuania for the Lithuanians, Poles to Poland, Yids to the Crematoria.*

Asleep in my room at the Savoy, I dreamed that I heard a loudspeaker blast through the hotel. The hotel management was shouting, howling, and screaming for all of the Jews to assemble in the courtyard. Then I dreamed of a horse that had fallen into a swimming pool. When it was hoisted up, it had no legs.

Chaotic times, strange, terrifying, wonderful. There were people who had no bread and people who talked to you fearlessly about politics and smiled at you in the subways just for the hell of it. I didn't get anywhere with Dean Reed's death, though, just the same rumors and whispers recycled, retailed, cranked up. It was driving me crazy. Back to Berlin.

In Berlin, most of the Wall was already gone, except for a few slabs, one that was a kind of backdrop for a snack bar in the Potsdamerplatz. On the road to the suburbs to see a homicide cop who had some information, or said he did, there were dozens of trashed Trabants, the Cold War cars nobody wanted anymore.

Thomas Sindermann, who had been East Berlin's chief homicide policeman, had sharp eyes and a pointy nose, and he occasionally sniffed when he talked, as if he had an allergy or smelled something bad. Private enterprise had allowed Sindermann to recycle himself as a private eye, a German Sam Spade with a fancy computer in the office in his house.

I wasn't expecting much. I'd half given up expecting answers about Dean's death, and then, in a matter-of-fact way, Sindermann calmly laid it all out.

In Sindermann's view the confusion surrounding Dean's death was that the Central Committee of the Communist Party got involved instead of the homicide police; but, then, he was a cop. And it was easy for Sindermann in hindsight to see what the problems were, to treat it as a straightforward case. Renate had, of course, been most of all worried about her husband during the events leading up to his death and never suspected a crime. As far as Renate and Gerrit List were concerned there was no reason to suspect anything other than that Dean had disappeared temporarily as he so often had. They had acted the way anyone would have done in their situation.

Sindermann felt the Central Committee had somehow attempted a cover-up; Dean Reed was an important person, Sindermann said, and it had been important to preserve his reputation.

"He was a well-known figure especially for youngsters. He'd been promoted as an idol, an American fighter for Communism. He also starred in films. Their quality was debatable," added Sindermann, with a faint smirk, "but the authorities didn't want to show young people and others that he had problems and had taken his own life."

Finally, according to Sindermann, Dean's death was a suicide. He was sure about it. Then, as if he'd opened the door a crack, more stuff came through and the alleged suicide letter I'd heard about surfaced. How did it happen? Where did it come from? No one was sure, but somehow Leslie Woodhead and I got hold of a copy in time to include it in the BBC documentary we were making.

It was addressed to Eberhart Finch, Dean Reed's friend on the Central Committee, and written in German on the back of Dean's movie script.

We got it translated. The letter said that he, Dean, could not take money for a film that might never be finished and death was the only way out.

To the end, though, he was still Comrade Rockstar. He ended his letter saying, "May all progressive people create a better and more just and more peaceful world, Dean Reed."

Was it authentic? Was it the real thing? I believed it was. And that was it. All the months and years of looking, and then I knew: Dean had killed himself.

Handwriting experts confirmed as best they could—they were dealing with a dead man, after all—that Dean Reed had written the letter. Renate only saw it four years after he died and she suffered terribly. It was as if a hand had reached from the grave to hurt her one last time.

In 1991, Dean's mother took his ashes back to Colorado, and Renate rubbed his name off his gravestone in the little cemetery near their house in East Berlin.

* * *

330

"I would never have believed the Wall would come down in my lifetime," Johnny Rosenburg wrote to me. "I wonder what Dean would have thought. I sort of feel he would have adjusted real quick and went along with the flow . . . Why in God's name did he have to die at this point in time? With things changing the way they are, he could have played such an important part in the whole affair. What a waste."

What Johnny couldn't see was that, without the Berlin Wall, Dean Reed had no role. When Dean crossed to the East he seemed seditious, foreign, sexy, American.

The Cold War raged; Dean sang. He was wonderful propaganda, this American true believer they could sell to their own people. Dean was rock and roll and good times; for twenty years behind the Iron Curtain Dean Reed seemed to be a force for life or at least the illusion of it.

As things changed, even in the short time I had been looking for him, Dean Reed seemed to recede towards some far horizon defined by the Cold War.

"There was no profit in a dead man," Vaclav Nectar said in Prague, where a million portraits of Vaclav Havel replaced a million pictures of Vladimir Lenin. In a record store up a cobbled street near Havel's castle, an old lady in carpet slippers searched the bins in vain.

"Dean Reed? I am so sorry, but it was a very long time ago," she said.

Still, the little Dean Reed industry cranked up by Dean's death hummed along. Dean's first wife, Patty, was said to be writing a book and so were half a dozen other people. I heard that Martin Scorsese was interested in making a movie and so was Stewart

Copeland, the drummer for the Police. At some point I read in the *Los Angeles Times* that Ed Pressman, the producer, was thinking of making a movie about Dean. Alive, Dean couldn't get an agent in Hollywood; dead, he was a hot property.

Nothing happened.

And so it went. A first version of my book was published in England and the documentary for the BBC's *Arena* was aired, both in 1991. Occasionally, Mona Rosenburg sent me a Christmas card or some of her pickled beets.

And then, about seven years later, my agent and friend Brian Siberell, in Los Angeles, said, "Remember that book of yours, *Comrade Rockstar?*" And I said, sure, of course I remembered it. And he said, "Mind if I send it around?"

"Why not?" I said, and forgot about it.

A year or so later, I was in a missile silo in Wyoming, working on a BBC documentary about America's Missileers, when my cell phone rang. It was Brian.

"I've sold *Comrade Rockstar* to Tom Hanks," he said.

On a subsequent trip to California, I went to visit Playtone and met up with Gary Goetzman, who runs the company with Tom Hanks. I was having lunch with Gary, who gives lie to the idea that Hollywood producers are crass or dull—Gary was neither of these, but warm and smart—when a tall man appeared. He put out his hand and said, "Hi, I'm Tom." I tried to remain cool.

Tom Hanks sat down and talked about the Cold War and Dean Reed for a while and what thrilled and astonished me, apart from the fact that I was sitting and drinking Cokes with Tom Hanks, was that he got it. He understood the story better than I ever had.

But what did I make of it? What did I make of Dean Reed? The music was nothing special. The movies were silly and the politics naive. I also knew he could not have existed without the Berlin Wall or the Iron Curtain. He was a tale from the Cold War. It was his frontier.

I was ultimately convinced that his death was suicide or at least a bumbled self-willed accident, not because of letters or autopsy reports or a homicide cop, but because of something I heard in Moscow. It was the most persuasive, most Russian account of how Dean Reed died and why.

After Dean died, Xenia Golubovich, the young woman in Moscow who kept a poster of Dean on her wall, said, "Dean's death was not a surprise for me. It was not a shock for me. And I think he committed suicide because that's what a hero must do. In a way, Dean represents this very strange idea. When a human really wants to become something, he does. And it demands enormous strength. Dean died having absolutely ruined himself. Dean, in his very minor way according to his strength, became what he wanted."

Reggie Nadelson is a journalist and documentary filmmaker. She is also the author of five thrillers, including the recently published *Disturbed Earth* and *Red Hook*. She lives in New York City.